C

PROGRAMMING

IN THE

BERKELEY UNIX ENVIRONMENT

R. Nigel Horspool

Department of Computer Science
University of Victoria

Prentice-Hall Canada Inc., Scarborough, Ontario

Canadian Cataloguing in Publication Data

Horspool, R. Nigel, 1948-
    C programming in the Berkeley UNIX environment

Includes index.
ISBN 0-13-109760-1

1. C (Computer program language). 2. UNIX (Computer operating system). 3. Programming (Electronic computers). I. Title.

QA76.73.C13H67 1986   001.64'24   C86-093525-6

© 1986 **Prentice-Hall Canada Inc.,** Scarborough, Ontario

Prentice-Hall Inc., *Englewood Cliffs, New Jersey*
Prentice-Hall International, Inc., *London*
Prentice-Hall of Australia, Pty., Ltd., *Sydney*
Prentice-Hall of India, Pvt., Ltd., *New Delhi*
Prentice-Hall of Japan, Inc., *Tokyo*
Prentice-Hall of Southeast Asia (Pte.) Ltd., *Singapore*
Editora Prentice-Hall do Brasil Ltda., *Rio de Janeiro*
Prentice-Hall Hispanoamericana, S.A., *Mexico*
Whitehall Books Limited, *Wellington, New Zealand*

ISBN 0-13-109760-1

Production Editor: David Jolliffe
Manufacturing Buyer: Sheldon Fischer
Cover Design: Marilyn Swallow

Printed and bound in Canada by John Deyell

         3   4   5   JD   90   89   88

To Nicole and Daniel

CONTENTS

PREFACE

As an intelligent reader should have noticed from the cover, this book proclaims itself as an introduction to C programming in the Berkeley UNIX operating system evironment. The material in the book is applicable to the versions of the Berkeley UNIX system known as 4.2bsd and 4.3bsd. Except for one chapter and a few sections of other chapters, the material is also applicable to 4.1bsd. (The abbreviation *bsd* is short for *Berkeley Software Distribution*.)

The contents of this book have evolved from a short C language summary written for computer science students at the University of Victoria. The students would normally take a course in a topic, such as compiler construction, for which they would have a regular text book. Assignments for such a course, however, would involve programming in C. The C summary was therefore provided as supplementary material for the compiler course and for a couple of other courses. The process of converting the original summary into book form has given me the opportunity to add a lot more material. As well as giving a reasonably comprehensive treatment of C, this book includes much material about the Berkeley UNIX operating system itself, particularly information that a novice user of the UNIX system would need. In fact, so much information about the system has been added, it would be inaccurate to describe this book as just a C book. About two thirds of the material is on the Berkeley UNIX system itself – how to use system functions and how to use various system programs.

This book is not in any way intended to teach how to program. It certainly teaches the C language but it does not explain how to perform the basic steps of taking a vaguely defined problem stated in English and converting this problem description into an algorithm. Nor does this book explain the fundamental concepts of a programming language, like what a variable is or what an assignment statement does. It is assumed that anyone using this book is already reasonably proficient in using some other programming language – and it does not really matter what that other language is. This assumption helps keep the material short and focused on C. There are occasional comparisons between C features and features of the PASCAL language in this book, but a reader unfamiliar with PASCAL will not be at a disadvantage.

It might be argued that the Berkeley UNIX system is not sufficiently different from other UNIX implementations to deserve a text specifically tailored to C programming for that system. However, the version of the UNIX system developed at the University of California at Berkeley is a popular system, especially with educational institutions, and is used by tens of thousands of students. The Berkeley UNIX system does have its differences from other UNIX variants, particularly in its command language (the *C shell*). Most books on the UNIX operating system try to cover all varieties of UNIX – either by restricting their coverage to a more or less standard UNIX subset or by adding extra chapters and appendices describing each UNIX variant. My feeling is that **a book tailored to the actual system used by the student will be more usable**, requiring less searching through appendices and providing fewer surprises.

If C programs are carefully crafted, they need be no harder to read than an equivalent program in another language. The preprocessor facilities of the C compiler can also be used to good effect in rendering programs easier to read. Another advantage of C is that C programs are easy to separate into files which can be compiled separately. This book tries to encourage a particular philosophy for organizing a large program into separate files. It is intended to follow the precepts of good software engineering design and to minimize the risk of interfacing errors.

Acknowledgements

I wish to thank Gary Duncan at the University of Victoria who read the first draft of each chapter as it was written and caught many early mistakes. I also thank Vince Manis of the University of British Columbia for his constructive comments, Michael Bauer of the University of Western Ontario for his encouraging review, and an anonymous reviewer for many good suggestions.

Of course, I do not wish to forget the developers of the UNIX system, both at Bell Laboratories and the University of California at Berkeley, who gave me both the subject matter and the word-processing software which produced the camera-ready copy for this book. Yes, this entire book was produced using *troff*, augmented by *tbl*, *pic* and the *-me* macro package. In spite of a nasty bug in the footnote macros which caused no end of trouble, I extend special thanks to Eric Allman, the author of the *-me* macro package.

R. Nigel Horspool
Victoria, B.C., Canada

C

PROGRAMMING

IN THE

BERKELEY UNIX ENVIRONMENT

CHAPTER 0

INTRODUCTION

0.1. HISTORY

C is a language developed at Bell Laboratories and is closely associated with the UNIX* operating system. Indeed, almost all the source code for UNIX is written in C. A knowledge of C is more or less essential for anyone who wants to become a serious user of UNIX. This is not just because a serious user will need to read system source code but also because some UNIX programs use a C-like syntax for their inputs (*csh*, *awk* and *bc* are examples that come to mind).

The person most responsible for designing the C language is Dennis Ritchie, one of the UNIX pioneers. His language design was developed in light of his experiences with a predecessor language, B, which had also been intended for use in the UNIX project. B, in turn, was based on the programming language BCPL. The BCPL language, developed by Martin Richards at the University of Cambridge in England, is still used for portable software applications. And, in case you want to follow the family tree even further back, BCPL is a simplified version of the CPL programming language. CPL was also developed at the University of Cambridge. The article by Ritchie cited at the end of this chapter provides an interesting and amusing account of the early history of the UNIX operating system and the C language.

Since Ritchie's original language design, C has undergone some further evolution. The changes that have occurred over the years have tended to make the language syntax more consistent and have also added a few features

---

* UNIX is a trademark of AT&T Bell Laboratories

1

borrowed from other programming languages.

Following its original implementation on the PDP-11, C has been implemented for most other computers – both large and small. Furthermore, it has become available with operating systems other than UNIX. There are some minor differences between the various implementations. Different hardware characteristics, such as word size, account for the most visible differences. The versions of C provided with the 4.1bsd, 4.2bsd and 4.3bsd versions of the Berkeley UNIX system on the VAX-11, Sun and Pyramid series of computers are described in this book. If C is used carefully, implementation differences can be isolated to a few definitions and thus a very high degree of software portability can be achieved. For advice on how to construct portable C programs, the book by Plum (cited at the end of this chapter) is recommended.

0.2. LANGUAGE CHARACTERISTICS

C has been described as being a high-level assembly language. Two of the operators, for incrementing and decrementing variables, certainly appear to be based on memory-addressing modes of the PDP-11 computer series. (These modes are also found in the VAX-11 series of computers.) As a general principle, a principle that has directed the language design all along, C only contains constructs that are capable of being translated into efficient machine code sequences.

With the exception of special control lines handled by the C preprocessor, C programs are written in a free format style. To make programs more readable, it is normal to indent statements that are nested within loops or or other language constructs. There are two system utilities, *cb* and *indent*, that can be used to reformat a C source file to produce a consistent indentation of statements. Details of these two programs are given later in the book.

The C language itself does not provide any input-output operations. However, there is a standard library of I/O functions to which programs may refer. The library also includes functions for performing various string handling operations, converting characters from upper case to lower case or vice versa, and numerous other operations. The book by Kernighan and Pike provides a good introduction to system functions in UNIX and their use from within C programs. But it should be noted that the book is oriented towards the standard AT&T UNIX operating system (System V UNIX) and therefore does not mention the many extra features of the Berkeley UNIX system.

0.3. SOME BASIC TEXTUAL RULES

In a moment, we will take a look at a small sample C program. But, before doing that, we should state some of the lexical rules that govern the structure of a C program.

First, any line that has the # character (often called the *hash* character or *pound* character) appearing in the first column is a line that is extracted and processed by the C preprocessor. The contents of such a line do not form part of the C program. Instead, such lines contain directives that cause the C preprocessor to include C source code from other files or to modify C source code in the remainder of the current file. A full explanation of the C preprocessor and of the various directives appears later in Chapter 6.

A C program is composed of lexical units or *tokens*. Examples of tokens include identifiers, decimal integers, keywords (like **if** and **while**), special symbols (like + and <=), and punctuation symbols. A full list of these symbols appears in the C syntax description provided in Appendix C. Two consecutive tokens may be separated by an arbitrary number of *white space* characters and comments. White space characters include blanks, tabs, newline characters, and form-feed characters (typed as *Control-L*). While it is not usually necessary to separate two adjacent tokens, there are circumstances when it is necessary. When a program is compiled, the C compiler tries to construct the longest possible token, reading from left to right. For example, a C declaration such as

```
int counter;
```

cannot be written without white space after the keyword **int**, because the compiler would then assume that you had written the identifier *intcounter*.

Identifiers may have a practically unlimited length in Berkeley UNIX implementations. As is usual for programming languages, identifiers are composed from sequences of letters and digits, where the first character must be a letter. The underscore character is considered to be a letter. Upper and lower case letters are differentiated, thus *Num* and *num* are two distinct identifiers. It is a fairly standard style in C programming to use lower case for normal program identifiers and to use upper case for identifiers handled by the C preprocessor. This convention is to be recommended because an upper-case identifier stands out and gives a warning to the reader. As we shall see, an identifier can be transformed by the preprocessor into an arbitrary piece of C source code. Keywords are composed only of lower-case letters. For example, **int** is a keyword to denote the *integer* type, whereas *Int* and *INT* are taken as identifiers by the C compiler.

Comments begin with the character pair /* and are terminated by the first occurrence of the character pair */. Of course, comments can range over many lines. Comments may not be nested inside each other. For example,

```
/*    The following statement is commented out
/*         i = 0;                 */
```

represents a complete comment. Unfortunately, there are some C compilers on other computers that let comments be nested. This difference can cause problems if a C program is transferred to the other computer. If you should ever temporarily desire to comment out a section of program that itself includes

comments, the best approach is to use the C preprocessor and the **#ifdef** directive to cause this section of code to be ignored by the compiler. (See Chapter 6
for preprocessor details.)

Comments may be used to separate textual elements of a C program, in
the same way as space characters and new-line characters. Therefore,

```
jack/*and*/jill
```

does not represent a single identifier named *jackjill*, but two separate identifiers.

0.4. A SAMPLE C PROGRAM

To demonstrate that C can be quite readable and to give some feel for the
language, let us examine a short program. The program shown in Figure 0.1
does nothing more than read one line of text from the terminal keyboard and
then display that line backwards. It is hard to imagine why anyone would ever
want to look at program output in a mirror but, in case they do, this is just the
program they need.

The program is considerably longer than it need be if we were to take full
advantage of the C language and of the input-output functions in the C library.
However, it would not then serve as such a good introductory example.

In the example program, the line beginning **#include** is a preprocessor
directive specifying that a file named "stdio.h" is to be read and included in the
program at this point, replacing the line containing the preprocessor directive.
The "stdio.h" file contains declarations for various input-output functions that
exist in the C library. The file does not contain the actual source code for these
functions, since it would be grossly inefficient to re-compile these functions
every time somebody needed to use them. Instead it just contains declaration
information telling the compiler how to invoke the various input-output functions and defining the data types needed to work with files. If you want to look
and see what is in the file, just execute the command

```
more /usr/include/stdio.h
```

The line beginning **#define** is another preprocessor directive that tells
the preprocessor to substitute the two characters **80** for every occurrence of
the identifier *MAXLENGTH* in the remainder of the program. Our usage of
#define achieves an effect similar to a **const** definition in the PASCAL
language.

The line beginning **void main()** and all the following lines form a
definition for a function named *main*. This function is the main program. It is
that part of the C program which is the first to receive control from the UNIX
system. A complete C program must always contain a function named *main*.
Since the function *main* has no result to return, the result type for the function
is declared as **void**, a special type that denotes the absence of any usable value.
Left and right brace characters (commonly called *curly brackets*) surround the

FIGURE 0.1. A Sample C Program

```
#include <stdio.h>

#define  MAXLENGTH  80    /* limit on line length */

void main( ) {
    char   line[MAXLENGTH];
    int    ch, length;

    /*  Read up to the end of line, or up to a maximum
        of 80 characters, whichever occurs first  */
    length = 0;
    while( length < MAXLENGTH ) {
        ch = getchar();
        if (ch == '\n') break;
        line[length] = ch;
        length++;
    }

    /*  Output the line backwards  */
    while( length > 0 ) {
        length--;
        putchar( line[length] );
    }
    putchar( '\n' );
}
```

body of the function definition. In this function, some local variables are defined. There is a character array, named *line*, and integer variables named *length* and *ch*.

The function contains two major parts. The first part uses a loop, introduced by the keyword **while** and whose body is delimited by matching brace characters, to read one line of text from the keyboard. This form of loop is similar to the **while** loop of PASCAL. Our C loop repeatedly executes a group of statements as long as the controlling expression after the keyword **while** has the value *true*. In our program, the loop would continue until the character array has been filled. However, we should not assume that the input line will necessarily contain *MAXLENGTH* (80) characters. Therefore, after a statement to read the next input character (the *getchar* function returns the next input character), the loop contains a test to see if we have reached the end of a

line. The line end is indicated by the *newline* character. This character is a
standard character in the ASCII character set but one which would tend to destroy the program layout if it could directly appear as a character constant. In
C programs, a character constant whose value is the newline character is written as '\n'. If the test for a newline character is successful, the **break** statement causes the loop to be exited immediately. This statement operates like a
goto statement whose target is the statement that immediately follows the
loop. If the test is unsuccessful, we plant the input character into the array and
increment the variable used as the array index. A special increment operator,
++, is used to add one to the variable.

The second loop in the program uses another **while** loop to run through
the array elements in reverse order, outputting each character. As you might
guess, the *putchar* function outputs a character and the operator, $--$, is used to
decrement a variable. Finally, our program completes the output line by printing a newline character.

0.5. RUNNING A C PROGRAM

Before you can run a program, the program must be compiled. The C compiler
is invoked by the *cc* command in the UNIX system. The compiler requires that
an input file containing C source code must have a name that ends with the two
characters '.c'. Let us assume that you have created a file, named "reverse.c",
which holds the program of Figure 0.1. (If you do not know how to create such
a file, you should read Appendix A which covers the *vi* editor.) A session at the
computer terminal to compile and test our program might proceed as shown in
Figure 0.2.

Initially, the command prompt (which we have shown as a percent symbol) is displayed on the screen. We then type the *cc* command, as shown. We
provide three arguments for this command. The first is the name of the file
containing the source code. The second argument is a flag, '-o', which indicates
that the following argument, 'reverse', is to be used as the name of the compiled

FIGURE 0.2. Running the Sample Program

```
% cc reverse.c -o reverse
% ls -F
reverse*        reverse.c
% reverse
Hello World!
!dlroW olleH
%
```

program. If we omit the two arguments, '-o reverse', the compiled program will be stored in a file called "a.out".

If there are no errors in the program, the C compiler does not send any output to the terminal. We just see the prompt for the next command as soon as the compilation is completed. As a result of the compilation, a new file named 'reverse' has been created. We can check this by entering the *ls* command, which lists the names of the files in the current directory. The '-F' argument to *ls* asks that files with special characteristics be flagged in the output. The asterisk after the name 'reverse' in the output indicates that the file is *executable*.

Since 'reverse' is an executable program, we can execute it by typing its name as a command.[1] When we do this, nothing happens – the cursor just sits at the beginning of the next line. The reason for this lack of activity is that our program is waiting for some input. If we now type a line like 'Hello World!', the program immediately wakes up and outputs the reverse of our input line. After doing this, the program is finished and we receive the prompt for the next command.

FURTHER READING

- B.W. Kernighan and R. Pike. *The UNIX Programming Environment.* Englewood Cliffs, N.J.: Prentice-Hall, 1984. For a gentle introduction to system calls and systems programming, this book is strongly recommended. Although the work is intended to be a companion to System V UNIX, almost all the material is applicable to the Berkeley UNIX system too.

- S.P. Harbison and G.L. Steele Jr. *C: A Reference Manual.* Englewood Cliffs, N.J.: Prentice-Hall, 1984. This manual is an up-to-date and definitive description of the C language, applicable to almost all implementations.

- T. Plum. *C Programming Guidelines.* Englewood Cliffs, N.J.: Prentice-Hall, 1984. Plum's book contains hints on how to write C programs that can be easily transferred from one kind of computer to another. Even if you have no intentions of ever running the program on another machine, these guidelines will help you achieve more readable and consistent C code.

- D.M. Ritchie. "The Evolution of the UNIX Time-Sharing System," *ATT Bell Laboratories Technical Journal* 63, Issue 8, Part 2 (October 1984), pp. 1577-1593. The article describes the origins of C and UNIX. (This particular issue of the journal is entirely devoted to articles about the UNIX system.)

---

[1] This will work only if the current directory, referenced by the name '.', is in the command search path used by the shell. This is almost always the case. For a fuller explanation of search paths, see the appendix on the *csh* command shell.

CHAPTER 1

BASIC DATA TYPES

1.1. THE STANDARD DATA TYPES

The basic data types provided in C are integers (in several varieties), characters, reals and double-length reals. With one exception, we defer the more complicated data types, such as pointers and arrays, until a later chapter. The
exception is that we include string constants in this chapter. Strings in C are
just arrays of characters, the same as in PASCAL. However, since the notation
for a string constant is very similar to the notation for a character constant, it
is more convenient to consider it here.

The standard integer type, named **int**, is implemented as a signed 32-bit
longword on the VAX, Sun and Pyramid computers. Although C provides a
data type named **long int**, this is also implemented as a signed 32-bit longword.
The **long int** type is mostly useful for 16-bit machines, where **int** means a 16-
bit word and **long int** means a 32-bit double-word. There is a **short int** type
which is implemented as a signed 16-bit word on all three of the computers.

The integer types may also be designated as **unsigned**. In this case, the
range of integer values represented by the type does not include any negative
values. In a compound type name, such as **short int**, the keyword **int** may be
omitted. In the source code for the UNIX system, it appears to be standard
practice to take advantage of this option. Whether or not you wish to abbrevi-
ate in this way is a matter of personal style.

The **char** type is implemented as an 8-bit byte on the computer. It is, of
course, intended for holding character values. ASCII characters have values in
the range 0 to 127. However, as we shall see later, you are not restricted to

using **char** variables to hold only ASCII characters. In C, values of type **char** and values of type **int** are practically interchangeable. Thus, **int** variables can be used to hold character values and **char** variables may be used to hold small integer values. With the implementations of C on the VAX, Sun and Pyramid, the range of integers that may be held in a **char** variable is -128 to 127. But if you have plans to transfer your C programs to other computers, you have to be careful in this regard. Not all computers provide *signed-bytes*. Some computers, notably those with the IBM/370 architecture, provide *unsigned-bytes* only. Thus, **char** variables in C programs on those machines can hold integer values only in the range 0 to 255.

The **float** type is implemented as a 32-bit word and the **double** type as a 64-bit doubleword on the VAX, Sun and Pyramid computers. For the VAX and Pyramid computers, the magnitude of a **float** value lies between the approximate bounds, 2.9×10^{-37} and 1.710^{+38}, and has about 7 decimal digits of precision. The **double** type gives the same approximate range of values but with much greater precision, about 16 decimal digits. The Sun computer is different because it uses formats for floating-point numbers that follow the IEEE standard. Although **float** and **double** values occupy the same amount of storage (32 bits and 64 bits respectively), normalized **float** values have magnitudes lying between the approximate bounds, 1.2×10^{-38} and $3.4 \times 10^{+38}$, and have about 7 decimal digits of precision. Normalized **double** values have magnitudes lying between the approximate bounds, 2.2×10^{-308} and $1.8 \times 10^{+308}$, and has about 16 decimal digits of precision. The IEEE formats also provide representations for *infinity* and for *Not-a-Number* (NaN), which is generated as the result of an erroneous operation.

The basic types are summarized in Table 1.1.

TABLE 1.1 Basic Data Types

Type Name	Size (bits)	Range of Values
int	32	-2^{31} to $2^{31} - 1$
long	32	-2^{31} to $2^{31} - 1$
short	16	-2^{15} to $2^{15} - 1$
unsigned	32	0 to $2^{32} - 1$
unsigned long	32	0 to $2^{32} - 1$
unsigned short	16	0 to $2^{16} - 1$
char	8	-128 to 127
float	32	(see text)
double	64	(see text)

1.2. INTEGER CONSTANTS

Integer constants may be written in decimal, octal or hexadecimal notation. A sequence of digits, where the first digit is not a zero, is assumed to represent a decimal integer. For example,

12345

represents a value of type **int** and is, of course, equal to 12345 in decimal.

If the first digit in a sequence of digits is a zero, the integer constant is assumed to be written in octal. For example,

0456

is a value of type **int** equal to 302 decimal (computed as $4 \times 8^2 + 5 \times 8^1 + 6$). Although it is unlikely that you will have much need for octal constants, there are many source code programs for the UNIX system which use them. Octal constants are most often encountered when dealing with ASCII characters. If you look up *formfeed*, say, in a table of ASCII characters, you are more likely to see that its value is listed as 014 (octal) than as 12 (decimal).

A hexadecimal constant begins with the two characters `0x` or `0X` and is followed by one or more hexadecimal digits. The normal convention is followed, namely that the letters *a* to *f* (or, equally, *A* to *F*) represent the hexadecimal digits with (decimal) values 10 to 15. For example,

0x5ac

is an **int** constant with decimal value 1452 (computed as $5 \times 16^2 + 10 \times 16^1 + 12$).

In the full C language, any integer constant can be suffixed by the letter *L* to indicate that it should be a **long int** constant. (The suffix may also be written as the lower-case letter *ell*, but this is easily confused with the digit 1 and so its use is not recommended.) An example of a **long int** constant is

12345L

But, since the **int** and the **long int** types are implemented identically on the VAX, Sun and Pyramid computers, this feature may be safely ignored. It would be useful only if there is some possibility that the C source program might be transferred to another computer.

1.3. FLOATING-POINT CONSTANTS

Floating-point constants must fit one of the following patterns:

> *integerpart . fraction* **e** *sign exponent*
> *integerpart . fraction*
> *integerpart*   **e** *sign exponent*
> *integerpart .*   **e** *sign exponent*
> *integerpart .*
>   *. fraction* **e** *sign exponent*
>   *. fraction*

where *integerpart*, *fraction* and *exponent* represent sequences of one or more decimal digits, and *sign* represents an optional plus or minus sign. The exponent symbol *e* may be written in upper case if desired. Here are a few simple examples of floating-point constants:

> 123.4   12.   .23   2.3E5   033e+10   1e-2

     All floating-point constants are automatically stored in the computer memory in double-precision format. Thus there is no need for a special notation to represent double-length floating point constants (as is provided in FORTRAN). Of course, the fact that all the constants are kept in double-length format does not mean that all variables are too. If a variable is declared with the **float** type and an assignment statement assigns a floating-point constant to it, the value is truncated as part of the assignment operation.

1.4. CHARACTER CONSTANTS

Values of type **char** are delimited by single quote characters. Here are three straightforward examples:

> 'a'   '5'   '%'

Certain, exceptional, character constants must be written using an escape notation. A complete list of these exceptional constants is listed in Table 1.2. Finally, any character constant may be written using its *octal* equivalent. The constant is written as '\d', '\dd' or '\ddd', where *d* represents any octal digit. For example,

> '\033'

represents the ASCII escape character (which has the octal value 33 or decimal value 27).

1.5. STRING CONSTANTS

String constants are delimited with the double-quote character. For example,

> "Don't"

is one such constant. Note that a string containing just one character is not the

TABLE 1.2 Special Character Constants

`'\n'`	--	newline	(NL)
`'\t'`	--	tab	(HT)
`'\b'`	--	backspace	(BS)
`'\r'`	--	carriage return	(CR)
`'\f'`	--	formfeed	(FF)
`'\\'`	--	backslash	(\)
`'\''`	--	single quote	(')
`'\"'`	--	double quote	(")

same as a character constant. For example,

> `'X'`   and   `"X"`

have different data types and, in fact, occupy differing amounts of storage.

The type of a string constant is an array of **char**. The number of elements in the array is one greater than the number of characters contained in the string. This is because the compiler places an extra element at the end of the array which holds the value `'\000'` (the ASCII character NUL). The presence of this null byte at the end of the string is required by most of the library functions that work with strings. You, too, will find that a special value to mark the end of a string can greatly simplify programming.

The same escape combinations as listed above for character constants may be used inside strings. The escape combination (\") is needed so that strings may contain the double-quote character. When using the octal notation for characters inside the string, you will occasionally need to provide one or two leading zeros to avoid an ambiguity problem. Suppose, for example, that we wish to define a string that consists of two characters: the character with octal value 001 followed by the digit 5, say. We cannot code this string as

> `"\15"`   or as   `"\015"`

for obvious reasons. However, it can safely be coded as

> `"\0015"`

because no character requires more than 3 octal digits.

Finally, there is a provision for writing strings which do not fit onto one line of the program. If the last character on the line is a single backslash, that backslash and the newline are ignored. For example,

```
    "abcd\
efghijk"
```

is another way of writing the string constant `"abcdefghijk"`. Note that the letter *e* must be in the first column on the second line. If it were not in the first column, the string constant would contain some blank characters immediately before the letter *e*. You may split string constants across several lines, but this does not imply that you can make your string constants as long as you like. The C compilers impose a limit, albeit a fairly large limit, on the maximum number of characters in a string constant.

1.6. SIMPLE DECLARATIONS

The simplest form of declaration statement has the structure

typename   identifier-list   ;

where *typename* covers all the simple types that we have seen so far. There are some other possibilities for *typename*, but we will leave those until a later chapter. The construct *identifier-list* represents a list of variable names separated by commas. In actual fact, more complicated objects than simple variables can be intermingled in the list, but we will look at that later too.

Here is a sample group of declarations:

```
int        i, j, k;
short      flag1;
char       ch1, ch2;
int        byte_count;
short int  digit_seen,
           current_column;
```

QUESTIONS

The questions here and at the end of subsequent chapters are provided so that you can check your comprehension of the material.

1.   Is the following a valid way to write the decimal constant 9999?

```
99/* a comment */99
```

2.   What decimal values do the following integer constants have?

```
0100    -077    0xabc    -0X0F0
```

3.   How many bytes of storage does the following string occupy? (Hint: the answer is not 7.)

```
"\n\n\n"
```

4. How many bytes of storage does the following string occupy? (Note: this string is correct C.)

    " "

5. Which of the following floating-point constants is the odd one out?

    1.5e2   15e1   1500e−1   .15e4   0015e+1

6. How many bytes of storage does the following floating-point constant occupy?

    1.0e0

CHAPTER 2

ASSIGNMENTS AND EXPRESSIONS

2.1. LVALUES AND RVALUES

Before we look at the various expression operators in the C language, it is a good idea to introduce two important concepts. In C, an *lvalue* is any object or expression which can be assigned to. In other words, an *lvalue* always represents a memory location (or a register if the object is declared with the **register** attribute). Similarly, an *rvalue* represents any object or expression that may be written on the right-hand side of an assignment. The names *lvalue* and *rvalue* are, of course, just contractions of the terms *left-hand value* and *right-hand value*.

The name of a variable in a C program is both an example of an *lvalue* and of an *rvalue*. However, a constant such as 99 has only an *rvalue*. It is non-sensical to make an assignment to the constant 99 (although some early FOR-TRAN compilers were reputed to permit this!). Similarly, an expression like (I+3) is an *rvalue* but is not an *lvalue*.

The essential difference between an *lvalue* and an *rvalue* is that an *lvalue* represents a memory location whose contents may be changed. An *rvalue*, on the other hand, may only be inspected, not changed.

2.2. THE ASSIGNMENT OPERATOR

The C assignment operator is = and may be used in the same way as the assignment operator of PASCAL or FORTRAN. Here is a sample assignment statement:

```
n = 10;
```

C is a little unusual in that it also considers an assignment to be a form of *expression*. This is quite useful if you want to set two or more variables to the same value. For example, it is possible to write:

```
m = n = 10;
```

or

```
m = (n = 10);
```

They both mean the same thing. When considered as an expression, n = 10, returns the result 10 (this is the value of the expression appearing to the right of the assignment operator) and also has the side effect of changing the variable on the left-hand side, *n*, to 10.

As a final example, consider

```
i = (j = 1) + (k = 2);
```

It has the same effect as three separate assignments:

```
j = 1;
k = 2;
i = j + k;
```

As you can see, statements with assignments embedded inside expressions are not as easily readable.

By definition, the left operand for an assignment must be a *lvalue*, whereas the right operand need be only an *rvalue*.

2.3. ARITHMETIC OPERATORS

C provides the standard arithmetic operations that are found in other programming languages. The binary infix operators are

+	addition
−	subtraction
*	multiplication
/	division
%	modulus or remainder

All the above operators, except for %, may be used with *rvalue* operands of int, float and double types.[1] If / is used with two integer operands, an integer division (yielding an integer result) is performed (like the div operator of PASCAL). The % operator may only be used with integer operands. It

---

[1] One or both operands for addition and subtraction may also have *pointer* types. This will be explained in a later chapter.

returns the remainder on dividing the first operand by the second (it is similar to the mod operator of PASCAL).

The only unary arithmetic operator is −, used for negation. (No unary + operator is provided.) The − unary operator may be used with an integer or floating-point *rvalue* operand, as in the assignment

```
i = -(i + 2);
```

2.4. COMPARISON OPERATORS

The comparison operators are

==	equal
!=	not equal
<	less than
<=	less than or equal
>	greater than
>=	greater than or equal

These comparison operators may be applied to *rvalue* operands with any of the basic data types. Where necessary, automatic type coercions are performed to force both operands to the same type before the comparison is performed.

The result of a comparison is either the integer 0 (to represent *false*) or the integer 1 (to represent *true*). Thus, an assignment like

```
flag = j >= 0;
```

will cause the variable *flag* to be assigned 0 if the condition $j<0$ holds, and to be assigned 1 otherwise.

It is a common programming error to use = (assignment) instead of == (equals) in an equality comparison. Unfortunately, this error does not cause a syntax error (remember that = may be embedded in expressions) and the program simply behaves in a strange way. For example, we might accidentally write an **if** statement as

```
if ( n = 5 ) {   ... /* etc. */ }
```

and find that this statement changes *n* to 5, as well as always executing the *then* part of the *if* statement. (Any non-zero value is interpreted as *true* in this context.)

2.5. LOGICAL VALUES AND LOGICAL OPERATORS

There is no Boolean type defined in the C language. For most purposes (in an **if** statement for example), any non-zero value may be used to mean *true*. However, the integer 1 is the normal choice for representing *true*. Zero is always used to represent *false*. The results produced by the three logical operators, introduced below, and by the comparison operators are always zero or one.

If you wish to store a logical value in a variable, the data type of that variable may have any integer type. If you are not very concerned about the amount of storage required, the **int** type or **short int** type will be quite adequate. However, if you wish to achieve the ultimate in (convenient) storage efficiency, you should use the **char** type. Since C automatically converts small integers to character values and vice versa, the **char** type is eminently suitable. You can make your C programs a little more readable by including these three definitions at the beginning of a program:

```
#define Boolean char
#define TRUE   1
#define FALSE  0
```

(The hash character must be in the first column on each line.) Then you can proceed to declare variables with the type *Boolean*[2] and use the constants *TRUE* and *FALSE* in the rest of your program.

The binary infix logical operators are

    &&   logical 'and'
    || logical 'or'

and may be used with *rvalue* operands of type **int** (or of a type convertible to **int**).

These operators do not necessarily evaluate their second operands. If the left-hand operand of **&&** evaluates to 0, the **&&** operator immediately returns its zero result without inspecting or evaluating the right-hand operand. Similarly, if the left-hand operand of **||** evaluates to a non-zero value, the operator immediately returns the result 1 (meaning true). In many programming languages, both operands are evaluated before the **and** or **or** operator is applied. In PASCAL, some compilers will always cause both operands to be evaluated and other compilers may not.[3] In C, the behaviour is guaranteed and it is common to take advantage of it. For example,

```
if ( n != 0  &&  m%n == 2 ) { ... /* etc. */ }
```

can never cause a divide-by-zero error. But the equivalent statement in PASCAL is quite likely to generate that error when *n* is zero.

The logical negation (or logical inversion) operator is **!**. Its operand is an *rvalue*. If the operand is any non-zero integer, the result is 0; if the operand is zero, the result is 1. For example,

---

[2] A **typedef** definition for *Boolean* is preferable to a preprocessor definition. Details are given later in Chapter 6.

[3] The PASCAL Standard deliberately leaves the choice of implementation up to the compiler implementer.

```
flag  =  ! flag;
```

is an assignment statement that inverts a logical flag.

2.6. INCREMENT AND DECREMENT OPERATORS

The increment operator ++ adds one to its operand and the decrement operator -- subtracts one from its operand. Thus, the line

```
++n;
```

can be used as a stand-alone statement that is identical[4] in effect to

```
n = n + 1;
```

Clearly, the operand for either operator must be an *lvalue*. The data type of the operand may be any type for which the addition is meaningful.

Just as with the assignment operator, there is a result that can be used. For example,

```
m = ++n;
```

means the same as

```
m = (n = n + 1);
```

which, in turn, has the same effect as

```
n = n + 1;   m = n;
```

Similarly, --n means exactly the same as (n = n-1).

The ++ and -- operators, used above as prefix operators, are sometimes called preincrement and predecrement operators. That is, the variable used as the operand is first incremented (or decremented) and then the new value of the variable is used as the result from the expression. These two operators may also be written as postfix operators, e.g. n++ or n--, in which case, they are called the postincrement and postdecrement operators. The difference is that the result of the expression is first taken from the variable specified as the operand and then the variable is incremented (or decremented). The difference between n++ and ++n can be quite confusing. If the following line is executed

```
n = i-- * 2;
```

the effect is exactly the same as

```
n = i * 2;   i = i - 1;
```

When the postincrement or postdecrement operators are used, the increment or decrement action is simply delayed until some moment after the value of the operand variable has been used. The C language definition does not

---

[4] If, instead of *n*, we had written an *lvalue* expression that has side effects when evaluated, this expansion would be inapplicable.

define the exact time at which the increment or decrement is applied. Thus, some C expressions can have implementation dependent results. For example,

```
n = 1;   m = n++ * n++ ;
```

could result in *m* being assigned either 1 or 2. It is inadvisable for programs to contain uses of ++ or −− similar to the above.

2.7. BITWISE OPERATORS

Almost all assembly languages include instructions for "and-ing", "or-ing", "exclusive-or-ing" and shifting sequences of bits. Few high-level languages, however, have equivalent operators. C, in its role as a high-level assembly language, does provide them. The binary infix bitwise operators are

&	bitwise and
|	bitwise or
^	bitwise exclusive-or
<<	shift left
>>	shift right

For example,

```
n = n | 0x00000003;
```

could be used to force the two rightmost bits of *n* to ones. Similarly,

```
n = n & 0xfffffffc;
```

could be used to clear those same two bits to zero. And,

```
n = n ^ 0x00000003;
```

inverts just the two rightmost bits. All the other bits in the variable *n* are unaffected.

The two shifting operators shift the left operand by the number of places specified in the right operand. For example,

```
n = 1;   n = n << i;
```

would assign 2^i to the variable *n* for any value of *i* between 0 and 30

If the left operand of << or >> is an unsigned integer type, a logical shift is performed. A logical shift to the right fills vacated bit positions on the left with zeros. If the operand is a normal signed integer type, the vacated bit positions on the left are filled with copies of the sign bit. (This is known as an *arithmetic right shift.*) For left shifts, there is no difference between a logical left shift and an arithmetic left shift, they both produce the same result. The right-hand operand of << or of >> should not be negative. The effect is not defined in the C language and depends on the computer and compiler implementation that you are using.

The remaining bitwise operator, the unary operator ~ (negate), is used to invert every bit in its operand. That is, every 0 bit is changed to 1 and every 1 is changed to 0.

Novice C programmers are often confused by the difference between the **&** and **&&** operators (and between **|** and **||**). This confusion is compounded by the fact that both operators usually seem to produce the same results. For example, the **if** statement

```
if ( a > 0 && b > 0 ) {  ... /* etc. */ }
```

and the **if** statement

```
if ( a > 0 & b > 0 ) { ... /* etc. */ }
```

never behave differently (as long as *a* and *b* are simple variables). This is because both the comparisons return a result of zero or one and a bitwise *and* produces the same zero or one result as a logical (or Boolean) *and* operation. Timing the speed of the program should reveal, however, that the first form executes a little faster. The difference between the **&** and **&&** operators is revealed when an operand has a value other than zero or one, or when the evaluation of the second operand has side effects (division by zero being an extreme form of side effect). For example, the *true* clause of the following statement is always executed

```
if ( 2 && 5 ) { ... /* etc. */ }
```

whereas it is never executed if the **&** operator is used.

2.8. EXTENDED ASSIGNMENT OPERATORS

The designers of C recognized that statements similar to

```
n = n + x;
```

occur very frequently in programs and that some computers (notably the PDP-11 and VAX computers) have instructions for "in-place" addition that can be used directly. Thus, a combined addition and assignment operator, +=, was incorporated into the language. The statement,

```
n += x;
```

has exactly the same effect[5] as the preceding example.

For reasons of generality, most of the binary operators can be combined with the assignment operator in this way. (However, not all combinations can be implemented as a single machine instruction.) The complete list of allowed combinations is as follows:

+=	add to left operand
-=	subtract from left operand
*=	multiply left operand
/=	divide the left operand
%=	take remainder of left operand
&=	bitwise 'and' left operand
|=	bitwise 'or' left operand
^=	bitwise 'exclusive-or' left operand
<<=	shift left operand to left
>>=	shift left operand to right

For any such combination,

$$x \; op= \; y;$$

is defined to have exactly the same effect[5] as

$$x = (x \; op \; y);$$

For example,

```
n = 3;   n <<= 4;
```

will result in the variable n having the value 48. (A left shift by 4 places is equivalent to multiplying by 16.)

2.9. CONDITIONAL EXPRESSIONS

A conditional expression involves three subexpressions and has the form

$$expr1 \; ? \; expr2 \; : \; expr3$$

The first subexpression *expr1*, representing a logical expression, is evaluated. If the result is non-zero (recall that this is interpreted as **true**), then the second subexpression *expr2* is evaluated and its value is returned as the result of the entire conditional expression. In this circumstance, the third subexpression is not evaluated. If the first subexpression evaluates to 0, however, then the third subexpression *expr3* is evaluated and its value is returned as the final result.

As a simple example,

```
sign = i<0 ? '-' : ' ';
```

assigns the minus sign character to the variable *sign* if i is negative and assigns a blank otherwise. Of course, the same effect can be achieved with an **if** statement, as in

```
if (i<0) sign = '-'; else sign = ' ';
```

There is nothing to choose between these two versions in terms of program

---

[5] Again, this form of expansion would be incorrect if x were to be replaced by some lvalue whose evaluation has side effects. The operand x is evaluated only once.

efficiency. If, however, the object of the assignment had been more complicated, as in

```
line[index++] = i<0? '-' : ' ';
```

then the conditional expression form would usually translate into fewer machine instructions (depending on how much optimization is performed by the C compiler). Some people also consider the conditional expression form to be easier to read. On the other hand, there are people who consider it harder to read, so its use by you should be a matter of personal preference.

Unlike ALGOL60 and ALGOL68, a conditional expression may be used only as an expression. It cannot, for example, be used on the left-hand side of an assignment statement. The following statement is not legal C:

```
( (i == 0)? i : j ) = 10;
```

In other words, the result of a conditional expression is always an *rvalue* in C.

2.10. THE COMMA OPERATOR

The comma character, with two operands, is regarded as being an operator in the C language. Because few programming languages have an operator with similar properties, there is no name for this operator other than *comma operator*. The following assignment statement is silly, but quite legal C:

```
i = ( j+1, 2 );
```

The statement assigns a value to *i*, where the value being assigned is the result of the comma operator. The operator evaluates its left operand and ignores the result. Then it evaluates the right operand and uses that value as its own result. So our example is just a silly way of assigning 2 to *i*.

There are more sensible uses of the comma operator, particularly in controlling **for** loops. This is because the evaluation of the left operand may have side effects. However, the code is likely to be less readable than code that does not contain any uses of the comma operator. If you do use the comma operator, you should be careful to parenthesize the expression, because the comma operator has the lowest precedence of all the operators. (The meaning of *precedence* is explained in the next section of this chapter.)

2.11. TABLE OF OPERATORS

Table 2.1 shows all the operators in the C language, including several that have not yet been mentioned. These new operators have uses in pointer handling, type coercions and the like. They will be explained in later chapters. Italicized words in the "Syntax" column of the table indicate various constructs of the C language. The term *rvalue* denotes an expression, including elementary expressions like variable names or constants. The term *expr-list* represents a list of zero or more rvalues, separated by commas. And as explained earlier, an *lvalue* represents a variable or expression that may legally appear on the left-hand side

TABLE 2.1 C Operators

Precedence	Syntax	Meaning
15 L	*rvalue* (*expr-list*)	function invocation
	rvalue [*rvalue*]	array indexing
	rvalue -> *field*	pointer qualification
	lvalue . *field*	structure qualification
14 R	! *rvalue*	logical negation
	˜ *rvalue*	bitwise complement
	++ *lvalue*	pre-increment
	-- *lvalue*	pre-decrement
	lvalue ++	post-increment
	lvalue --	post-decrement
	- *rvalue*	arithmetic negation
	(*type*) *rvalue*	type cast
	* *rvalue*	pointer dereferencing
	& *lvalue*	take address of
	sizeof *rvalue*	take size of
13 L	*rvalue* * *rvalue*	multiplication
	rvalue / *rvalue*	division
	rvalue % *rvalue*	remainder
12 L	*rvalue* + *rvalue*	addition
	rvalue - *rvalue*	subtraction
11 L	*rvalue* << *rvalue*	shift left
	rvalue >> *rvalue*	shift right
10 L	*rvalue* < *rvalue*	compare less than
	rvalue <= *rvalue*	compare less or equal
	rvalue > *rvalue*	compare greater than
	rvalue >= *rvalue*	compare greater or equal
9 L	*rvalue* == *rvalue*	compare equal
	rvalue != *rvalue*	compare not equal
8 L	*rvalue* & *rvalue*	bitwise **and**
7 L	*rvalue* ^ *rvalue*	bitwise **exclusive or**
6 L	*rvalue* | *rvalue*	bitwise **or**
5 L	*rvalue* && *rvalue*	logical **and**
4 L	*rvalue* || *rvalue*	logical **or**
3 L	*rvalue* ? *rvalue* : *rvalue*	conditional expression
2 R	*lvalue* = *rvalue*	assignment
	lvalue += *rvalue*	add and assign, *etc.*
1 L	*rvalue* , *rvalue*	comma

of an assignment. The word *type* signifies the name of some C data type, like **int**, and *field* stands for the name of a field in a structure (**struct** type).

To understand how complicated expressions are decoded by the C compiler, it is necessary to introduce two concepts known as the *associativity* and the *precedence level* of an operator. The importance of the precedence level concept is illustrated by any expression that contains an unfamiliar operator, such as

        a << i + 1

Does this expression mean that the value of *a* should be shifted left by *i* binary places and then one added to the result, or does it mean that *a* should be shifted left by one plus *i* binary places? In other words, should the shift be performed first or should the addition be performed first? The precedence levels of the two operators involved answer this question. The rule is that operators are evaluated in order of their precedence levels, with the highest numbered levels being evaluated first. Therefore our expression gives the same result as

        a << (i + 1)

because shifting is at level 11, while addition is at level 12. If we had actually wanted to perform the shift first, we should have placed parentheses around the appropriate subexpression. That is, we should have written

        (a << i) + 1

This illustrates an important fact, that parentheses can always be used to force a particular order of evaluation. Rather than memorizing the table of operators, the easiest policy is to use parentheses liberally. There is little point in risking having a program go wrong just to avoid typing a few extra characters. As you become experienced with the C language, you may gain enough confidence to start dropping some of the superfluous parentheses. However, even programs written by professional C programmers contain redundant parentheses.

The other sort of information, associativity, is needed to know how the C compiler decodes complicated expressions involving two or more operators with the same precedence level. For example, the expression

        a - b + c

is normally understood to mean that the value of *a* minus *b* is first computed and then *c* is added to the result. In other words, the left operation is performed first. The letter *L* after the precedence level in the table of operators means *left-associative* or *evaluate from left to right*.

The letter *R* after the precedence level in the table, however, indicates that the operator is *right-associative*. Here is an example of right-to-left evaluation:

        a = b += 2;

Because the operations involved are right-associative, this statement has the same effect as

```
a = (b += 2);
```

which, in turn, has the same effect as the two statements

```
b += 2;   a = b;
```

All the unary operators are evaluated from right to left. Here is another example of right-to-left evaluation, this time involving some unary operators:

```
! * p++
```

This expression is decoded to mean that the pointer p is first incremented, then the original pointer value is dereferenced and finally the resulting value is logically negated. That is, the expression is equivalent to

```
! ( *( p++ ) )
```

QUESTIONS

1.   What value is assigned to i by the following statement?

```
i = 1 << 2 >> 1 ;
```

2.   The effect of the following statement is undefined because the increment and decrement operations can be applied in different orders. If i has the initial value 2, what result values are possible for i ?

```
i = i++ * --i + i++ ;
```

3.   Almost all binary operations may be combined with the assignment operator to produce another kind of C operator. For example, % may be combined to give the operator %=. Why do you think the comparison operators cannot be combined with the assignment operator in C?

4.   Insert parentheses into the following expression so that its value does not depend on the precedence levels or associativities of any of the operators involved.

```
x |= *y++ >= a - b & 1;
```

5.   Does the statement

```
*++ip += 3;
```

have the same effect as

```
*(ip+1) = *(ip+2) + 3;   ip += 2;
```

or as

```
ip += 1;   *ip = *ip + 3;
```

or as something different?

CHAPTER 3

EXECUTABLE STATEMENTS

3.1. SIMPLE STATEMENTS AND BLOCKS

Any expression can become a statement by appending a semicolon to it. Indeed, this is exactly how an assignment statement is obtained. If we write

        (i = 1)

we have an expression (with the value 1) that has the side effect of assigning 1 to i whenever the expression is evaluated. If, however, we write

        i = 1;

we have an assignment statement. If you like, you can think of the semicolon as being an operator which means, "Evaluate the expression on the left and throw away the result." Of course, this rule implies that a statement like

        1+2;

is legal, and indeed it is. It simply does nothing when executed.

Other than simple assignments, statements like

        i++;   and   i--;

occur frequently in programs. As a general rule, a statement must have some side effect to be useful. The increment and decrement operators do have the side effects of changing the value of some variable.

When several statements need to be grouped together (as required for **if** statements), curly braces are used. For example,

        { i = j * k;   k = 0; }

is a group containing two statements. Note that a semicolon is required after the second statement, **k** = 0. This is because there is a value (zero) which needs to be *thrown away*. No semicolon appears after a right brace. And this absence can be justified by noting that there is no residual value to be discarded.

Statement groups may, optionally, begin with a group of declarations. Identifiers declared inside a group are only visible within that group. Here is a simple example that uses an embedded declaration:

```
n = read_number();
{          /* force n to a multiple of 10 */
           int remdr;
           remdr = n % 10;
           n -= remdr;
}
print_number( n );
```

Outside the bracketed group of statements, the identifier *remdr* is unknown and cannot be used (unless there happens to be a declaration for another variable with the same name).

3.2. IF STATEMENTS

An **if** statement is written in the form

```
if ( expression )
    statement1
```

or in the form

```
if ( expression )
    statement1
else
    statement2
```

The expression after the keyword **if** is evaluated and if it is non-zero, *statement1* is executed. Otherwise, *statement2* (if it is provided) is executed. Both statements 1 and 2 may themselves be **if** statements. If there is any ambiguity as to which **else** associates with which **if** statement, it is resolved by matching an **else** with the closest unmatched **if**. (This is the usual rule, adopted in PASCAL and PL/I for instance.) If you want to force a different matching, you should enclose the nested **if** in curly braces.

Here is a simple example of an **if** statement:

```
if ( i < n )
    i++;
else {
    n++;
    i = n;
}
```

Note that the semicolon after `i++` is required.

Here is a second example, showing nested **if** statements:

```
if ( i < n ) {
    if ( i != 0 )
        i--;
} else
    if ( n != 0 )
        n--;
```

Without the braces, the group of statements would have a different meaning.

3.3. WHILE LOOPS

The structure of a **while** loop is

```
while ( expression )
    statement
```

PASCAL programmers should take note that there is no **do** keyword after the controlling expression. Otherwise, the **while** loop in C is used in just the same way as in PASCAL and other programming languages. The expression is evaluated; if it is non-zero the statement is executed, then the expression is re-evaluated and so on. The body of the loop may, of course, be a group of statements enclosed in curly braces. Even if the loop body consists of only a single statement, it is probably better to use braces because the extent of the loop is then made immediately apparent to the eye.

As an example, here is a use of a **while** loop for searching an array:

```
found = i = 0;
while( i < NUM_ELEMENTS && !found ) {
    if (arr[i] == value)
        found++;
    else
        i++;
}
```

3.4. DO-WHILE LOOPS

The normal **while** loop performs its test at the beginning, a fact which implies that zero iterations through the loop body may occur. The **do-while** form of loop places the test at the bottom, so that at least one iteration through the loop body must occur. The **do-while** loop corresponds to the PASCAL **repeat-until** loop, but with the difference that the sense of the controlling test is reversed.

The general structure is

```
do
      statement
while ( expression )
```

The statement which forms the loop body is executed and then the expression after the keyword **while** is evaluated. If the expression is non-zero (implying *true*), the statement is re-executed and so on. Braces must be used to enclose the loop body if the body consists of several statements. As with the **while-do** form of loop, it is good practice to always use these curly braces.

The following example of a **do-while** loop counts input characters excluding spaces and line-feeds:

```
do {
    ch = getchar();
    if (ch != ' ' && ch != '\n')
        chcnt++;
} while( ch != EOF );
```

3.5. FOR LOOPS

The **for** loop in C corresponds to the PASCAL **for** loop, but is more general. The general syntactic structure is

```
for ( expr1; expr2; expr3 )
      statement
```

where *expr1* is an expression that has the side effect of performing loop initialization, *expr2* is an expression that performs a test to determine whether the loop should be repeated, and *expr3* is an expression that has the side effect of performing loop re-initialization (typically an action like incrementing a loop index variable). The general **for** loop form, above, is defined to be exactly equivalent in effect to

```
expr1;
while ( expr2 )  {
    statement
    expr3;
}
```

For example, a **for** loop to step the index variable *i* through the values 1 to 10 and print these values and their squares could be coded as

```
for ( i = 1; i <= 10; i++ )  {
    printf( "%d  %d\n", i, i*i );
}
```

The C **for** loop is very general because the three controlling expressions are not restricted in any way and may have arbitrary side effects. As further extensions, any or all of *expr1*, *expr2* or *expr3* may be omitted. If *expr1* or *expr2* is omitted, the corresponding expression in the expansion of the loop is simply omitted. If *expr2* is omitted, the value 1 (for *true*) is substituted in the expansion.

If all three expressions are omitted, the loop will repeat forever. Such a loop would presumably contain a construct such as **break, goto** or **return** to actually exit from the loop. A small example appears in the next section of this chapter.

Sometimes a loop has two index variables. As a trivial example, consider the problem of reversing the order of elements in an array. We can certainly make do with one index, but logically we need one index counting upwards while a second index counts downwards. The general nature of the **for** statement makes it easy to program such a loop:

```
/* Reverse order of N element array */
for( i=0, j=N-1;  i<j;  i++, j-- ) {
    temp = a[i];
    a[i] = a[j];
    a[j] = temp;
}
```

This example code also illustrates one of the few genuine uses of the comma operator.

3.6. BREAK AND CONTINUE IN LOOPS

The **break** statement may be used to exit a loop from within the loop body. Executing a **break** statement inside a loop simply causes control to be transferred to the statement that immediately follows the bottom of the loop. Only one level of loop nesting can be exited with **break**.

The **continue** statement has an opposite effect. When used inside **while** or **do-while** loops, it causes control to be transferred to the top of the loop. When the **continue** statement is used inside a **for** loop, control passes to the loop re-initialization expression. In the expansion of the **for** loop given in the previous section of this chapter, control is transferred to the code for *expr3*.

The **break** and **continue** statements can handle most situations in which a **goto** statement might be used in other programming languages. However, they cannot be used to break out of a doubly-nested loop and so a case can still be made that the **goto** statement is occasionally useful in C.

A small coding example that illustrates the use of both **break** and **continue** statements follows:

```
/* count lines and non-blank characters */
for( ; ; ) {
    int ch;
    ch = getchar();
    if (ch == ' ' || ch == '\t')
        continue;
    if (ch == '\n') {
        line_cnt++;
        continue;
    }
    if (ch == EOF) break;
    char_cnt++;
}
```

3.7. SWITCH STATEMENTS

The **switch** statement is the analogue of the **case** statement in PASCAL. Its general structure is

```
switch ( expression ) {
case constant :
        statement-list
case constant :
        statement-list
case constant :
        statement-list

            .
            .
            .

default :
        statement-list
}
```

The constants used after the keyword **case** must be constants that have the

char type, **int** type or any enumerated type. When the **switch** statement is executed, the selecting expression is first evaluated. Control is then transferred to the **case** label which has the matching value. If no **case** label has a matching value and if a **default** label is provided, control is passed to the **default** label. If no value matches and if no **default** label is provided, control is simply passed to the end of the entire **switch** statement.

The **default** label is shown above as being the last label. Being last is not a requirement; the label may be placed anywhere within the **switch** statement. Similarly, the **case** labels may be given in any order.

When control is passed to a **case** label or **default** label, the statements appearing after that label are executed. After these statements have been executed, control normally passes to the statement-list provided for the following case (if there is one). Sometimes, this *drop-through* effect is desired. (One of the questions at the end of the chapter illustrates the *drop-through* nature of case clauses.) In most cases, however, the effect is unwanted, and therefore the last statement in each statement-list is usually a **break** statement. When used inside a **switch** statement, **break** causes control to exit immediately from the **switch** statement. A **break** statement at the end of the last clause in the **switch** statement is optional, but it is probably wise to include it. Including it reduces the chance of making an error if you later add cases to the **switch** statement.

Unlike the **case** statement of PASCAL, it is not possible to give a list of values or a range of values on a C **case** label. If one wishes to execute the same statements for several values of the selecting expression, several **case** labels may have to precede the statements.

Figure 3.1 contains a basic example of the use of a **switch** statement. The function *print_width* calculates the maximum number of print columns that the argument string *s* would occupy if it were printed. The problem is complicated by the assumption that the string can contain backspaces, tab characters, line feeds and carriage returns.

The **for** loop steps through all the characters in the argument string. All ordinary characters are covered by the **default** label of the **switch**. When an ordinary character is printed, it occupies one column and therefore the column position is incremented. On the other hand, a backspace reduces the column position by one. A tab character advances the column to the next tab stop. Like much UNIX software, our code assumes that there are tab stops at every eighth column. And since 8 is a power of two, we can use the masking operator **&** to truncate a number to a multiple of 8. (The expression ˜7 produces a bit string containing ones in all but the rightmost three positions.)

FIGURE 3.1. An Example of a switch Statement

```
/* A function to determine how wide a screen or
   printer needs to be if string 's' is output */
int print_width( s )
char s[];
{
    int  width, column, i;

    column = width = 0;

    for( i=0;  s[i] != '\0'; i++ ) {
        if (column > width) width = column;
        switch ( s[i] ) {

        case '\n':   /* line-feed       */
        case '\r':   /* carriage-return */
        case '\f':   /* form-feed       */
            column = 0;
            break;

        case '\b':   /* backspace */
            if (column > 0) column--;
            break;

        case '\t':   /* tab */
            column = (column + 8) & ~7;
            break;

        default:        /* other characters */
            column++;

        }
    }
    return( width+1 );
}
```

3.8. GOTO STATEMENTS

Any executable statement may be prefixed by a label, which consists of an identifier followed by a colon. An example is

```
incr:  x += 10;
```

A **goto** statement elsewhere in the program may be used to transfer control to that label, as in

```
goto incr;
```

The only restriction on the use of **goto** statements is that control must be passed to a label within the same function. It is, for example, permissible to jump into the middle of a loop from outside (but probably unwise to do so).

QUESTIONS

1.   What is the value of i after the following **if** statement is executed?

```
i = 0;
if (1 > 2)
    if ('a' > 'b') i = 1;
  else i = 2;
```

2.   How many lines of output does the following loop print? (Each call of *puts* prints one line.)

```
j = 20;
for( i = 1;  i <= j;  i++ ) {
    puts( "Hello Folks!" );  j--;
}
```

3.   Is the following a legal statement in C? If so, what does it do?

```
-99 ;
```

4.   How would you set up a **for** loop so that the control variable i takes on the values 1, 4, 9, 16, 25 ... 256 (i.e. the squares of the integers up to 16 squared)?

5.   Using the function in Figure 3.1 as a guide, can you program a function that modifies its argument string so that all overstriking of characters is eliminated? For example, the character string "X\bY" should be coalesced to just "Y" because Y would print on top of X. (The *col* program, available as a UNIX command, performs a similar function.)

6.   What mathematical function is computed by *fn* below?

```
int fn( n ) int n; {
    int r;   r = 1;
    switch( n ) {
      case 7:   r *= 7;
      case 6:   r *= 6;
      case 5:   r *= 5;
      case 4:   r *= 4;
      case 3:   r *= 3;
      case 2:   r *= 2;
    }
    return( r );
}
```

CHAPTER 4

COMPOUND DATA TYPES

4.1. ARRAYS

A one-dimensional array (often called a *vector*) is declared by simply giving size information after the array name in a declaration. For example,

```
int  a[20], b[5];
```

declares *a* to be an array of 20 integers and *b* to be an array of 5 integers. Somewhat surprisingly to C beginners, however, the first element of an array is defined to have the subscript position 0. This means that the elements of *a*, above, have subscripts ranging from 0 to 19.

Vectors may be accessed with normal subscript notation. For example, the array *a* declared above, could be initialized to hold the first 20 Fibonacci numbers with the following code:

```
a[0] = a[1] = 1;
for ( i = 2; i < 20; i++ ) {
    a[i] = a[i-2] + a[i-1];
}
```

Two-dimensional arrays (and higher dimensions) are formed by taking arrays of arrays (and so on). For example,

```
int  table[10][5];
```

and elements of such an array can be accessed by writing separate subscripts after the array name, as in the statement

```
table[i][j]++ ;
```

If we were to write just

```
table[i]
```

the result would be a vector with 5 elements. This vector can be understood as being the *i*-th row of the table. When the second subscript is supplied, as in

```
table[i][j]
```

the result is an element of type **int**. It is this element which is incremented in our original example.

Unlike PASCAL, PL/I and many other languages, C does not permit arrays to be assigned. The C compiler would complain at the following code sequence:

```
int vec1[10], vec2[10];

/* The following statement is illegal */
vec1 = vec2;
```

If you want to copy one array into another, you must provide a loop to copy one element at a time or you must call a library function that performs block copies. The following code will perform the desired copy:

```
for( i=0; i<10; i++ ) {
    vec1[i] = vec2[i];
}
```

So will the following call to the appropriate library function:

```
bcopy( vec2, vec1, sizeof(vec1) );
```

Similarly, two arrays cannot be directly compared for equality or inequality. Again, you must either code a suitable loop or use a call to a library function that performs block memory comparisons, as in:

```
test = bcmp( vec1, vec2, sizeof(vec1) );
```

A common method of accessing array elements is through pointers. Pointers are discussed in the next section.

4.2. POINTER TYPES

Pointer variables hold values which are addresses of data objects in the main memory of the computer. The declarations

```
int  *ip;
char *cp1, *cp2;
```

declare three pointer variables. The first, *ip*, is declared to be a pointer to objects of type **int**; the other two, *cp1* and *cp2*, are pointers to objects of type **char**. When simply declared like this, these pointer variables are not initially pointing at any data objects at all; that is, they do not hold valid memory addresses.

One means of giving a value to a pointer is by assigning the address of a data object. The type of this data object should match the type declared for the pointer variable (otherwise the C compiler will warn of a possible error in the program). To obtain the address of a data object, we may use the unary operator **&**. The following C program fragment could be used to give values to *ip*, *cp1*, and *cp2*:

```
int    n;
char   linebuffer[10];
    .

    .
ip  = &n;
cp1 = &linebuffer[0];
cp2 = &linebuffer[4];
/* Now ip holds the address of n, while */
/* cp1 refers to the 1st element, and   */
/* cp2 to the 5th element of the array. */
```

To help visualize the states of pointers and other variables, it is often a good idea to draw a diagram. Figure 4.1 shows such a diagram. It represents the state of memory after the pointer assignment statements, above, have been executed. Memory locations corresponding to variables and array elements are drawn as boxes. Simple values (such as an integer or character value) can be written inside the boxes. Pointer values are shown as arrows, directed at the memory locations to which the pointers currently refer.

FIGURE 4.1. Pointers

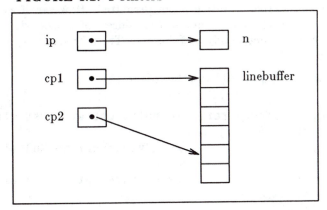

To return to the pointer assignment operations in our example, the assignment to *cp1* is unnecessarily complicated. The C language treats the name of an array, used without a subscript, as a pointer to the first element of that array. We can rewrite that assignment as

```
cp1 = linebuffer;
```

The array name *linebuffer*, standing alone, has the same status in C as a constant; it is not an lvalue and cannot be used on the left-hand side of an assignment operator. Because character strings are treated as arrays of **char**, an assignment such as

```
cp2 = "A String";
```

is also quite acceptable. This does not copy a character string. The pointer variable, *cp2* is merely assigned the address of the first character in the string.

When a pointer variable has been given the address of some data object, that object may be accessed by dereferencing the pointer. The dereferencing operator is a unary asterisk, *****, appearing before the pointer value. Thus, if the the situation depicted in Figure 4.1 currently exists, writing ***ip** would be the same as writing the identifier *n*. For example, the assignment

```
*ip = 5;
```

has exactly the same effect as

```
n = 5;
```

Pointer values are simply addresses in the computer memory, and addresses are implemented as integers in the computer hardware. It is reasonable, therefore, to expect that some operations applicable to integers may also apply to pointers. Two straightforward operations are assignment and comparison. Pointer values may be assigned and they may be compared. All the comparison operators are legal. What about the addition and subtraction of pointers? If we add two memory addresses together, we do not get anything very sensible and so this operation is not permitted. However, if we add a constant, say 1, to an address, we obtain the address of a succeeding location in memory and this is a potentially useful effect. The following is a legal fragment of C program:

```
char   *cp1, linebuffer[100];
        .
        .
cp1 = linebuffer;   /* point cp1 at first element */
*cp1 = 'A';
cp1++;              /* advance cp1 to 2nd element */
*cp1 = 'B';
cp1++;              /* advance cp1 to 3rd element */
*cp1 = 'C';
cp1++;
```

The state of memory after executing these statements is shown in Figure 4.2. Our code illustrates how a character string may be constructed from individual character values. The variable *cp1* always points at the array element to place the next character of the string. To reduce the number of C statements, it is usual to combine dereferencing with postincrementing. Thus, the next character can be appended to the string with a statement like

```
*cp1++ = 'D';
```

Eventually, after we have stored the last character into the string, a null byte must be appended to terminate the string. That is, the statement

```
*cp1 = '\0';
```

is needed. (There is no need to increment *cp1* if no more characters are to be added to the end of the string.)

FIGURE 4.2. Constructing a String

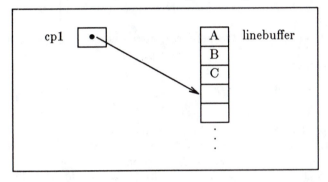

Adding one to the memory address held in variable *cp1*, above, simply gives the memory address of the next array element. As a general rule in C, the addition of one to a pointer always has the effect of advancing the pointer to the next element of an array. This effect is quite independent of the size of the elements of the array. (If the array is an array of **int**s, and *ip* is declared as a pointer to **int**, then an action like `ip++` actually causes 4 to be added to the memory address held in *ip*.) Thus, when an expression with one of the forms

$$pointer + integer \quad \text{or} \quad integer + pointer$$

is evaluated, the integer is implicitly multiplied by the size of the data object referenced by the pointer before being added. The result type is a pointer of the same type as before. An expression with the form

$$pointer - integer$$

works similarly.

As well as allowing addition and subtraction between pointers and integers, C permits the subtraction of one pointer value from another. We can subtract a pointer from another pointer of the same type and yield an integer. Thus, if *p1* and *p2* point at different elements in the same array, `p1-p2` gives the number of array elements lying between the positions referenced by *p1* and *p2*. This subtraction operation is sensible only if the pointers do refer to elements within the same array. If they refer to other kinds of objects or to elements of different arrays, the results are undefined.

There is an equivalence between pointer dereferencing and the action of subscripting an array. If an unsubscripted array name, like *linebuffer*, is considered to be a pointer to the first element of the array, then

```
*linebuffer    and    linebuffer[0]
```

must mean the same thing. It then follows that

```
*(linebuffer+5)    and    linebuffer[5]
```

also mean the same thing. In fact, array indexing is considered to be a redundant concept in C and is provided only because it is a convenient notation. In general, the construction

arrayname [*expr*]

is defined to mean

(arrayname + expr)

As already mentioned, there is a very close correspondence between arrays and pointers. This will seem to be particularly true when we look at dynamically allocated arrays. It frequently happens that we do not know how many elements an array should have until the program has begun execution. If we are programming in PASCAL or FORTRAN, we would probably declare the array with the largest conceivable size and then use a small part of the array. In C we can allocate storage for the array at execution time and give it exactly the right number of elements. The fragment of code shown in Figure 4.3 allocates an array with *n* elements, where *n* is a value read from input. Notice that after storage for the array has been allocated by *calloc*, we can refer to this array with the same notation as for any other array in the program.

The code in Figure 4.3 uses a few features of C for the first time. Two functions, *printf* and *scanf*, are standard functions in the library of Input-Output routines. *Printf* has an obvious effect, though it has rather more power than our usage might suggest. *Scanf* is used for the input of data items. Both functions will be explained more fully in Chapter 7.

Storage for arrays is allocated by the system function *calloc*. The first argument to *calloc* is the number of elements in the array; the second argument is the size (in bytes) of one array element. The result from *calloc* is a pointer to a fresh area of memory that is large enough to accommodate the array. The funny construction in front of *calloc*, namely

```
(float *)
```

is known as a *type cast*. Because *calloc* simply returns the address of a block of

FIGURE 4.3. Dynamic Array Allocation

```
int    n;        /* number of elements in array */
float *f;        /* pointer to 1st element of array */
int    i;
    .
    .
for( ; ; ) {
    printf( "How many elements do you want?\n" );
    scanf( "%d", &n );   /* read a decimal number */
    if (n > 0 && n <= 10000) break;
    printf( "Invalid input, try again...\n\n" );
}
f = (float *)calloc( n, sizeof(float) );

/* Initialize the array */
for( i=0; i<n; i++ ) {
    f[i] = 1.0;
}
    .
    .
```

storage without regard to its data type, the C compiler should be given this information. The cast tells the compiler to convert the returned result (whose data type, in the absence of any declarations to the contrary, is **int**) to the data type "pointer to float." Without the cast, the program still works but the C compiler would generate a warning message. A more complete explanation of *casts* is given later in this chapter.

The second argument to *calloc* uses another new feature of C – the **sizeof** operator. When applied to the name of a type, like **float**, it returns the number of bytes that an object with that type occupies.

Two examples of working with arrays and pointers will close this section. The first example copies one array of integers to another:

```
int array1[100], array2[100];
register int *ip1, *ip2, cnt;
    .
    .
```

```
/* copy contents of array2 into array1 */
ip1 = array1;   ip2 = array2;
for (cnt = 0; cnt < 100; cnt++) {
        *ip1++ = *ip2++;
}
```

The second example copies a character string constant into a character array:

```
char string[100], *sp, *tp;
             .
             .
             .
/* point tp at the target array,
        sp at the source string */
tp = string;
sp = "The Source String";
while ( *sp != '\0' ) {
        *tp++ = *sp++;
}
*tp = '\0';
```

In this second example, we assume the C convention that there is a null character (i.e. a byte containing zero) at the end of every string. The final assignment
is to put this null byte at the end of our copy of the string. It is possible to
recode the string copying logic more economically than shown above. The
entire copying code in the last four lines of the above example can be replaced
by the single line:

```
while( *tp++ = *sp++ );
```

Note that the body of this loop is an empty statement. It works because the
while condition is an assignment expression which evaluates to the value just
assigned. As long as we are copying non-zero bytes, the **while** expression is
considered to be *true*. As soon as a zero byte has been copied, the expression is
considered to be *false* and the loop terminates.

On the other hand, the shortest way and the most readable way of coding
the string copy operation is

```
strcpy( string, "The Source String" );
```

This code uses a library function for copying strings. This one line of C code
replaces all six executable statements in our original example. Similarly, the
code for copying the array of integers in the preceding example could, and
probably should, be replaced by

```
bcopy( array2, array1, sizeof(array1) );
```

4.3. STRUCTURES

Structures in C are equivalent to records in PASCAL. A structure is a data aggregate, possibly containing data values of many different types. Structures may contain arrays or even other structures. The following is a sample declaration of a structure:

```
struct namedata {
        char name[35];
        char address[100];
        int  age; } ;
struct namedata employeelist[500], *emplptr;
```

There are actually two declarations here, both beginning with the keyword **struct**. The first declaration serves only to introduce a name, *namedata*, for this particular structure layout. This identifier, which has a role somewhat analogous to a type name in PASCAL, is called a *structure tag*. The second declaration uses the structure tag to declare some data objects. It declares both an array of these structures and a pointer to structures of this type.

It is possible to combine the two declarations into one, as follows:

```
struct namedata {
        char name[35];
        char address[100];
        int  age;
    } employeelist[500], *emplptr;
```

It is also legal to omit the structure tag from this form of declaration. However, it would not then be possible to declare more objects with the same structure later in the program.

Fields of a structure may be accessed with so-called *dot* notation. This notation should be familiar to PASCAL or PL/I programmers. Thus, we might initialize one of the elements of the *employeelist* array as follows:

```
strcpy( employeelist[5].name, "Ms. Joan Jones" );
employeelist[5].age = 27;
strcpy( employeelist[5].address,
                    "102-2222 Rainy Blvd.\n\
Vancouver\nB.C. V6J 2X5\n" );
```

Similarly, if *emplptr* is pointing at some element in the *employeelist* array, we could access fields in that element with code similar to

```
(*emplptr).age = 43;
```

The parentheses are necessary to override the precedence levels of the dereferencing operator and dot operator. Without the parentheses, the C compiler would expect to find a field named *age* in the variable named *emplptr* and then it would want to dereference the contents of that field. Fortunately, C provides an equivalent, but neater, notation. This preceding assignment can be rewritten as

```
emplptr -> age = 2;
```

PASCAL programmers can interpret this arrow symbol, ->, as being equivalent to the two operators, ↑. , appearing consecutively.[1]

Just as in PASCAL, structures may be assigned and they may be passed as arguments to functions. A function may also return a structure as its result. (This is a facility that is not provided in standard PASCAL, though it is allowed by the Berkeley PASCAL compiler.) Using the employeelist array declared earlier, we can write assignments such as

```
employeelist[10] = employeelist[11];
*emplptr = employeelist[0];
```

There is no equivalent of the PASCAL **with** statement in C. If we want to reduce the amount of code that we must write when accessing several fields in a structure, we must use pointers. The code to initialize the fifth element of the *employeelist* array can be rewritten in this manner:

```
emplptr = &( employeelist[5] );
strcpy( emplptr->name, "Ms. Joan Jones" );
emplptr->age = 27;
strcpy( emplptr->address,
        "102-2222 Rainy Blvd.\n\
Vancouver\nB.C. V1J 2X5\n" );
```

Since structures may contain pointers to structures, we can create *recursive* or *self-referential* data structures. The simplest example of this concept is a linked list. If we needed a list of real numbers, we could declare the list element structure and two list pointer variables as follows:

```
struct listelement {
        float value;
        struct listelement *next; } ;
struct listelement *headptr, *tempptr;
```

To be able to build up the list, we need to be able to obtain storage for new elements as required. We could certainly declare a large array of these structures and use it as a storage pool. However, it is probable that most of the array would remain unused. Therefore, it is preferable that we should dynamically allocate storage for elements as needed. Previously, we used *calloc* to dynamically allocate storage. The *calloc* is tailored specially for allocating array storage and is inappropriate for our present need. To allocate storage for a single structure, the *malloc* function should be used. The single argument to

---

[1] The up-arrow has to be entered as a *carat* symbol, ⌃, in most PASCAL implementations.

malloc is an integer that specifies the amount of storage, in bytes, to be allocated. We can build a list in a manner similar to the following:

```
float r;
       .
       .
       .
headptr = 0;
for ( r = 0.0;  r <= 1.0e2;  r += 1.5 ) {
    tempptr = (struct listelement *)
              malloc(sizeof(struct listelement));
    tempptr->value = r;
    tempptr->next = headptr;
    headptr = tempptr;
}
```

The state of memory in the middle of the fourth iteration of the loop is shown in Figure 4.4. The diagram shows the state immediately after the call of *malloc* and the assignment to *tempptr* has been performed. The next three statements in the loop body set the *value* field of the new structure (the structure referenced by *tempptr*); link the new structure to the front of the list; and then change *headptr* to make it refer to the new structure.

FIGURE 4.4. Building a Linked List

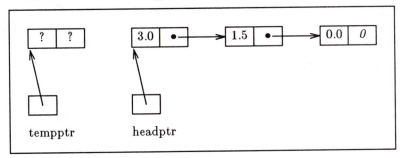

There is an important point to be covered in the example code. We are assigning an integer (zero) to a pointer variable. The assignment of zero to a pointer, an apparent exception to the type rules, is explicitly permitted by the C compiler. An attempt to assign any other integer constant (or even an integer variable) will cause a warning message to be printed. The integer value 0 is used to indicate a null pointer, and is used in the same way as **nil** in PASCAL or **null** in PL/I. There are no implementation problems with using zero since no data object can have memory address zero in the computer. Also, zero is a convenient value to test for. For example, we could traverse the linked-list, created above, to find its length in the following way:

```
tempptr = headptr;
len = 0;
while ( tempptr != 0 ) {
    len++;
    tempptr = tempptr->next;
}
```

However, the use of zero as a null pointer value does not stand out in the same way as a keyword would and may even be non-portable when transferring a program to another computer. The identifier *NULL* is conventionally used to represent the null pointer value in C programs. Of course, *NULL* must be defined to be the integer zero somewhere in the program. You could insert the preprocessor definition

```
#define NULL 0
```

near the beginning of the program. However, such a definition is automatically included in any program that uses the standard package of input-output functions, "stdio.h". Therefore, you will rarely see an explicit definition for *NULL* in any program.

It is sometimes necessary to have two kinds of structures in a program, where each structure contains a pointer to the other kind of structure. Since one structure must be declared before the other, we must use a structure tag identifier before it has been declared. The C language allows such a forward reference as long as the size of the structure does not need to be known. A pair of structure definitions that refer to each other is shown in Figure 4.5.

A diagram showing how just a few of these structures might be interrelated appears in Figure 4.6. Presumably, there would be a head pointer (not shown) referring to the first *person_info* structure in the list of persons. We have cheated slightly in this diagram. There are several strings, such as `"Chevrolet"`, which we have written directly inside boxes. If you examine the declarations of the structures, however, you will see that the structures contain only pointers to the strings (not the strings themselves). Therefore, a perfectly accurate storage diagram should show one or more separate character arrays for the strings and pointers into these arrays should be drawn.

It is easy to imagine much more complicated networks of structures and pointers being constructed. For example, we add extra pointer fields to the *car_info* record so that all cars with the same make are linked into lists, all cars of the same model year are linked together, etc.

A structure definition is nothing more than a template for accessing a block of contiguous memory locations. No memory is actually allocated for the structure unless an object with the structure type is declared in the program or unless the program explicitly allocates memory with a function like *malloc*. The fields of a structure have addresses within a block of storage allocated to the

FIGURE 4.5. Self-Referential Structures

```
/* Each 'car_info' structure contains information
   about one car.  Each 'person_info' structure
   contains information about one person.
   A 'car_info' structure contains pointers to the
   current owner and the previous owner.
   A 'person_info' structure contains a pointer to
   the current car owned by this person, and a
   pointer to the next person (so that 'person_info'
   structures are linked to form a list).         */

struct car_info {
        char    *make, *model, *colour;
        int     model_year;
        struct person_info *current_owner,
                           *previous_owner;
    };

struct person_info {
        char    *last_name, *first_name, sex;
        short   age;
        struct car_info     *car_owned;
        struct person_info *next_person;
    }
```

structure. These addresses, which are relative to the address of the start of the block of memory, are commonly called *offsets*. These offsets are calculated by the compiler so that each field has a size suitable for its data type. Storage for fields in a structure is allocated in the same order that the fields are declared. For example, the fields of the *person_info* structure defined in Figure 4.5 have the following sizes and offsets on the VAX, Sun and Pyramid computers (these numbers may be different on other kinds of computer):

$$\text{offset} = 0, \text{size} = 4: \quad \text{last\_name}$$
$$\text{offset} = 4, \text{size} = 4: \quad \text{first\_name}$$
$$\text{offset} = 8, \text{size} = 1: \quad \text{sex}$$
$$\text{offset} = 10, \text{size} = 2: \quad \text{age}$$
$$\text{offset} = 12, \text{size} = 4: \quad \text{cars\_owned}$$
$$\text{offset} = 16, \text{size} = 4: \quad \text{next\_person}$$

Note that although the field named *sex* is at offset 8 and requires only one byte of memory, the next field is placed at offset 10 rather than 9. The compiler has

FIGURE 4.6. Linked List Structures

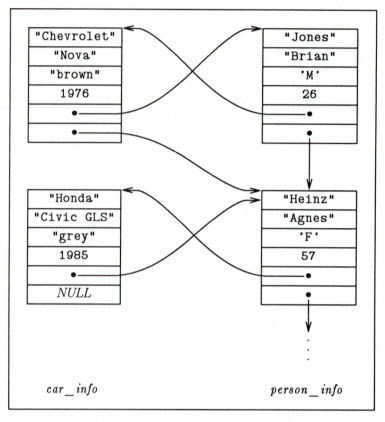

left one byte unused in the structure so that the *age* field can have an even offset, since access to a two-byte integer is faster on a VAX or Sun computer if that integer is located at an even address in memory. On a Pyramid computer, the address must be even or else the data item cannot be accessed at all in a single machine instruction.

The compiler assumes that the block of storage for the structure begins at a memory address divisible by a suitable number (2, 4 or 8 depending on the data types of the fields in the structure) and then inserts padding bytes as necessary into the structure layout so that each field has the correct alignment in memory. Therefore, the total size of the structure may be larger than you might expect from just adding the sizes of the component fields. You can usually reduce the size of a structure by ordering the fields carefully. If you just order the fields in decreasing size order, no padding bytes will be inserted.

4.4. UNIONS

Sometimes it is desirable for values of different types to share storage. For example, a word in the computer memory might sometimes be used to hold **int** values and sometimes to hold **float** values. Compilers and storage allocators (like the *malloc* function) frequently need this freedom to look at data values in different ways. Just as the PASCAL language has this flexibility (with its variant records), the C language has something similar. The construct in C is a **union** type.

The syntax of a **union** is similar to that of a structure. Whereas the fields of a structure represent consecutive memory locations, the fields of a union all represent the same location or group of locations. A sample pair of declarations for a **union** is

```
union overlay {
        float r;
        int   i;
        int   *ip;
} ;
union overlay ol1, *olptr;
```

As with the earlier example of a **struct** declaration, the first declaration above defines a union tag (called *overlay*). The second declaration uses the tag to define one instance of this union and a pointer to instances of this union. The result is that the fields, *ol1.r*, *ol1.i* and *ol1.ip*, all occupy the same memory locations. Thus, it would be technically legal but probably meaningless to execute sequences of statements similar to

```
ol1.r = 0.5;
k     = ol1.i;
```

In reality, the only difference between a **struct** and a **union** is in the calculations of offsets for the field members. (All field offsets in a union type are zero.) As with structures, it is possible to assign union type values and to have functions that accept arguments with union types and return results with union types.

A more practical example of the use of a **union** structure is shown in Figure 4.7. The example shows code to build a balanced binary tree data structure. A call such as

```
root = build_tree( 8 );
```

will construct a tree of depth 8 and containing a total of 255 nodes (127 interior nodes and 128 leaf nodes). Interior nodes in the tree contain pointers to the left subtree and the right subtree. Leaf nodes of the tree have no descendants and so do not contain pointers. Instead, they might have other kinds of information associated with them. In the example, each leaf node just has a single associated integer, but it would be easy to provide for additional fields.

FIGURE 4.7. A union Structure Example

```
struct node {
        char tag;   /* 'L' = leaf, 'N' = non-leaf */
        union {
            struct {
                struct node *left, *right;
            } non_leaf;
            struct {
                int leaf_number;
            } leaf;
        }
    } *root;

int leaf_cnt;

struct node *build_tree( depth )
int depth;
{
    struct node *new_node, *malloc();
    newnode = malloc( sizeof(struct node) );
    if (depth > 1) {        /* allocate non-leaf node */
        new_node->tag = 'N';
        new_node->non_leaf.left  = build_tree(depth-1);
        new_node->non_leaf.right = build_tree(depth-1);
    } else {
        new_node->tag = 'L';
        new_node->leaf.leaf_number = ++leaf_cnt;
    }
    return( new_node );
}
```

The structure used for a tree node in Figure 4.7 has been deliberately designed to imitate a PASCAL record type. The fields applicable to a non-leaf version of the node are overlayed on the single field that is applicable to a leaf version. Because the C run-time system does not keep track of which version of a union type is currently in effect, we must record this information ourselves. That is why the node structure contains a field named *tag*. (This field is used in a similar manner to a tag field in a variant record in PASCAL.)

4.5. ENUMERATED TYPES

After the apparent success of enumerated types in PASCAL, they were added to C. Enumeration declarations are modelled after **struct** and **union** declarations. Here is a simple example:

```
enum truth_state {false, dontknow, true};
enum truth_state flag1, flag2, flag3;
```

The identifier *truth_state* is called an enumeration tag (with a status similar to that of a structure or union tag). There are three variables which are declared to have the enumeration type, namely *flag1*, *flag2* and *flag3*.

The range of directly available operations on enumeration variables is somewhat limited. Values of an enumeration type may be assigned or compared; they may be used as selecting values and case labels in **switch** statements, but that is all. What follows are some examples, using the variables declared above:

```
flag1 = true;  flag2 = dontknow;
if (flag1 < flag2)
        flag3 = true;

switch ( flag2 ) {          /* invert flag2 */

case true:
        flag2 = false;
        break;

case false:
        flag2 = true;
        break;
}
```

Variables of an enumerated type are implemented as unsigned integers. The constants of the enumeration are, by default, implemented as the integers, 0, 1, 2..., corresponding to their order of appearance in the declaration. If a variable has an enumeration type, this variable cannot directly be stepped through the values of this type. The variable must be cast to the **int** type to perform the addition. For example, to program a loop that steps through the values of our *truth_state* enumeration type, we must code a loop similar to

```
for (flag1=false; flag1<=true; ((int)flag1)++) {
        /* body of loop omitted */
}
```

As we have stated, the C compiler normally implements the enumeration constants with a sequence of integer values starting at zero. If you wish, you can force other integer values to be used. For example,

```
enum numbers {
        one = 1, ten = 10, hundred = 100,
        thousand = 1000, million = 1000000 };
```

associates values in the obvious way. If you provide values for some enumeration constants and not for others, the compiler will supply a value for a constant by adding one to the internal value of the previous constant in the list. (If there is no previous constant, the value zero is provided.)

By providing explicit values for the enumeration constants, it is possible to make two or more of these constants have the same internal value. Therefore, they would compare as equal.

4.6. GENERAL DECLARATION SYNTAX

Suppose that we wish to declare an object which is an array of pointers to arrays with **float** elements. A correct C declaration would look something like

```
float   ( *apf[10] )[20] ;
```

Here our object, called *apf*, is an array with 10 elements; each of these elements is a pointer; each pointer refers to an array containing 20 elements of type **float**. At first sight, the declaration appears to be inside-out. The key to understanding the declaration is to realize that the declaration exactly mirrors the usage syntax for this object in the subsequent program. For example, we might later use the array *apf* in a statement such as

```
x = ( *apf[i] )[j] ;
```

In this statement, the first operation to be applied to *apf* is the act of indexing by i. (Why indexing and not dereferencing first? Because indexing has higher precedence: see the table given at the end of Chapter 2.) Thus *apf* must be an array. After indexing, the next operation to be applied is dereferencing. Thus *apf* must be an array of pointers. The final operation to be applied is that of indexing by j. Thus we conclude that *apf* is an array of pointers to arrays. The relationship between this sequence of operations and the declaration syntax should now be a little clearer.

In case declarations are still a mystery, here are a few more examples:

```
char    *fn( );
int     **abc[15];
float   (**def)[25];
double  *(*gh)[35];
```

In the first example, *fn* is a function which returns a pointer to an object of type **char**. That is, *fn* is a string valued function. The need for a declaration like this will be explained later. Next, *abc* is an array of pointers to pointers to **int** values. The variable *def* is a pointer to a pointer to an array with **float** elements. Finally, *gh* is a pointer to an array whose elements are pointers to **double** values.

To reiterate a statement made earlier, the declaration of an object *exactly* mirrors the correct syntax for a reference to that object in some subsequent statement. If, for example, we wanted to use object *def*, declared above, then one correct usage is:

```
(**def)[i+1] = 99.99;
```

That is, writing the exact same construction as in the declaration and replacing the array size with an array subscript expression must give access to a memory location with the **float** type.

4.7. NAMING DATA TYPES WITH typedef

A relatively modern concept in programming language design is that of *type encapsulation*. Let us consider an example, say a matrix. We might implement a matrix as a two-dimensional array or, if the matrix is known to be sparse, we might use a complicated linked-list representation. Now, one principle of type encapsulation is that we should be able to declare objects of type *matrix* without being concerned with any such implementation details. The constructs of C seen so far do not give us this ability. If we want to use an array implementation, we must use one form of declaration; if we use a linked-list implementation, we would probably use a declaration for a different form of declaration involving a structure. In other words, we need information about the data structure in order to declare objects of this type.

C partially solves the problem by providing the **typedef** feature. A **typedef** gives a name to a type. For example, suppose that we want to define the name *MATRIX* to correspond to an array implementation of a matrix. The definition is

```
typedef float MATRIX[20][20];
```

Note that without the keyword **typedef**, we would be declaring *MATRIX* to be a variable of this array type. When the **typedef** keyword is included, *MATRIX* is instead defined to represent the type that this variable would have had. Subsequently in the program, we can write declarations such as

```
MATRIX array1, array2, *arrp;
```

in which we declare two instances of the matrix type and a pointer variable for referring to matrices.

The **typedef** feature can be used to parameterize a program. With extensive use of **typedef**s and with conscientious use of *access functions* to access the internal fields of the defined data types, very little needs to be changed if we decide to adopt another implementation for our *MATRIX* type, say.

The feature can also be used to make programs more easily transferable from one computer to another. A major problem in transporting C programs is that a variable of type **int** may be 16 bits on one machine and 32 bits on another machine. If, however, the variable is declared as type *BIT32*, say, we can use a **typedef** like

```
typedef int BIT32;
```

for running the program on one machine and a different **typedef** like

```
typedef long BIT32;
```

for running on the other machine.

Another use for **typedef** definitions is to assist in constructing complicated declarations. Suppose that we would like to declare *f_table* to have the following type: "pointer to array of pointers to functions that return integers". It may take some time to work out the single C declaration that achieves the desired effect. However, if we do not mind writing several lines of C, there is a way to be certain of getting the declaration right. Looking at the type we need to declare, we can see that the next simplest type after **int** is "function of **int**". We can name this type using the definition

```
typedef int FI();
```

The type that is next in simplicity is now "pointer to *FI* ", which we can define with

```
typedef FI *PFI;
```

Now, we need to create a new type that represents an array of the *PFI* type, which we do with

```
typedef PFI APFI[];
```

And, finally, the desired type can be defined with

```
typedef APFI *PAPFI;
```

Therefore, we can conclude with the declaration of *f_table*:

```
PAPFI f_table;
```

4.8. TYPE CONVERSION RULES AND CASTS

C performs many type conversions automatically. Suppose, for example, that we have used an arithmetic operation like addition or subtraction in our program. Any operand with the **char** or **short int** type is automatically converted to **int**. An operand with the **float** type is automatically converted to **double**. (All floating-point arithmetic operations are performed in double precision.) Now, after these conversions, if one operand of the arithmetic operation is **double** and the other is **int**, the integer operand is converted to **double**. If one operand is a signed **int** and the other an unsigned **int**, the signed operand is converted to unsigned.

An automatic type conversion from any one of **char**, **short**, **int**, **float** and **double** to any other of these types is freely performed on assignment.

Type conversions can be forced in situations where they do not occur automatically. A construction of the form

(*type*) *expression*

forces the expression to be converted to the specified type. This construction is known as a *cast*. Type casting is needed most often when dealing with functions. For one thing, C does not always convert arguments in the proper way when they are passed to functions. C implements all arguments as either the **int** type or the **double** type. If you pass a **char** value to a function that expects an **int** argument (or vice versa), everything works. However, if you pass an **int** value to a function expecting a **float** or **double** argument, no conversion takes place. The conversion has to be forced, as in

```
x = fn( (double)n );
```

There is a similar problem if you attempt to pass a floating-point value to a function that expects an integer argument. Another frequent use for type casts is in dealing with results returned by the *calloc* and *malloc* storage allocation functions.

QUESTIONS

1. What single declaration statement should you write if you want object *papc* to be a pointer to an array of pointers to characters?

2. How would you repeat Question 1, but using several **typedef** definitions?

3. If *b* is declared in the statement

```
int *((*b)[10]);
```

what data type does *b* have?

4. In the section describing **union** types, a type called *overlay* was defined. How many bytes of storage does an object with this type (such as variable *ol1*) require?

CHAPTER 5

FUNCTIONS

5.1. FUNCTION DEFINITIONS

5.1.1. Functions versus Procedures

Many languages, including PASCAL and FORTRAN, provide both *functions* and *procedures*. (A *subroutine* in FORTRAN is equivalent to a procedure.) A function in a programming language is supposed to correspond to the mathematical notion of a function. That is, the function returns a result which is computed from its argument(s). An example of a function which everyone should be familiar with is the trigonometric *sine* function (abbreviated to *sin* in C and in most programming languages). It is a pure function because it returns a computed result without changing its argument. You would be (or should be) surprised if you found that the variable x has been altered after making the function call

```
result = sin(x);
```

A procedure, on the other hand, does not return a direct result. It is executed only for its side effects. Possible side effects include performing input-output, changing the values of global variables, changing the values of parameters, and changing the values of hidden (static) variables.

Unfortunately, most conventional programming languages blur this distinction between a function and a procedure because they permit functions to have exactly the same side effects as procedures. The C language cannot be accused of blurring the distinction because it does not provide both functions and procedures. All subprograms in C must be declared as functions, even if we intend to use a subprogram in the same way as a procedure. Therefore, every C function must be declared with a result type, even if the function does not actually return a result. A function that is used like a procedure (it does not return a result), should be declared with the type **void**. If a function is defined with this type, the C compiler will report an error if there are any subsequent attempts to provide return values for this function or to access a returned value.

The **void** type was added to C only after the language had been in use for several years. The previous convention had been to omit the type for any function used like a procedure. However, when the type is omitted, it simply defaults to **int**. A function with any type whatsoever may be used like a procedure because there is no requirement that functions must return a result and there is no requirement that the caller of a function must use a result returned by a function. Because old habits take a long time to die, most C source code you look at is likely to use **int**-valued functions instead of **void** functions. If you want to obtain the maximum benefit from the compiler's type checking, you should not imitate the old convention and should use the **void** type whenever appropriate.

5.1.2. Function Declaration Syntax

A function definition has the following structure:

>   *type function-name* (*parameters*)
>   *parameter-declarations*
>   {
>   *local-declarations*
>   *statement-list*
>   }

As mentioned above, the function type may be omitted, in which case it defaults to **int**. Declarations for parameters may also be omitted, in which case their types also default to **int**. Inside the function body, **return** statements may be used to exit from that function and return a result, if there is one. The return statement has the syntax

>   `return`   *expression* ;

or

>   `return` ;

depending on whether the function returns a result or not.

A simple example is the following definition for a function that counts the number of characters in a string:

```
int strlen( s )
char *s;
{
        int len;  char *t;
        len = 0;   t = s;
        while( *t++ )
                 len++;
        return len;
}
```

The first line specifies that the function name is *strlen*, that it accepts a single parameter *s* and that it returns a result of type **int**. The parameter *s* is declared to be a string type on the second line. To be slightly technical, *s* is called a *formal parameter* of function *strlen*. The remaining lines of our example form the function body. There are two local variables, *len* and *t*. These local variables cannot be directly accessed from inside any other function. (They could only be accessed if their addresses were passed, by some route, to another function.) Storage for these local variables is obtained from a stack on entry to the function and released again on exit. Therefore these local variables do not retain their values from one function invocation to the next.

Our sample function may be invoked with statements like the following:

```
char *cp1;
      .
      .
      .
cp1 = "a string of some sort\n" ;
i = strlen( cp1 );
```

Or like:

```
i = strlen( "a string of some sort\n" );
```

5.1.3. Parameter Passing Mechanism

The call-by-value parameter passing mechanism is used. (This is the parameter passing mechanism used in PASCAL when the keyword **var** is omitted from the parameter declaration.) The call-by-value mechanism implies that the caller of a function passes only a copy of each argument value to the function. Any assignments to a parameter inside the function change only the value of this copy. For example, our *strlen* function, given above, could have been written as

```
int strlen( s )
char *s;
{
        int len; len = 0;
        while( *s++ )
                len++;
        return len;
}
```

and a possible call of the *strlen* is

```
n = strlen( text_pointer );
```

where *text_pointer* could be a pointer variable (declared with the data type char *).

When the call to this new version of *strlen* is made, a copy of the *text_pointer* variable is made and stored into the formal parameter *s*. This version of the function changes the value of its formal parameter, *s*. It is safe to change this copy because these changes cannot affect the actual parameter provided by the caller. That is, the value of *text_pointer* is unchanged by the statements executed inside *strlen*.

There are, of course, situations where we want the function to alter one of its arguments. Such an alteration can only be accomplished by passing a pointer to a data object. The function then has the capability of dereferencing the pointer to access and change the data object. This capability allows the function to simulate the call-by-reference parameter passing mechanism (which is used for **var** parameters in PASCAL). As an illustration, the *swap* function exchanges the values of its two arguments:

```
void swap( a, b )
int *a, *b;
{
    register int temp;
    temp = *a;   *a = *b;   *b = temp;
}
```

If we wanted to call this function to exchange the values of the variables *m* and *n*, we would have to write the call as

```
swap( &m, &n );
```

Of course, this notation is sufficiently inconvenient and *swap* is sufficiently simple to make it desirable to implement *swap* as a macro. Macros are a feature of the C preprocessor that are discussed in the next chapter.

Array parameters to functions can, apparently, be changed without having to resort to explicit pointers and explicit dereferencing. However, the C convention that an unsubscripted array name is equivalent to a pointer to the first array element simply means that the pointers and dereferencing actions are implicit. The definition of a function for sorting an array of integers into ascending order appears in Figure 5.1. Our function uses a standard sorting technique invented by C.A.R. Hoare and known as Quicksort. Before discussing points in the C language raised by our example, it might be a good idea to explain the principle behind Quicksort.

Suppose that we have the following array to sort:

5   3   2   7   4   8   1   2

The algorithm picks one array element (we arbitrarily pick the first element) to be a *pivot* value. The array is now reordered so that all elements with values less than the pivot appear before the pivot and all values greater than the pivot appear afterward. Thus, if the pivot is chosen to be 5, Quicksort might rearrange the list to be

3   2   4   1   2   5   7   8

(Our implementation tries to avoid moving elements around unnecessarily, so it actually produces a different ordering that has the same property.) The pivot element is now in its correct position and need not be moved again. However, the five elements to the left of the pivot need reordering amongst themselves and, similarly, for the two elements to the right of the pivot. To reorder the five elements on the left, we recursively invoke Quicksort on a subarray of the original array. To reorder the two elements on the right, we also use a recursive call on Quicksort. The sequence of recursive calls halts when the subarray to be sorted has two or fewer elements.

Now we can return to a discussion of the C syntax. Figure 5.1 illustrates at least three points. First, it shows that the size may be omitted from an array declaration of a parameter. In actual fact, the declaration

```
int a[];
```

is completely equivalent to

```
int *a;
```

There is no difference in a parameter declaration.[1] The second point is that **return**, standing alone, is a statement to exit from the function without returning a result. And when the **return** statement would be the last statement in the function body, it may be omitted (as we have done). The third point is that recursive calls on a function are allowed.

It might appear that our *quicksort* function example conflicts with the statement that function parameters are passed by value. If this is the case, how does the function actually change the array being passed by the caller? Our function definition is correct. The explanation is that array names in C are actually implemented as pointers to the first element of the array. It is the

---

[1] There is a major difference if anything but a parameter is being declared.

FIGURE 5.1. A Sample Function Definition

```
/* Sort an array, a, with n elements */
void quicksort( a, n )
int a[], n;
{
    int lpos, rpos, pivot;

    if (n <= 2) {
        if (n == 2 && a[0] > a[1]) {
            int tmp = a[0];
            a[0] = a[1];
            a[1] = tmp;
        }
        return;
    }
    pivot = a[0];  lpos = 0;  rpos = n-1;
    while( lpos < rpos ) {

        /* Assertions true at this point:
            1.  a[0] .. a[lpos-1]   <= pivot
            2.  a[rpos+1] .. a[n-1] >= pivot
            3.  if we assigned a[lpos] = pivot,
                the array would be a permutation
                of the original array passed in.  */

        while( a[rpos] >= pivot ) {
            if (--rpos == lpos) goto EXIT;
        }
        a[lpos++] = a[rpos];

        while( a[lpos] <= pivot ) {
            if (++lpos == rpos) goto EXIT;
        }
        a[rpos--] = a[lpos];
    }
EXIT:
    a[lpos] = pivot;
    quicksort( a, lpos );
    quicksort( a + lpos + 1, n - lpos - 1 );
}
```

pointer which is being passed by value. The statements inside the function implicitly dereference the pointer *a* and can access or change the original array elements provided by the caller.

Suitable calling code for the *quicksort* function, above, might look like

```
int        table[100];
        .
        .
        .
quicksort( table, 100 );
```

As we just explained, we do not need to pass the address of an array argument explicitly. An unsubscripted array name is automatically considered to be an address in C. Of course, it would be perfectly correct to code the call, if you prefer to do so, as[2]

```
quicksort( &table[0], 100 );
```

But before you get carried away and copy the code for *quicksort* into all your C programs, you should know that the Berkeley UNIX system provides a sorting routine as a library function. The function is called *qsort*, an implementation of the *quickersort* algorithm. It is, as the name suggests, an improved version of *quicksort*. The C code needed to invoke *qsort* is shown in Figure 5.2.

The *qsort* function is designed to be very general. It is not restricted to sorting just arrays with **float** elements. To provide this generality, the caller must provide a third argument that specifies the number of bytes in an array element and a fourth argument that is the name of a function for comparing two array elements. (A more complete discussion of passing function names as parameters appears later in this chapter.) By redefining this compare function appropriately, *qsort* can be used to sort arrays of structures, arrays of strings, etc., into either ascending or descending order.

5.1.4. Forward Declarations of Functions

Identifiers should normally be declared before they are used in C programs. Function names represent the only exception to this rule. Thus it is permissible to write a call of a function that is not defined until later in the program. (It can even be defined in another C source program file.) However, the C compiler will automatically assume that that function returns a result of type **int**, unless told otherwise. A short declaration of the result type is needed to override the default assumption.

---

[2] It would, however, be incorrect to code the call as
```
quicksort( &table, 100 );
```
because *table*, without a subscript, has the same status as a constant, and you are never permitted to take the address of a constant.

FIGURE 5.2. Use of the qsort Function

```
/* The array to be sorted */
float table[100];

/* A function like the following must be provided by
   the caller of 'qsort'.  The function is needed to
   compare two elements of the array to be sorted.   */
int fcmp( a, b )
float *a, *b;
{
    if (*a > *b) return( 1 );
    if (*a < *b) return( -1 );
    return( 0 );
}
    .
    .
    .
    /* after storing values into 'table', the following
       call will invoke 'qsort' to sort the array.   */
    qsort( table, 100, sizeof(table[0]), fcmp );
```

For example, if our *quicksort* function were not defined in the same file as our calling code or if we wanted to define the function later in the current file, we would need to provide the declaration

```
void quicksort();
```

No other information about the function is provided (not even about how many parameters the function expects or what types they should have). As a second example, suppose that we want to code a call of a function named *getreal*, which takes two arguments and returns a result of type **double**, but the definition for *getreal* appears later in the same program. We would have to provide a declaration for *getreal* as in the following code fragment:

```
double x;
double getreal();
    .
    .
x = getreal(a,b);   /* call the function */
```

The importance of providing the declaration for *getreal* in the above example should, perhaps, be stressed. If the declaration is omitted, the compiler will translate the function call under the assumption that the function is to return an **int** result. This integer value is converted to **double** before being stored into x. Unfortunately, when this conversion operation is applied to a value that is already in floating-point format, it will produce nonsensical results. If the compiler finds a definition for *getreal* later in the C source file, an error message complaining about a "redeclaration of getreal" will be produced. If there is no definition for *getreal* in the file, as will be the case if *getreal* is a library function or if it is defined in another C source file[3], no error message is generated. The program would simply execute and produce incorrect results.[4]

We should also point out that a type cast is not always an appropriate alternative to declaring the result type of a function. If statement

```
x = (double)getreal( a, b );
```

is used without any prior declaration for *getreal*, the compiler will again assume that *getreal* returns an **int** result and will convert this result value to **double**. The only difference between this version and the earlier version is that the conversion to **double** is explicit rather than implicit. Earlier examples of calls to the *malloc* and *calloc* functions that used type casts work only because integer values and pointer values are implemented identically. (This assumption does not necessarily hold on all computers.)

5.1.5. Parameter Conversion Rules

As mentioned in an earlier chapter, C implements function arguments as either **int** or **double**. (Pointer types and enumerated types are included as being kinds of integers.) This is usually transparent to the programmer. He or she can still declare the parameter types as being **char** or whatever, because all other (simple) types can be converted to **int** or **double** types without loss of information. For example, if the caller passes an argument with type **char**, the C compiler generates machine instructions to convert the argument value to an **int** value. This means that the character value gains three (high-order) bytes when it is expanded to fill a four-byte longword. If the argument of the function is declared as type *char*, then only the low-order byte of the longword is actually accessed by statements inside the function body. Thus, it appears to the programmer that a single byte is passed to the function and that a single byte is received in the function. (Passing *float* values and converting to *double* works similarly.)

A relatively recent extension to C is to permit arguments of functions and results from functions to have a **struct** or **union** type. Thus, the code fragment shown in Figure 5.3 could form part of a software package to implement complex arithmetic.

---

[3] A single C program can be split into several source files, as will be explained in Chapter 9.

[4] Although the compiler is unaware about this error in the program, the *lint* processor can find and report this kind of error in function usage.

FIGURE 5.3. Functions with struct Types

```
typedef struct {
                float x, y;
        } COMPLEX;

COMPLEX cadd( a, b )
COMPLEX a, b;
{
    COMPLEX rslt;
    rslt.x = a.x + b.x;
    rslt.y = a.y + b.y;
    return rslt;
}

COMPLEX cmultiply( a, b )
COMPLEX a,b;
{
        COMPLEX rslt;
        rslt.x = (a.x * b.x) - (a.y * b.y);
        rslt.y = (a.x * b.y) + (a.y * b.x);
        return rslt;
}
```

5.2. SCOPE RULES AND STORAGE LIFETIMES

A C function cannot be defined inside another function, as in some programming languages (such as PASCAL). This restriction considerably simplifies the rules for visibility and lifetime of storage for variables.

A complete C program is composed of a sequence of global, or external, declarations. These declarations define data objects and functions. The identifiers defined in these declarations are potentially visible throughout the program, from their points of declaration to the end of the file.[5] The storage for all of these global data objects persists for the entire lifetime of the program. These data objects are said to have the *static* storage class.

Identifiers declared within a function are visible only within that function. If declared within a group of statements enclosed by curly braces, they are visible only within that statement group. Variables declared inside a function are known as local variables. The usual case is that their storage is allocated (on a

---

[5] We are assuming, for the time being, that the program source code is held in a single file.

system stack) only when control enters the function, and their storage is deallocated when control exits the function. Such variables are said to be *automatic*. (That is, their storage is automatically controlled by C.) If you wish, you may explicitly provide the attribute **auto** in a declaration for a local variable and so specify that the storage is be automatic. A sample declaration with the **auto** attribute is

```
auto float fudge_factor;
```

However, automatic storage is assumed by default anyway and, therefore, it is rare to see **auto** used in programs.

It is possible to declare a local variable as having the **static** storage class. In this case, its storage will, as in the case of external data objects, persist for the lifetime of the program. Therefore, a **static** variable retains its value from one function invocation to the next.

All **static** variables are initialized to zero before execution of the program begins, unless some other initialization has been specified (see the following section). No such initialization takes place for automatic variables, unless explicitly specified.

5.3. STORAGE INITIALIZATION

External and **static** variables are, by default, initialized to hold binary zeros. For the VAX, Sun and Pyramid implementations, this implies that integer variables are initially zero; floating-point variables are initially equal to 0.0; character variables initially contain the ASCII NUL character ('\0'); and pointer variables are initially equal to the NULL pointer. These initial values do not necessarily hold for C implementations on other computers.

No default initialization occurs for **automatic** variables. It is possible to provide explicit initialization for **static** variables and for simple **automatic** variables (i.e. automatic arrays and structures are excluded).

Simple variables may be initialized when declared, as in the following examples:

```
int count = 20;
char escape = '\033';
float height = 3.85 * 12;
```

When the simple variable has the *automatic* attribute, any expression may be used for initialization. Otherwise, if the simple variable has *static* storage, only an expression comprised wholly of constants may be used as the initializer. Initialization takes place once only for static variables and occurs before the program begins execution; it takes place each time control enters the enclosing block for automatic variables.

Static arrays and structures may be initialized, as in the following examples:

```
int dayspermonth[13] = { 0, 31, 28, 31, 30, 31,
                 30, 31, 31, 30, 31, 30, 31 } ;
char errmsg[20] = "system error\n";
struct person { char name[30]; int age; };
struct person family[4] =
        { "John Johns", 39, "Joanie Johns", 35,
          "Jimmy Johns", 4, "Jackie Johns", 1 } ;
```

If fewer initializers are provided than are needed to initialize the entire array or structure, remaining elements or fields are filled with zeros. Too many initializers cause an error message. As a convenience, it is permissible to omit the size of an array from its declaration when initialization values are provided. The compiler simply counts the number of initializers and makes the array just large enough to hold them all. For example, we could have coded

```
int dayspermonth[] = { 0, 31, 28, 31, 30, 31,
                 30, 31, 31, 30, 31, 30, 31 };
char errmsg[] = "system error\n";
```

If a two-dimensional array is being initialized, the values in each row may be enclosed within curly braces. Thus, we can have a declaration like:

```
int table[5][4] = { {0}, {1,1,1,1}, {2,2,2,2},
                 {3,3,3,3}, {4,4,4,4} };
```

We should read the declaration to mean that there are 5 rows, each containing 4 columns. Since each inner pair of braces corresponds to one row of the matrix, the compiler can determine that three initializers are missing from the first row and it will supply zeros by default. The inner sets of curly braces are not mandatory; we could have written

```
int table[5][4] = { 0,0,0,0,1,1,1,1,2,2,2,2,
                 3,3,3,3,4,4,4,4 };
```

but this is less readable and a single missing initializer might cause chaos.

5.4. POINTERS TO FUNCTIONS

If you have ever programmed in assembly language, you know that instructions and data reside in memory together. Pointers in C are nothing more than memory addresses. A natural question to ask, therefore, is, if we can have a pointer to a data object, why not have a pointer to an instruction in memory? In fact, C provides exactly that. The C language allows you to take the address of a function (i.e. take the address of the entry point to the function in the computer memory) and treat that address as a data value.

Here is an example of a declaration for a variable whose type is *pointer to function*:

```
int  (*fp)();
```

FIGURE 5.4. **Example of Pointers to Functions**

```
double square(x)
double x; { return( x*x ); }

double sin(), cos(), tan();

double (*fns[4])() = { sin, cos, tan, square };
char    *names[] = {"sin","cos","tan","square"};

/* trapezoidal integration of fn from a to b */
double integrate( fn, a, b )
double (*fn)(), a, b;
{
    double h = 0.0001;
    double sum, x, y1, y2;
    sum = 0.0;  y1 = (*fn)( a );   x = a;
    while( x < b ) {
        x += 2*h;
        y2 = (*fn)( x );
        sum += (y1+y2)*h;
        y1 = y2;
    }
    return( sum );
}

void main() {
    double low, high;    int i;

    for( ; ; ) {
        printf( "Enter function number, low bound \
and high bound:\n" );
        scanf( "%d  %e  %e", &i, &low, &high );
        if (i < 0 || i >= 4) break;
        printf( "Integral of %s from %f to %f is %g\n",
            names[i], low, high,
            integrate( fns[i], low, high) );
    }
}
```

The declaration actually says a little more. It says that if we call the function whose address is held in variable *fp*, a result of type *int* is returned. The variable *fp* can be given a value with an assignment like

```
fp = somefunction;
```

provided that *somefunction* is the name of some function in the program that returns an **int** result (or is another variable in the program of type "pointer to function returning **int**"). If *fp* has been assigned the address of some function, we can call this function with a statement like

```
result = (*fp)( arg1, arg2 );
```

The parentheses are necessary because *fp* must be dereferenced (to obtain a function object) before calling the function.

There are only four actions that can be performed on function pointer variables: they may be assigned to; they may be compared for equality; they may be passed as arguments to other functions; and they may be called.

A simple, but complete, program to illustrate the use of pointers to functions appears in Figure 5.4. As the program shows, data objects such as arrays of pointers to functions may be constructed. Declarations of pointers to functions may include initialization too. The only point to watch is that the C compiler is not smart enough to deduce that the identifiers appearing in the list of initializers are the names of functions. Therefore, the prior declarations of the types of *sin, cos, tan* and *square* are required in this program.[6]

QUESTIONS

1. Some programming languages use the *call-by-value-result* parameter passing mechanism. For example, ALGOL-W and many FORTRAN implementations use it. This mechanism is like *call-by-value* in that a copy of the argument passed by the caller is manipulated inside the function. However, when the function returns, the copy is stored back to replace the original argument provided by the caller. How could you simulate *call-by-value-result* in C?

2. Would the program given in Figure 5.4 execute much faster if every occurrence of **double** were to be replaced with **float**? Explain your answer.

---

[6] If you want to try out this program, you must supply the −1m flag when you compile it. Otherwise the loader will not search the mathematical library for definitions of the *sin, cos* and *tan* functions.

3. Here is a complete definition for the factorial function:

    ```
    int fact( n ) { return (n==0)? 1 : n*fact(n-1); }
    ```

    Explain what happens if you make the function call:

    ```
    result = fact(-1);
    ```

4. How would you generalize the *quicksort* function of Figure 5.1 to make its interface the same as the library function *qsort*?

5. Can you explain the difference between the functions *f* and *g* as defined in the following C declaration?

    ```
    int *f(), (*g)();
    ```

6. The following short C program is wrong, but will be accepted by the C compiler. What is wrong? Can you suggest a suitable correction?

    ```
    void foo( x, y )
    char x;   float y;
    {
        printf( "%c%f\n", x, y );
    }

    void main() {
        foo( 3.5, 'c' );
    }
    ```

CHAPTER 6

THE PREPROCESSOR

6.1. THE PURPOSE OF THE PREPROCESSOR

A C source code file is read and processed by a program called the *C preprocessor* (or *cpp* for short) before it is passed to the C compiler proper. One of the jobs of the preprocessor is to remove comments from the source file. But the preprocessor also provides some very useful facilities.

The macro facility makes it easy to set up different versions of a program all in the same file. If we want to compile one version of a program for 80 column terminals and then compile another version for 132 column terminals, we should need to change only one preprocessor directive line in the program. This directive line might look like

```
#define NUM_COLS 80   /* width of screen */
```

Apart from providing a simple macro expansion facility, the preprocessor also provides a means of including source code from other files and a facility for ignoring chunks of program text.

Preprocessor control lines are flagged by having a hash character (#) in the first column. Following the hash character, some optional white space is allowed and then a keyword is provided. Arguments to the command, if any, occupy the remainder of the line. The directives recognized by the preprocessor are summarized in Table 6.1.

The output of the preprocessor must be syntactically correct C source code (conforming to the syntax rules given in Appendix C). The input to the preprocessor need not, and usually does not, satisfy the syntax of C.

TABLE 6.1. Preprocessor Directives

`#define`	Define a constant or macro.
`#undef`	Remove a constant or macro definition.
`#include`	Insert text contained in another file.
`#ifdef`	Either include or ignore the following lines in the program, depending on whether a name has a macro definition or not.
`#ifndef`	Similar to `#ifdef`, but with a reversed test.
`#if`	Either include or ignore the following lines depending on whether an expression evaluates to 0 or 1.
`#endif`	Close a `#if`, `#ifdef` or `#ifndef` construct.
`#else`	Terminate the text following a `#if`, `#ifdef` or `#ifndef` construct and introduce a new block of text to be included if the test failed.
`#line`	Specify a source file name and line number to be used in error messages from the compiler; ordinary programs should not use this directive.

6.2. THE #include DIRECTIVE

Programs may contain control lines of the form:

> `#include` <*filename*>

Or of the form:

> `#include` "*filename*"

With the first form, the compiler is directed to look in the standard program library (the directory "/usr/include" in the Berkeley UNIX system) for a file called "filename". The contents of this file are then read as part of the program in place of the line containing the `#include` directive. The second form is similar except that the compiler first looks for "filename" in the current working directory and then, only if it is not found there, does the compiler look for the file in the standard program library[1] In other words, you should use angle brackets around the names of include files supplied in some library, as in the case of the "stdio.h" header file for input-output, and use double quote

---

[1] Note that there is an option on the compile command (*cc*) to specify extra program libraries.

characters around the names of any other kind of include file.

Files that are included by a `#include` directive may themselves contain `#include` directives. The preprocessor can handle nested include files to a fairly large depth of nesting. If you construct your own include files, as you should when developing large programs, you may find it useful to nest some of the `#include` directives.

6.3. THE #define DIRECTIVE

The define directive is a control line which begins with `#define`. It provides a simple macro substitution facility. It is commonly used to parameterize a program, as in this example:

```
#define MAXLENGTH 100
. . .
char  linebuffer[MAXLENGTH];
. . .
for ( i = 0; i < MAXLENGTH; i++ ) {
    etc.
```

Here the identifier *MAXLENGTH* is defined to be the string consisting of the three characters: 100. Note that there must not be a semicolon appearing at the end of the control line. This is because all the text appearing after the identifier *MAXLENGTH* on the same line is taken to be part of the definition. Subsequently, every occurrence of *MAXLENGTH* in the following program is textually replaced by the characters 100. (If we had terminated the definition by a semicolon, the four characters 100; would be substituted for *MAXLENGTH*.)

Macros may be parameterized. For example,

```
#define MAX(a,b)  (a>b? a: b)
. . .
i = MAX( j, 20 );
```

will cause the sample assignment statement to be expanded to

```
i = (j>20? j: 20) ;
```

Parameterized macros are frequently used to make the program more readable, but without having to incur the inefficiencies of function calls.

To avoid a common pitfall with macros, it would be wise to make sure that a macro always expands to a parenthesized expression or a bracketed group of statements. If we had defined our *MAX* macro as

```
#define MAX(a,b)  a>b? a: b
```

then the following line of C program

```
n = MAX(n1,n2) + 1;
```

would be expanded by the preprocessor to

```
n = n1 > n2 ? n1 : n2 + 1;
```

Because of the relative precedences of the + and ?: operators, the compiler treats that expanded statement as being equivalent to

```
n = (n1 > n2)? n1 : (n2 + 1);
```

If you compare this version with the original, you can see that it does not quite do what you would want.

Similarly, if we define a *swap* macro to be

```
#define swap(x,y)  t=x; x=y; y=t;
```

we are likely to be surprised if we later use *swap* in a situation similar to the following:

```
if (a[i] > a[j]) swap( a[i], a[j] );
```

If you do not see what the problem is, try expanding the macro and taking another look. (Look at the entire line, not just the macro expansion.) The solution to the problem is to define *swap* as

```
#define swap(x,y) {float t=x; x=y; y=t; }
```

In this case, we can also take advantage of the curly braces to declare the temporary variable needed in the exchange.

The C preprocessor performs absolutely no syntax checking on macro definitions. It scans the definition removing comments and splitting it up into tokens. The preprocessor remembers this sequence of tokens as being the body of the macro definition. There is no requirement that the token sequence should correspond to a syntactically valid fragment of C code. It is therefore all right to define macros that do not expand to balanced units of C program. For example, if you prefer the look of PASCAL code, you can define a package of macros like the following:

```
#define BEGIN   {
#define END     ;}
#define IF      if(
#define THEN    )
#define ELSE    else
     etc.
```

Now you can write PASCAL-like (or ALGOL-like) code such as

```
IF a == b THEN
    BEGIN  a++;  b--  END
ELSE
    b = 0;
```

which expands into perfectly good C code. We do not, however, recommend that you actually create and use such a macro package. Macros tend to disguise the origins of coding mistakes and you are likely to find that it takes you longer to debug a program that makes extensive use of macros. Furthermore, macros like those given above are likely to render the program unreadable to anyone but the original author.

If you have a macro definition that does not conveniently fit onto one line, you may continue the definition over two or more lines. The continuation can be indicated by inserting a backslash character at the end of the line. Here is a sample definition:

```
#define  PUSH(x)                                    \
    { if (top >= STACKSIZE)                         \
        fprintf(stderr,"stack overflow!\n");   \
    else stack[top++] = x;   }
```

Many of the files that can be included from the standard libraries define macros. If, for example, you care to inspect "/usr/include/stdio.h", you will see that *getchar* is not a function but a macro without parameters. Its definition is

```
#define getchar() getc(stdin)
```

You will also see that *getc* is itself a macro, rather than a function. The preprocessor correctly handles macros that are defined in terms of other macros. It just keeps rescanning and expanding macros until it can find nothing left in the line to expand. Many other macro definitions can be seen in the "/usr/include/ctype.h" include file.

If macro definitions in an included file are conflicting with identifers in your program, there is a way to remove the offending definitions. A directive of the form

```
#undef identifier
```

has the effect of disabling macro substitutions for *identifier* in the remainder of the source program file.

6.4. CONDITIONAL INCLUSION OF SOURCE CODE

Frequently, there is a need to create more than one version of a program. Suppose that we wish to have two versions, one is a version which prints voluminous amounts of diagnostic output and the other is a smaller, faster, version which prints no diagnostic output. Therefore, there would probably be several sections of code which are required only for the first program version.

The directive

```
#ifdef identifier
```

indicates that the following lines of code are to be processed and output by the preprocessor only if *identifier* has a definition (made with a #define directive).[2] However, if there has been no definition for this identifier, all lines up to a matching directive line,

```
#endif
```

are ignored. The word *matching* is used here because `#ifdef-#endif` constructions may be nested inside each other. For example, our program might contain lines such as

```
#ifdef DEBUG
    printf( "x, y values are: %d, %d\n", x, y );
    fflush(stdout);
#endif
```

The directive `#else` may also be used with the `#ifdef` directive, so that one code sequence is compiled if the identifier is defined and the other sequence is compiled if it is not defined. A directive

```
#ifndef identifier
```

which makes the opposite test also exists. It causes the following lines to be compiled only if the identifier is currently undefined.

There is yet one more directive:

```
#if constant-expression
```

If *constant-expression* (i.e. an expression composed only of constants and macro identifiers that expand to constants) evaluates to non-zero, the following lines are compiled; otherwise they are ignored. For example, if the identifier *VERSION* has been defined to be some version number (an integer), our program might contain these lines:

```
#if VERSION==2
    /* the following lines are included
       in only version 2 of the program  */
    ...
#endif
```

The macro identifiers, like *DEBUG* and *VERSION* above, could be defined at the beginning of the program source code. Thus only one, easily found, line needs to be changed before a new version of the program is compiled. However, these identifiers are more easily defined in the UNIX command **cc** which performs the C compilation. The compilation directive

```
-DDEBUG
```

---

[2] You must not confuse a macro definition with C declarations for identifiers. For example, if the program begins with the two lines,

```
    int i;
    #ifdef i
```

the preprocessor considers *i* to be undefined.

causes the identifier *DEBUG* to be defined to the preprocessor (by default, equal to 1) before compilation begins. The directive

```
-DVERSION=2
```

causes the identifier *VERSION* to be defined equal to 2.

6.5. TROUBLE-SHOOTING

If the preprocessor outputs C code that contains syntax errors, you may have some difficulties in relating the syntax errors to the original source code. Such difficulties are likely if you have particularly complicated macros whose expansions are defined using other complicated macros, and so on.

If you are in trouble, it is useful to know that the −E compilation flag causes the compiler to execute only the preprocessor phase. Running the compiler with a command such as

```
cc -E program.c
```

causes the expanded version of the program to be sent to the standard output.

QUESTIONS

1. How might use of the following macro surprise you?

    ```
    #define increment(n)   n++
    ```

2. What will happen if you try to use this macro?

    ```
    #define self_refer   self_refer+1
    ```

3. The following macro defines a function that returns 1 if its argument is an upper-case letter and 0 otherwise.

    ```
    #define UPCASE(x) (x>='A' && x<='Z')
    ```

    But, when someone tried to use it in the statement

    ```
    if (UPCASE(*++s)) { ...etc.
    ```

    a problem was found. What is the problem? [Note: instead of defining his own macro, this person should have used the *upcase* function defined in the "ctype.h" include file.]

4. The following macros are intended to allow comments to be introduced by the word *comment* and closed by the word *tnemmoc*. Unfortunately, they do not work. Can you explain why not?

    ```
    #define comment  /*
    #define tnemmoc  */
    ```

5.   The *swap* macro was defined earlier in this chapter as

```
#define swap(a,b) { float t=a; a=b; b=t; }
```

However, this macro may give surprising results when supplied with some kinds of parameters. Can you find an example where this macro does not exchange its arguments?

CHAPTER 7

THE STANDARD C LIBRARY

7.1. STANDARD LIBRARIES

7.1.1. What is a Library?

Throughout this book, there has been an assumption that C programs can include calls to various standard functions. Now is the time to take a closer look at the standard functions, what services they provide to the user, the rules for accessing them and where they reside in the UNIX system.

Consider, for example, this C statement:

```
fprintf(stderr,"error in line %d\n", lineno);
```

The *fprintf* function used in this statement is not defined as part of the C language. In this matter, C does not follow the same path as PASCAL. In PASCAL, the equivalent operation, *writeln*, is defined as a standard procedure and has a special status in the language. The call on the *fprintf* function in C is treated like a call on any other function.

In principle, the source code of the *fprintf* function could be made available for inclusion in your program with a `#include` directive. However, this approach would be grossly inefficient because even the smallest C programs could easily require that several thousand lines of function definitions be included. In addition, much of the work would be repetitious because the same functions would be compiled over and over again by different users.

The normal solution to the problem, adopted in all major computer systems, is to precompile a large collection of useful functions. The compiled versions of these functions are in a form called *relocatable binary code*; in other words, as ".o" files. This is the form of file created when a C source file is compiled with the −c flag in effect. Since it is little inconvenient to have hundreds of tiny ".o" files, collections of these compiled functions are combined into larger files called *libraries* or *archive libraries*. These libraries are identified by having the special suffix ".a". To speed up searches for functions within an archive, a special section, similar to a table of contents, can optionally be inserted at the front of the file.

If you have a directory containing a large number of ".o" files, you can create your own archive library by executing commands similar to the following:

```
ar rv mylib.a *.o
ranlib mylib.a
```

The *ar* command creates the archive library and the *ranlib* command inserts the table of contents at the front.

It is unlikely that you will need your own private archive libraries. They are likely to be useful only in the largest software projects. For normal programming, it is only necessary to know of the existence of the standard archive libraries provided with the UNIX system. The most important library is the C library which is automatically searched for functions whenever you use the *cc* command to create an executable program. This library is the file "/lib/libc.a", which contains almost all the standard functions mentioned in this book. If you are interested, you can obtain a list of all the ".o" files that were merged to create this library by executing this command:

```
ar t /lib/libc.a
```

(This list is very long.) You can also see the table of contents section by executing this command:

```
ar p /lib/libc.a __.SYMDEF | od −c
```

7.1.2. Loading Functions from a Library

If you wish to use one of the many standard functions and if you do not require a result from that function or if its result has type **int**, no declaration for the function need appear in your program. For example, you can simply code

```
length = strlen( somestring );
```

in the middle of your program. This code works because the C compiler assumes that undeclared functions have the attributes **extern** and **int**. Although few programmers actually bother to do so, you should insert the explicit declaration

```
extern int strlen();
```

in your program. Declarations like this help document the program better and also eliminate many of the nuisance messages generated by the *lint* checker.

If the function you want to use returns a result with a type other than **int**, you will normally have to include some typing information in the program. An example of such a function is *getenv*.[1] If you wish to call this function in such a statement as

```
term_type = getenv( "TERM" );
```

you should provide the declaration

```
char *getenv();
```

Some standard functions operate on structures with particular formats. For such functions, there is usually a special *include* file which contains the necessary type and structure definitions. For example, the identifier *FILE* (an important feature of input-output processing) is defined by a **typedef** statement in the include file "<stdio.h>". This header file also includes type declarations for the various input-output functions. The input-output functions and the "<stdio.h>" header file is discussed more fully later in this chapter.

The standard functions are documented in section 3 of the UNIX on-line manual. You may see succinct one-line descriptions of all these functions by executing

```
man 3 intro
```

If you have a spare hour or two, you can browse through all these manual entries and see what is available by executing

```
cd /usr/man/cat3;   more *
```

The directory named in the *cd* command normally holds preformatted copies of all the on-line manual entries. If this directory does not exist or is empty, you will have to read through the unformatted versions instead. To see the unformatted entries, execute

```
cd /usr/man/man.3;   more *
```

Each manual entry gives a brief synopsis of how to call the function and tells you if there is any associated include file.

In addition to the on-line manual files, the manual entries are also available in hard-copy form. Your system administrator should be able to help you obtain a copy. This person may also be able to direct you to supplementary documentation that is available for many system programs.

It should be noted that there are several archive libraries. When you use the C compiler, only the standard C library (in the file "/lib/libc.a") is actually searched for the functions that you use. If you use mathematical functions, such as *sin* or *sqrt*, you must ask for the mathematical library to be searched.

---

[1] Use of the *getenv* function is covered in Chapter 8.

This library is normally held in the file "/usr/lib/libm.a". You can request that the mathematical library be searched by supplying the −lm flag to the *cc* command when it is used to create the final executable program. For example, the command

```
cc *.o −lm −o math_problem
```

will suffice if you have already compiled several C source files to produce object files.

Similarly, there is a library of functions for terminal handling, which is searched if you provide the flag −ltermcap and there is a library of functions for full-screen I/O (the *curses* screen package), searched by including the flag −lcurses. If you browse in the "/usr/lib" directory, you will find many archive libraries. They are, of course, easily identifiable by the ".a" suffix.

7.2. FILES, DIRECTORIES, AND LINKS TO FILES

This section of the chapter provides a brief introduction to the implementation of files and directories in the Berkeley UNIX system. This material can be skipped if you just need to know how to perform simple input-output. The Ritchie and Thompson paper, cited at the end of the chapter, provides additional reading on the file system structure.

7.2.1. Implementation of Files and Directories

The data in a file is organized as a collection of blocks, which are not necessarily contiguous on the disk surface. Each file has a special disk block, called an *inode* (for *index node*), which gives the disk addresses of the data blocks and which contains other information needed by the system. In theory, all you need know to access a file is the *inode* number for that file. But, of course, users would be unhappy if files had to be referenced by numbers. Directories are therefore used to maintain a correspondence between names (character strings provided by users) and inode numbers. A directory is little more than a list of names and matching inode numbers. The fact that a directory is itself a disk file should not confuse you. An implication is that one directory file can contain the inode number of another directory file, and so the familiar tree-structured hierarchy of files can be built up.

When a directory is created, it is automatically provided with two entries. One entry has the name ". " (a single period) and gives the inode number of this directory. The other entry has the name ". ." (two periods) and gives the inode number of the parent directory in the hierarchy. These two entries cannot be changed or deleted.

If a directory *D1* contains the name and inode number for a file *F*, *D* is said to contain a link to *F*. There is no inherent restriction in the UNIX system which prevents a second directory *D2*, say, from containing a link to *F*. The *D2* directory might even associate a different name with the inode number for *F*.

Thus, we can have one file which has two, quite different, pathnames. (The shell command *ln* can be used create extra links to files.) Figure 7.1 illustrates a directory structure which permits a file to be accessed with two different pathnames. If the current working directory is the directory file at the left of the figure, the data file at the right of the figure then has the two names "D1/F1" and "D2/F2".

The directory links that we have just described are sometimes known as *hard links*. The term *hard link* is used whenever it is necessary to distinguish this kind of link from another kind of link, the *symbolic link*, that is available in the Berkeley UNIX system. Symbolic links are covered later in this chapter.

A disk is normally divided into separate regions called *file systems*. (You can see a list of all the file systems on your computer by executing the *df* command.) Each file system has its own set of inodes, numbered from one upwards. An inode number, therefore, does not completely specify a file unless you also state which file system it refers to. Names in directories are associated only with inode numbers, and so these inode numbers are assumed to belong to the

FIGURE 7.1. A Directory Structure

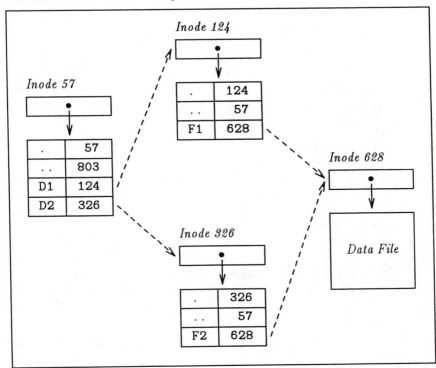

same file system as the directory itself. This assumption implies that a directory cannot contain links to arbitrary files; only links to files in the same file system are allowed. Another restriction is that links to directory files cannot be created by the *ln* command. This restriction is imposed to eliminate the possibility of cycles in the file system structure. If directory *A* could contain a link to directory *B* and *B* contain a link to *A*, many system programs would fail.

7.2.2. Symbolic Links

Although all the files owned by a single user are likely to be contained in the same file system, the user may wish to make links to files owned by other users. Such links would simplify project management in cases where individual project members let others access their files. Often, however, the files may be resident on different file systems. To get around this problem and around the restriction that *ln* must not create links to directories, Berkeley UNIX has another kind of directory link, called a *symbolic link*. When a symbolic link is stored in a directory, a correspondence is still made between a name and an inode. However, the file corresponding to this inode contains the pathname of the file that we are symbolically linking to, and the mode bits contained in the inode indicate that this file is a symbolic link. An example should make symbolic links a little clearer. If you execute the command

```
ln -s /usr/include/stdio.h io_header
```

an entry in your current directory is created. This entry contains the name *io_header* and the inode number of a new file. The new file contains only the string "/usr/include/stdio.h" and nothing else. The mode bits of the new file, held in a field of the inode block on disk, specify that the new file is a symbolic link. If you now execute a command, such as

```
pr io_header
```

the *pr* program will request that the file "io_header" be opened for input. When the UNIX system processes this request, it finds that the file mode indicates a symbolic link. It therefore reads the value of the symbolic link, the string "/usr/include/stdio.h" and repeats the file open process using this name instead. Hence, the user obtains access to the file without being aware that there is anything special about the route taken to locate the file. It is quite possible for the pathname found as the value of a symbolic link to lead to another symbolic link, and so on. This implies that there must be a limit on how many symbolic links that the system will follow when trying to access a file. It should also be clear that it is inherently less efficient for the system to follow a symbolic link than a hard link.

Each file has, stored in its inode block on disk, information about the file owner, the file size, when the file was last changed, when it was last accessed, and who has permission to access this file and in what manner. The *mode* bits for the file control access to the file and say a little about what kind of file it is (e.g. a directory or a symbolic link). The mode bits are set when a file is created and can be changed with the *chmod* command or the function of the same name.

7.2.3. Current Working Directory

The UNIX system remembers a current working directory for each executing process. This directory provides a starting point for following file pathnames if the path does not begin with the slash (/) character. The full pathname of the current working directory can be determined by calling the *getwd* function. The current working directory can be changed with the *chdir* function.

7.2.4. Miscellaneous File Handling Functions

We will briefly list, but not fully explain, some of the operations and corresponding system functions which are applicable to files. Details about the usage of these functions should be obtained from the on-line manual entries.

1) Testing a file to see if you have permission to read it, write it, execute it or just to see if it exists is performed with the *access* function.

2) The access modes on a file may be set with the *chmod* function.

3) Creation of a hard link in a directory is performed with the *link* function. This function does not create a new file, it simply makes an extra link to an existing file.

4) Creation of a symbolic link with the *symlink* function.

5) A file may be renamed with the *rename* function.

6) New files are created with the *creat* function. However, a file may also be created as a side effect of the *open* or *fopen* function. These two functions are described later in this chapter.

7) A link to a file may be deleted with the *unlink* function. (When the last hard link to a file has been deleted, the file is physically deleted from the disk.)

8) Directory files may be created with the *mkdir* function and removed with the *rmdir* function.

7.3. STREAM-ORIENTED INPUT-OUTPUT FUNCTIONS

The UNIX system provides two families of functions for handling input-output and for managing files. One family is relatively low-level and is best suited for handling large blocks of data, say 1024 characters at a time. These functions are used mostly by systems programmers who are striving to achieve extraordinary efficiency. The other family of functions deals with input-output on a character-by-character or line-by-line level, known as *stream* input-output. The stream input-output functions are actually implemented in terms of the low-level routines.

The stream I/O functions should be used in normal applications. As well as having a more usable interface, they also provide automatic blocking of data, so that file input-output is performed efficiently. Another reason to use the stream I/O functions is that this makes your program more portable. Most implementations of C on non-UNIX computer systems provide the standard library of stream I/O functions, but most do not provide a compatible library of low-level I/O functions.

We will now go through most of the stream I/O functions in some detail. For more information about any of these functions, you should, of course, consult the on-line manual entry.

7.3.1. Preliminaries

Any program that intends to perform stream input-output should contain the directive

```
#include <stdio.h>
```

somewhere near its beginning. The included file defines several macros, several constants and a special data type called *FILE*, which is needed for processing files.

Every program started from the shell automatically has access to a standard input stream and two standard output streams. One output stream is intended for use in normal program output; the other is intended to be used for error messages and other exceptional output. Suppose that we have compiled a C program and saved the resulting executable code in the file called "cprog". If we simply type

```
cprog
```

at the terminal, this program will read characters from the terminal keyboard (up to a *control-D* character) and it will print all its output at the terminal. If we type

```
cprog < datafile > results
```

the program will read its input from "datafile" and write its normal output into the file "results". Any error messages are still printed at the terminal. Finally, if we are using the *csh* command shell (see Appendix B) and if we should want error messages to be saved in a file along with the normal output, we could type the command

```
cprog < datafile >& results
```

This last form is most suitable for running *cprog* as a background process, while the terminal is being used for other things.

Since the UNIX shell command processor, *csh*, provides the I/O redirections described above (and the *pipe* facility), there is no great need for the simpler C programs to make explicit accesses to disk files. That is, they can usually get by with just the standard input and output streams that are provided automatically.

The three standard I/O streams are defined to have the names *stdin*, *stdout* and *stderr* in the "stdio.h" include file. These names correspond to "standard input", "standard output" and "standard error output", respectively. These three identifiers are declared to be pointers to a type with the name *FILE*. *FILE* is a **typedef** name for a complicated structure, whose inner details are irrelevant to normal programmers.

The stream input-output functions automatically provide buffering. Buffering of I/O is performed in order to improve efficiency. If a program is reading a continuous stream of characters from a disk file, it would be extremely inefficient to access the disk each time the program needs the next character. The usual approach is to begin by copying a large chunk of the file, 1024 bytes on the Berkeley UNIX system, into an area of main memory called a *buffer*. Then when the program asks to read individual characters with the *getc* function, the characters are taken from the buffer instead of from the disk. In this manner, slow and expensive accesses to the disk occur only once per 1024 characters read by the program. Similarly, if a program is outputting characters to a disk file, the characters are normally accumulated in a buffer until the buffer is full. When the buffer is full, the entire contents of the buffer are written to the disk in a single operation.

If the program is reading from a keyboard and writing to a terminal instead of using disk files, it still makes sense to buffer the input and output. Again, the reason for buffering is efficiency. If input is unbuffered, the program must be suspended from execution each time it requests an input character and the program must be made to wait until the user types a character. The system overhead involved in suspending and restarting the program for each character is fairly high, although there are some programs, such as the *vi* editor, where unbuffered input is necessary. Similarly, the software overhead is reduced if output characters destined for the terminal screen are accumulated in a buffer and transmitted in small chunks.

By default, standard output to a terminal is line-buffered. Output characters generated by the program are accumulated in the output buffer until either the buffer is full or until a *linefeed* character is output or until the program attempts to read from the terminal. (This last reason for transferring the buffer contents to the output terminal is to simplify interactive prompting for input.) Standard error output is, by default, not buffered at all. One consequence is that error output is performed inefficiently. It is unsuitable for large volumes of data. A second consequence is that if a program crashes, we can be fairly confident that we have not lost any messages that were in the buffer when the program failed. Input is also, by default, buffered. However, input from a terminal is actually buffered by a program (the tty driver) that is not part of the stream I/O functions. Control over terminal input buffering is performed with a function, *ioctl*, which will not be described until Chapter 11.

If buffering defaults are unsuitable for your application, they are fairly easy to change. The occasions when they need to be changed, however, are relatively rare.

7.3.2. Character-by-Character I/O

The simplest functions perform input and output of a single character. The function call

getc(*fp*)   returns the next character read from the file referenced by the pointer *fp*, and the call

putc(*c*,*fp*)   outputs the character *c* to the file referenced by the pointer *fp*.[2]

Because input from the standard input and output to the standard output are so common, the "stdio.h" include file defines two macros:

getchar()   returns the next character read from the standard input. It is defined to be the same as *getc(stdin)*, and

putchar(*c*)   outputs the character *c* to the standard output. It is defined to be the same as *putc(c,stdout)*.

Given these functions and given the fact that *getc* (and *getchar*) return the special code *EOF*[3] at the end of input we can code a simple program to strip comments from C source code. It is reproduced in Figure 7.2. (Use of this program on your source files is *not* recommended!)

7.3.3. Line-by-Line I/O

Another group of functions, *gets*, *fgets*, *puts*, and *fputs*, handle input/output of entire lines. To read a line, you must supply a character array to receive the line. If, say, your program declares the array as

```
#define MAX_LENGTH 256
char input_line[MAX_LENGTH], *result;
```

you can read a line from *stdin* with the call

```
result = gets( input_line );
```

If the line has been read successfully, *result* will be assigned the address of the array *input_line* and the array will contain the input line. The line is supplied as a string terminated by a null byte (the character '\0'). The string does not contain the *newline* character. If the read operation fails because we are at

---

[2] Actually, *putc* and *getc* are defined as macros in the "stdio.h" include file.

[3] *EOF* is defined as a constant with the value −1 in "<stdio.h>")

FIGURE 7.2. A Comment Stripper Program

```c
#include <stdio.h>

main() {
    int ch;

    for( ; ; ) {     /* loop forever */
        ch = getchar();

        /* copy non-comment text to output */
        while( ch != '/' && ch != EOF ) {
            putchar( ch );
            ch = getchar();
        }
        if (ch == EOF) break;

        ch = getchar();
        if (ch == '*') {
            /* output a blank instead
               of the comment */
            putchar( ' ' );
            /* search for end of comment */
            do {
                do {
                    ch = getchar();
                } while( ch != '*' && ch != EOF );
                if (ch == EOF) break;

                do {
                    ch = getchar();
                } while( ch == '*' );
            } while( ch != '/' && ch != EOF );
        } else
            putchar( '/' );

        if (ch == EOF) break;
    }
}
```

the end of input, *NULL* is assigned to *result*.

When using the *gets* function, you must be sure to supply an array that is guaranteed to be larger than the longest input line. It is preferable and safer to use the *fgets* function instead. We can read into the same array as before with the call

```
result = fgets( input_line, MAX_LENGTH, stdin );
```

This statement reads input characters up to the next *newline* character (but at most *MAX_LENGTH*-1 characters are read) into the *input_line* array. If the *newline* character is read, it is stored in the array too. (This behaviour is incompatible with *gets*.) As with *gets*, the function result is either the address of the array or *NULL* (to indicate end-of-file).

There are two corresponding routines for output of lines. One, *puts*, outputs its argument string on *stdout* and then outputs an extra *newline* character. The other, *fputs*, outputs its first argument, a string, on the stream indicated by the second argument. No extra *newline* character is output. For example

```
puts( "TABLE OF RESULTS" );
```

sends a complete line, terminated by a *newline* to the standard output. This is the same effect as is obtained with

```
fputs( "TABLE OF RESULTS\n", stdout );
```

Notice that we had to supply our own *newline* character here.

7.3.4. Formatted Output Functions

A further group of functions handles formatted input-output. The formatted output functions convert data values into character strings for output according to format specifications. The formatted input functions perform the opposite conversions. These functions are unusual in that they do not have a fixed number of arguments, and the arguments do not have to have predefined data types. Let us begin with one of the output functions, *fprintf*. Its first argument is a file pointer (like *stdout* or *stderr*); its second argument is a format specification; all subsequent arguments are values which are to be converted to character strings and printed according to the format specification. Here is an example call of fprintf:

```
fprintf(stderr,
        "error at line %d, input value is %d\n",
        lineno, invalue );
```

All the characters appearing in the format specification are printed as written, except where there is a percent symbol followed by a special code (the letter *d* here). The **%d** combination indicates that an integer is to be printed in decimal notation. The first use of **%d** corresponds to the print-out of the variable *lineno*; the second use corresponds to *invalue*. Thus if *lineno* has value 10 and *invalue* has value -99, the function call will output the message,

>   error at line 10, input value is -99

with a skip to a new line at the end. The message will be transmitted to the standard error stream.

The valid output format codes are listed in Table 7.1. Between the percent symbol and the format code, optional further information may be included. The format code may be immediately preceded by the letter *l* (*ell*) which acts as a modifier to indicate that the data item has the **long** attribute. For example, a possible format specification is

>   fprintf(stderr, "Big number = %ld\n", bignum);

Since the **int** and **long int** types are identical in the Berkeley UNIX system, this modifier is redundant. It is, however, important to use the modifier if you wish to make your programs portable to other computers and to other versions of UNIX. In addition to the *l* modifier, field width and precision information may be specified. This optional information has the following structure:

1) A minus sign may be given to specify left adjustment within the output field.

TABLE 7.1. Output Format Codes

%d	Decimal output of an integer.
%o	Unsigned octal output of an integer.
%x	Unsigned hexadecimal output of an integer.
%u	Unsigned decimal output of an integer.
%c	Output of a single **char** value.
%s	Output of a string; the argument must be a pointer to a null-terminated string.
%e	Output of a **float** or **double** value in exponent notation.
%f	Like **%e** except that fixed point notation is used.
%g	Output of a **float** or **double** value, using whichever of **%d**, **%e** or **%f** produces the shorter output without dropping significant digits.
%%	Output a single percent symbol.

2) A decimal number which specifies the minimum field width. By default, output items will be padded with blanks to achieve this minimum width. Padding with zero digits will be performed if the field width is written as an integer with a leading zero.

3) A period to separate the preceding number from the following one (if it is provided).

4) A decimal number (the precision) which specifies the maximum number of characters to be printed from a string or the number of digits to be printed after the decimal point (for output of **float** or **double** numbers).

The *printf* routine is like *fprintf* except that the standard output file *stdout* is used. Its argument structure is

```
printf( format-specification, arg1, arg2, ... )
```

A third function, *sprintf*, is very used very similarly to *fprint*, but does not actually perform any output. (It is mentioned here only because this seems to be the most appropriate place.) It generates a formatted string and stores it in a character array that is supplied as the first argument. For example,

```
char buffer[128];  int cpu_secs, total_secs;
       .
       .

sprintf(buffer, "CPU usage = %.2f%%\n",
          cpu_secs * 100.0 / total_secs );
```

We close this description of the formatted output functions with a warning. A very common mistake in C programming is to match data arguments with the format codes used in the format string argument incorrectly. A failure to match the arguments properly will, at best, cause garbage to be printed. More likely, however, it will cause the program to abort with a bus error or segmentation fault.

7.3.5. Formatted Input Functions

Formatted input of data is performed by the *fscanf* and *scanf* functions. A sample use of *fscanf* is

```
nd = fscanf(stdin, "%d%c", &n, &ch);
```

where *n* has type **int** and *ch* has type **char**. The *fscanf* function reads the specified file (standard input) looking for a decimal integer (as required by the %d format code). It will skip white space (blanks, tabs and *newline* characters), but no other characters when seeking this number. The number is read and assigned to variable *n*. The very next character (matched by the %c format item) is assigned to variable *ch*.

The *fscanf* function requires that it be passed pointers to variables in the third and following argument positions. (The word *pointers* must be stressed, because this represents a major difference in usage between the formatted input and output functions.) The function result returned by *fscanf* is the count of how many input items have been successfully read and assigned. Thus, if *nd* does not have the value 2 after executing the statement above, we know that there has been an error in the input. (Perhaps a character that is not a decimal digit has been found when reading the number to be assigned to *n*.) The result assigned to *nd* would be *EOF* if the end-of-input is reached.

The valid input format items are listed in Table 7.2. A modifier may optionally precede the format code. A modifier which may precede the d, o and x format codes is the letter *l* (*ell*) to indicate that the corresponding variable has the **long int** type. The *l* modifier may also precede the e or f codes to indicate that the corresponding argument has the **double** type.[4] A second possible modifier is the letter *h* which may precede the d, o and x codes to indicate that the corresponding argument has the **short int** type. Between the percent symbol and the format code, a maximum field width can be specified. This defines a limit on the number of characters which will be read, converted and assigned to the corresponding argument. An example is

TABLE 7.2. Input Format Codes

%d	Input a decimal integer and assign to an **int** variable.
%o	Input an octal integer and assign to an **int** variable.
%x	Input a hexadecimal integer and assign to an **int** variable.
%c	Input a single character. Unlike the other format codes, no white space is skipped before the character is read and assigned to the corresponding **char** variable. Thus, a blank can be read with the **%c** format.
%s	Input of a string of non-white space characters. The corresponding argument must be a character pointer pointing to a character array large enough to hold the string and a terminating null character. The null byte is supplied by *fscanf*.
%e %f	Input a floating-point number and assign to a **float** variable. The two format codes may be used interchangeably for input.

---

[4] These two format codes may also be capitalized to indicate that the corresponding argument has the **double** type. That is, the codes **%E** and **%F** are accepted as equivalent to **%le** and **%lf**.

```
        char linebuf[50];   int nd;
                  .
                  .
        nd = fscanf(stdin, "%49s", linebuf);
```

where a limit of 49 characters is imposed on the string to be read. (This leaves one element in the array to hold the null terminator.) Note that no ampersand prefixes the array name. This is because an unsubscripted array name is treated as being a pointer, a pointer to the first array element.

Format strings may include characters other than format codes. If these characters are not white space characters (blanks, tabs or *newline* characters), they must match characters found in the input. White space in the format matches optional white space in the input, but the kind of white space characters and how many are present is irrelevant. To match a percent symbol in the input, the format string may contain the code **%%**.

The *scanf* function is the same as *fscanf* except that the standard input file is assumed. Here is an example:

```
        nd = scanf( "%2d%2d", &n1, &n2 );
```

Finally, *sscanf* works similarly to *fscanf* except that the input characters are read from an array instead of from an input stream. For example, if the array *buffer* contains the string **"45677873 jones"** when the statement

```
        nd = sscanf(buffer,"%3d%d %s", &i, &j, s);
```

is executed, variable *i* will be assigned 456, *j* will be assigned 77873, the string **"jones"** will be copied into the array *s*, and *nd* will be set to 3.

Just as we closed the preceding section of this chapter with a warning, we should give a warning about *scanf* and its two companion functions too. It is a common error to forget that variables which are to receive values are not passed directly. Pointers to the variables are passed instead. If you forget to prefix an argument with the **&** operator, your program will probably fail with a bus error or segmentation fault.

7.3.6. File Handling

Input from or output to a disk file requires a file pointer variable and a call to the function *fopen* to allocate a buffer and prepare the file. This function takes two string arguments: the first argument is the name of the file, the second argument is a string specifying the access mode. The primary access mode strings are **"r"** for read access, **"w"** for write access, and **"a"** for writing to the end of a file (i.e. *append* mode). The *fopen* function returns a file pointer result, referring to a newly created stream, if it was able to access the file (or if it was able to create a new file to receive output). If *fopen* is unsuccessful, perhaps because the file is unreadable, it returns a null pointer as its result. (*NULL* is defined as the null pointer value 0 in the "stdio.h" include file.)

Thus, the following code will read the first line from the on-line manual file "/usr/man/cat1/ls.1":

```
#define MAXLEN 256
FILE *fopen(), *fp;
char line[MAXLEN];
    .
    .
    .
fp = fopen("/usr/man/cat1/ls.1", "r");
if (fp == NULL) {
    fprintf(stderr,"cannot read the file\n");
    exit(1);
}
fgets(line, MAXLEN, fp);
```

If the first character in the filename is not a slash (/) character, *fopen* will try to locate the file from within the current working directory, that is, the directory that was current when this C program began execution or that was made current by a call to the *chdir* function. Note that shell command language metacharacters, such as *, ? and ~, are not recognized as metacharacters if used in filenames that are passed to *fopen*.

It is possible to open a file for both input and output. But, because of buffering by the stream input-output functions, you will not get correct results if you freely intermingle input requests and output requests on a file. The rules are that you can only switch from reading to writing (or vice versa) if you have read up to the end-of-file indicator (*EOF*) or if you call *fseek* or *rewind*. The simultaneous input-output modes are "r+" where the file is initially positioned for reading/writing at its beginning, "w+" where the file is created or emptied if the file already exists, and "a+" where the file is initially positioned for reading/writing at its end.

When you have finished working with a particular file, you may close the file with the *fclose* function. Its sole argument is a file pointer for an open stream. There is normally no necessity to close files in your program, open files are automatically closed when the program terminates. You only really need to close files if you wish to reuse a file pointer variable for some other file or if you are in danger of having too many simultaneously open files. (The limit on the number of open streams is at least 20.)

7.3.7. Binary I/O Functions

File are not restricted to containing only ASCII characters. Indeed, relocatable binary ".o") files contain mostly non-ASCII data. Such files can be read one character at a time with the *getc* and *getchar* functions. Use of other input functions such as *gets* would be inappropriate. Non-ASCII data can be written with any of the output functions discussed so far.

A small problem occurs when reading a file containing non-ASCII data or data in extended ASCII (extended by the addition of 8-bit codes). The special character code, *EOF*, does not work as an unambiguous indication of the end of file. ASCII characters have integer values in the range 0 to 127. On computers which have signed bytes, bytes hold values in the range -128 to 127. Thus, non-ASCII data values may correspond to integer values in the range -128 to -1. This clearly conflicts with the value -1, which is used for the end-of-file indicator, *EOF*. In other words, it is possible to read a byte from a non-ASCII file which has the same value as *EOF*. The way around the problem is to use a special function, *feof*, which tests for the end-of-file condition. The call `feof(`*fp*`)` returns non-zero if the stream referenced by the file pointer *fp* is at the end of file. If you are concerned with efficiency and wish to avoid the overhead of an extra function call for each character read, you need only write your program to call *feof* when the byte just read has the *EOF* value.

If you wish to read non-ASCII data in larger chunks than one byte at a time, you have a choice of two functions. The *get word* function, *getw*, returns an integer composed of the next four bytes from an input stream. The *fread* function can be used to read an arbitrary amount of data into an array. Similarly, *putw* is used to output one word (four bytes) at a time, and *fwrite* is used to output an arbitrary amount of data from an array.

7.3.8. Other Stream I/O Functions

If you wish to reread a file, referenced by the file pointer *fp*, that is currently open, the call

        rewind(fp);

will suffice. The next call to *getc* on this file would read the first character in the file again. A call to the *rewind* function performs just a particular kind of file positioning. General positioning capabilities are provided by the *fseek* function, which permits an arbitrary file position to be specified. A file position is defined by an integer, which represents an offset in bytes. This offset can be made relative to the start of the file, to the current position in the file or to the end of the file. A typical call is

        status = fseek(fp, offset, kind);

where *kind* is 0, 1 or 2 to indicate that the offset is given relative to the file start, current position, or end of the file, respectively. The result returned by *fseek* is zero if the seek is successful and −1 if not.

When writing to a file, you can freely seek to a position way beyond the current end of the file. For example,

        fseek(fp, 1000000, 2);
        putc('*', fp);

seeks to a position one million bytes past the current end of file and writes a single character there. This does not cause the UNIX system to waste one million bytes of disk space. Holes in files, created by seeks similar to the above, consume very little storage. If you later attempt to read from a region in a file within a hole, the system will supply null bytes as the characters read, but these null bytes are not physically present on the disk. You should note, however, that the ability to create holes in files is peculiar to the UNIX system. If you transport your C program to a non-UNIX system, you should not expect files to have quite the same properties.

If you ever need to know the current position within a file, the *ftell* function should be used. The result of a call like `ftell(fp)` returns an offset relative to the start of the file.

Another useful function is *ungetc*. It can be used in conjunction with character-oriented input to "unread" one character. Frequently, program functions have to read one character too many. For example, a function to input a decimal number cannot determine that it has read the entire number unless it reads one extra character appearing after the number. This extra character may, perhaps, be a significant (non-blank) character that should be read in another part of your program. Rather than introducing extra flags and tortuous logic into the program to handle the situation, C lets us simply "unread" the extra character. This is accomplished with

```
ungetc(c, fp)
```

where *c* is the character and *fp* is the appropriate file pointer (such as *stdin*). The very next character to be read, by *getc* or *gets* etc., will be *c*. Note that *c* need not be the same as the excess character that was originally read. There are naturally some restrictions on the use of *ungetc*. There cannot be two successive calls to *ungetc* without a read operation in between. Also, *ungetc* will not permit you to unread the end-of-file marker (*EOF*).

7.4. LOW-LEVEL FILE HANDLING FUNCTIONS

7.4.1. Introduction to Low-Level I/O

As explained in the previous section, all the stream I/O functions are implemented in terms of lower level functions. A few of these functions, such as *chdir* and *chmod*, are useful in programs that use the stream I/O interface. Many others are not. However, it is probably still a good idea to know what the low level functions do and what their interface is.

The low level functions maintain a table called the *object reference table* or, sometimes, the *descriptor table*. This table contains, amongst other things, information about all open files in use by the current process. Each open file is identified by its index in the table. The files corresponding to standard input, standard output and standard error output initially have indexes 0, 1 and 2. These indexes are known as *file descriptors*. File descriptors are small integers, in the range 0 to 19 or so,[5] and should never be confused with streams or file pointers, which are pointers to structures maintained by the stream I/O functions. We will now examine some of the functions for manipulating files at the level of file descriptors.

7.4.2. Opening and Closing Files

A file may be opened (and created if necessary) through the use of the *open* function. Its first argument is the pathname of the file, just as it is for the first argument of the *fopen* function. The second argument is an integer containing flags that control the mode that the file should be opened in. The third flag defines the file access modes that should be given to the file if the file is created by this call to *open*. An example of a call follows:

```
#include <sys/file.h>
int fd;
     .
     .
     .
fd = open( "/tmp/junk", O_WRONLY|O_CREAT, 0644 );
if (fd < 0) {
    perror( "temporary file" );
    exit( -1 );
}
```

The names *O_WRONLY* and *O_CREAT* are flag values defined as `#define` constants in the include file. They indicate that we wish to open the file for output and to create the file if it does not already exist.[6] If the file is created, it will be assigned the access modes 0644 (an octal constant).[7] These particular modes permit reading by anyone but writing only by the current user. The result returned by *open* is a file descriptor. If the file could not be opened, an error code is set in the external variable *errno* and the function returns a negative integer as its result. The *perror* function may be used to output a message corresponding to the error code set in *errno*. The argument to *perror* is a string that will be prefixed to the error message.

When we have finished using the file, it can be closed with the *close* function.

---

[5] Berkeley UNIX guarantees only that each process has at least 20 slots in the object reference table. The table may be a little larger at your installation. The *getdtablesize* function may be used to find out what the actual size is.

[6] The full list of flags can be found in the manual entry for *open*.

[7] The full list of file mode values can be found in the section 2 manual entry for *chmod*. Execute the command: `man 2 chmod` to see this entry.

7.4.3. Reading and Writing

Only functions for reading and writing blocks of data are provided. To read a large number of bytes of data from the file with descriptor *fd*, a code sequence like

```
char inbuffer[1024];
int  fd, nread;
...
nread = read( fd, inbuffer, 1024 );
```

may be used. The result returned by *read* is the count of characters actually read. This count may be smaller than the size of the input buffer (specified in the third argument) if we reach the end of file or if the input is being read from a terminal. An error is indicated by a negative result. The buffer size used in our example is a size that leads to fairly efficient I/O. The actual size specified in the call can be any number from one upwards. But specifying a buffer size of one makes file processing quite inefficient, because the system overhead involved in reading one character is about the same as for reading 1024 characters. If you really wish to read characters one at a time, you should probably use the stream input-output package.

Output via a file descriptor proceeds similarly. The code sequence looks like

```
char outbuffer[1024];
int  fd, nwritten;
...
nwritten = write( fd, outbuffer, 1024 );
```

The result of the function call is the count of bytes that were actually written. This number will equal to the buffer size specified in the third argument unless there has been an I/O error. If there is an error, the result is -1.

7.4.4. Other Functions

We should mention here that the *lseek* function is available for changing the current position within a file. It is used in a way that is very similar to the *fseek* function in the family of stream I/O functions. Another useful function is *fdopen* which can be used to convert a low-level file descriptor to the higher-level stream interface. If *fd* is a descriptor for a file open for input, we can execute

```
int  fd;
FILE *fp;
...
fp = fdopen( fd, "r" );
```

to obtain a stream file pointer. The read-write mode used in the *fdopen* call should match the mode of the file descriptor. The opposite conversion, finding the file descriptor corresponding to a stream file pointer, is performed by the *fileno* macro.

7.5. STRING AND CHARACTER HANDLING

7.5.1. String Handling

There is a large family of string handling functions. These functions require that input strings be terminated by a null byte (as per normal C conventions). There are functions for copying (*strcpy*), comparing (*strcmp*), catenating (*strcat*), searching (*index* and *rindex*) and for finding the length (*strlen*). Suitable declarations for all these functions are provided in the header file "strings.h".

A couple of these functions are used in the program example of Figure 7.3. This program, called *addalias*, is trivial. If invoked with a command line like

        addalias jack jsmith@trashvax

it will add a line of the form

        alias jack jsmith@trashvax

to the ".mailrc" file in your home directory. (The ".mailrc" file contains commands and definitions for use by the *mail* program.) Our *addalias* program is so trivial, in fact, that we could replace it with the following *csh* alias in our ".cshrc" file:

        alias addalias 'echo \"alias \!*\" >> ~/.mailrc'

(Refer to Appendix B for more information about *csh* aliases.)

The program uses *strcpy* to copy the string referenced by the second argument into a character array referenced by the first argument. The function returns immediately after a null byte is copied. The *strcpy* function does not check whether the target array is actually large enough to receive the copied string. If there is a danger of overflow, you should use the *strncpy* function.

The *strcat* function is similar. The string referenced by the second argument is appended to the string referenced by the first argument. The first argument string must be contained in an array that has sufficient space after the null byte for the appended string. Again, if there is a danger of overflow, there is a function, *strncat*, which may be used instead.

Another string function is *strcmp* for comparing the first argument string with the second. The result is -1, 0 or $+1$ to indicate whether the first string is less than, equal to, or greater than the second string. The *strlen* function returns the length of the argument string. The *index* function searches its first argument (a string) for an occurrence of its second argument (a character). The result is a pointer to the first occurrence, or *NULL* if the character cannot

FIGURE 7.3. The addalias Program

```c
#include <stdio.h>

char filename[256];

void main( argc, argv )
int argc;   char *argv[];
{
    FILE *fp;   char *hp;

    if (argc < 3) {
        fprintf(stderr,
            "Usage: %s name path\n", argv[0] );
        exit( -1 );
    }
    hp = (char *)getenv( "HOME" );
    if (hp == NULL) {
        fprintf(stderr, "No HOME env. variable!!\n");
        exit( -1 );
    }
    strcpy( filename, hp );
    strcat( filename, "/.mailrc" );
    fp = fopen( filename, "a" );
    if (fp == NULL) {
        perror( filename );
        exit( -1 );
    }
    fprintf(fp, "alias %s %s\n", argv[1], argv[2] );
    fclose( fp );
}
```

be found in the string. The *rindex* function works the same way, except that it returns a pointer to the last occurrence of a character.

The *getenv* function used in Figure 7.3 will be fully explained in the next chapter. For now, it is sufficient to know that the result of the call getenv("HOME") is the same string as is printed by the shell command

          echo $HOME

This string is the full pathname of your home directory where the ".mailrc" file should reside, if it exists.

7.5.2. Character Handling

There is a large family of macros for testing and converting single characters. To use these macros, the C program must include the directive

```
#include <ctype.h>
```

These macros implement functions for testing if a character is alphabetic (*isalph*), is a decimal digit (*isdigit*), is a white space character (*isspace*), etc. In addition, there are macros for converting a letter from lower case to upper case (*toupper*), converting a string of decimal digits to an integer (*atoi*), etc. The full list of macros appears in Appendix D.

These macros are particularly useful if you intend to transport your program to another computer. For example, the test for a character being a letter of the alphabet must be coded differently on machines that use the ASCII and EBCDIC character sets. If you use the *isalph* macro to perform the test, you do not have to worry about how the test should be coded.

7.6. STORAGE ALLOCATION FUNCTIONS

Storage can be dynamically allocated by the *malloc* function. Its argument is the number of bytes to allocate, its result is a pointer to the newly allocated storage. If *malloc* cannot obtain sufficient storage, it returns a null pointer result. A typical code sequence for using *malloc* is

```
struct tagname *sp;
...
sp = (struct tagname *)malloc(
                 sizeof(struct tagname) );
if (sp == NULL) {
        fprintf(stderr,"insufficient storage\n");
        exit(1);
}
```

Dynamically allocated storage can be de-allocated through the *free* function. Its argument is a pointer to an area of storage that was previously obtained from one of the allocation functions. For example, to release the storage obtained in the code sequence above, we can execute

```
free(sp);
```

Of course, once you have released the storage, you should not subsequently attempt to access it in your program.

A useful alternative to *malloc* is the *calloc* function. This function is intended for allocating storage to arrays. The storage it returns contains zeros (or *NULL* pointer values), exactly the same as static storage that has no explicit initialization in C programs. The *calloc* function requires two arguments. The first is the number of elements in the array, the second is the size of each element in bytes. We might, for example, use *calloc* in a program as follows:

```
#define ARRAYSIZE 256
int *array1;
...
array1 = (int *)calloc( ARRAYSIZE, sizeof(int) );
if (array1 == NULL) {
        fprintf(stderr, "insufficient storage\n");
        exit( -1 );
}

/* initialize the array */
for(i=0; i<ARRAYSIZE; i++ )
        array1[i] = -1;
```

Storage obtained via *calloc* can be returned to the system with the *free* function, just as for *malloc*.

There is one more storage allocation function, *realloc*, but it is effectively obsolete and provided only to maintain compatibility with older versions of the UNIX system. If you browse through the on-line manual entries, you will find two more functions called *brk* and *sbrk*. These are the low-level routines which obtain storage directly from the operating system; *malloc* and the other functions listed above are implemented as calls to *brk* and *sbrk*. Normal programs should not call them directly.

7.7. MISCELLANEOUS USEFUL FUNCTIONS

Any *sh* shell command may be executed from within a C program. The argument to the *system* function is a string containing the command. If this command creates output, it writes directly to the standard output and, possibly, the standard error output. If the command expects input, it will read from the standard input. For example, if we would like a program to include a directory listing in its output, we might write the following code:

```
fflush( stdout );
system( "ls -alx" );
```

The call to *fflush* is usually required so that any previous output generated by the program actually appears before the output of the command executed by *system*.

If we are not content to have the output of the system command sent to the terminal, that is, if we need the output returned to our program for further processing, a *pipe* must be created. To read the output of the system *ls* command, code similar to the following could be used:

```
FILE  *lspipe;
...
lspipe = popen( "ls -alx", "r" );
if (lspipe == NULL) {
    fprintf(stderr, "\"ls\" command failed!\n");
    exit(1);
}
...
/*  Now the program can read the output
    of "ls" using the file pointer "lspipe".
    At the end of input, the character
    value EOF will be read, as usual.      */
...
pclose( lspipe );
```

The first argument to *popen* is the command to be executed. It is passed to the *sh* shell for interpretation and execution. The second argument indicates the I/O direction. If we specify `"r"`, as above, then we will be reading the standard output generated by that command. If we specify `"w"`, we would be writing to the pipe and thus providing standard input for the command. The result of the call to *popen* is a stream which may be used like any other stream (except that a few operations, such as *fseek* cannot be performed). When we have finished reading from or writing to a pipe, *pclose* is used to terminate it.

Pipes involve the creation of parallel processes. The command passed as an argument to *popen* is executed by a separate process. We will be looking at the creation and management of parallel processes in more detail in Chapter 11.

FURTHER READING

- D.M. Ritchie and K. Thompson, "The UNIX Time-Sharing System," *Communications of the ACM* 17, Issue 7 (July 1974), pp. 365-375. The paper provides a brief overview of the UNIX system and of its implementation. The description of the file system is particularly relevant to the material in this chapter.

QUESTIONS

1.   Although the *printf* and *scanf* functions have similar, but opposite, effects, their usage is inconsistent. For example, a call of *printf* to output an integer and a string variable looks like

```
printf( "%s  %d", str, n );
```

whereas the call to input these variables looks like

```
scanf( "%s %d", str, &n );
```

Why is the **&** operator required for variable *n* and not for *str* ?

2.   The program displayed in Figure 7.2 was intended to remove comments from C source code. Can you find an example of C source code which will be processed incorrectly by this program?

3.   What happens if, after we create a hard link to a file owned by someone else, the owner deletes the file? Can we still access the file via our directory link?

4.   What happens if after we create a symbolic link to a file owned by someone else, the file is deleted?

5.   The *getwd* function works by reading the "..." entry in the current directory to find the parent directory; then it reads the "..." entry in that directory, and so on until it reaches the root directory of the system. In this way, it can build up the full pathname of the current working directory. Under some circumstances, *getwd* fails. What are these circumstances?

6.   Name one system function which may fail to work properly if a group of hard links in a file system form a cycle.

CHAPTER 8

INTERFACING C WITH THE UNIX SYSTEM

8.1. ACCESSING COMMAND LINE ARGUMENTS

All UNIX commands typed at the terminal consist of a command name followed by zero or more arguments. The command name is just the name of an executable program (most often a compiled C program) that is invoked by the system. The arguments are simply strings which the C program can access.

A C program must always have a function named *main*. This function is directly invoked by the UNIX system. The *main* function has two arguments, conventionally named *argc* and *argv*.[1] The *argc* argument has **int** type and corresponds to the number of arguments provided on the UNIX command line. The command name (i.e. the program name) counts as one argument. If we type the command

        prog -x fred

to run the program *prog*, the *argc* argument passed to the *main* function inside program *prog* will have value 3. The second argument, *argv* is an array of strings. Each argument in the command line (including the command name) is a string in the array. For the command line given above, the *argv* array that is passed to the program would contain the following values:

---

[1] Actually the UNIX system provides three arguments. The third argument, often named *envp*, is a pointer to a list of environment variable definitions. Few programs use this third argument, and the environment is accessible by other means, so we will ignore its existence for now.

```
argv[0]  is  "prog"
argv[1]  is  "-x"
argv[2]  is  "fred"
```

Some code which is fairly typical of command line processing in C programs appears in Figure 8.1. The premise is that our program expects optional flag arguments (-b or -x) and expects an optional file name (which does not start with a minus sign) where input can be found. If a file name argument is not provided, the program will read from the standard input.

Inside this program, all input will be read via the *fp* pointer. For example, it will read a single character with the function call `getc(fp)`. The global variable *pgmname* is created and maintained solely for use in error messages. It is good practice to include the program name in error messages, as above. Also, by obtaining the program name from the command line, we make our program immune to any renaming of the file containing the executable program. It might also be a good idea to have this program print an error or warning message if it finds a flag other than -b or -x.

8.2. RETURNING A STATUS CODE FROM A PROGRAM

When a program completes execution, a status code is returned. The status code is usually a small integer, where zero is conventionally used to indicate that the program terminated normally. Sometimes the status code value is used to indicate a simple result. For example, the *cmp* program with the -s flag compares two files and sets the status code to zero if the files are identical and to one otherwise. Nothing is printed. The *cmp* program is useful in shell scripts, where the shell command language includes a means of testing the status of a command. For example, the *csh* command

```
if ( { cmp -s file1 file2 } ) rm file2
```

will delete "file2" if it is identical to "file1".

It is good practice to make sure that the status code of a program is meaningful before it terminates. A misleading status code value can cause problems when shell scripts or makefiles (see Chapter 9) are developed. If you simply let control reach the bottom of the function called *main* in your program, control returns to the system with an undefined status code. But setting the status code of a program is easy. If the main program executes a **return** statement, the status code can be specified in that. For example,

```
return( 1 );
```

would set the status code to one. If you wish to terminate the program while some function other than *main* is being executed, you may halt the program and set the status code by calling *exit*. For example,

```
exit( -1 );
```

FIGURE 8.1. **Accessing Command-Line Arguments**

```
#include <stdio.h>

char *pgmname;     /* name of this program */
short bflag = 0;   /* -b flag on command line? */
short xflag = 0;   /* -x flag on command line? */
FILE *fp;

void main( argc, argv )
int argc;  char *argv[];
{
    int i;  char *cp;

    pgmname = argv[0];
    fp = stdin;
    for( i=1; i<argc; i++ ) {
        cp = argv[i];
        if (*cp == '-') { /* a flag */
            if (*++cp == 'b')
                bflag++;
            else if (*cp == 'x')
                xflag++;
        } else {  /* a file name argument */
            if (fp != stdin) {
                fprintf(stderr,
                    "%s: too many arguments\n", pgmname );
                exit(1);
            }
            fp = fopen(cp, "r" );
            if (fp == NULL) {
                fprintf(stderr, "%s: unable to read %s\n",
                    pgmname, cp );
                exit(1);
            }
        }
    }

    /*  remainder of program omitted  */
```

may appear in any function in your program. Control will never return from a call to *exit*.

8.3. COMPILATION AND CHECKOUT

A C compilation proceeds in several stages. First, the C preprocessor reads the program source text. It performs all the operations implied by compiler directive lines (those beginning with the # character). Thus, it merges all included files into the source code, performs macro substitutions, and skips source text as required by #if and #ifdef directives. The preprocessor also evaluates constant expressions and it strips comments from the source code. Second, the C compiler reads the output of the preprocessor and translates this simplified C source code into assembler code. Next is an optional optimization step, in which an optimizer program attempts to improve the quality of the assembler code. These optimizations are mostly concerned with control flow; for example, jumps to jump instructions are redirected and jumps over jumps are simplified. Next, the system assembler program *as* reads the output of the preceding step and translates it into relocatable binary object code. In the final step, the system loader *ld* reads the object code file (or files), merges them with the object code for any system functions that are referenced, and creates an executable program.

All these steps are implied by the single UNIX command *cc*. Options on this command determine whether or not the optimization phase is included and can cause the last one or two steps to be suppressed. To use *cc*, the C program source must be contained in a file whose name has the suffix ".c". (If you forget to use this suffix, the *cc* command will give you the extremely strange error message "bad magic number"!) Supposing that this file is called "prog.c", we can compile it with

```
cc prog.c
```

If there are no errors, the executable version of this program is created in a file called *a.out*. The program can now be executed by typing

```
a.out
```

at the terminal. If you prefer to use another name for your program (which is likely), you can rename the program to *prog* (or whatever) by executing

```
mv a.out prog
```

Alternatively, we can make the *cc* command create the executable program in a file with this name directly if we type

```
cc prog.c -o prog
```

The flag -o represents just one of many compilation options. The full list of options can be obtained by executing the command

```
man cc
```

The more useful options are:

-c   causes cc to generate the relocatable object code version of the program and stop there. The object code file(s) have the same names as the source code files, except that the ".c" suffixes are replaced by ".o". This option is most useful in dealing with multi-file programs.

-g   causes cc to output extra symbol table information for use by the *sdb* and *dbx* debuggers. Note that to use *dbx* on the Pyramid computer, the necessary compilation option is −**gx**. For the SUN computer, −**go** must be provided if *adb* is to be used (instead of *dbx* or *dbxtool*).

-D   is used to define an identifier (a macro) to the preprocessor. It is useful for controlling the conditional inclusion of source code.

-o   is followed by the name of the file that should hold the final executable program.

-O   causes the optimization pass to be performed.

The C compiler is notorious for its poor handling of syntax errors. The error messages often seem to bear absolutely no relation to the mistake that was made. Furthermore, the line number reported in the message may not correspond to where the mistake was made. The only safe assumption is that the mistake was made on or before the reported line number.

There is another processor *lint* whose purpose is to check C source code for errors. If you execute

```
lint prog.c
```

where "prog.c" represents the name of your program file, you will be given better quality syntax error messages and your program will be subjected to a detailed analysis to check for type mismatches and probable errors. It is in the nature of the C language that many errors cannot definitely be determined to be errors by a static analysis (i.e. execution is needed); therefore *lint* will normally report only probable errors.

Another disadvantage of *lint* is that it tends to generate warning messages for C constructions that are perfectly valid. For example, if you sometimes use the *malloc* function to obtain storage for one kind of structure and at other times use it to obtain storage for another structure type, *lint* will complain. It complains because there is an inconsistent usage of the *malloc* function in the program. Indeed, *lint* would be quite correct; the usage is inconsistent. If you wish to eliminate warning messages about usage of the *malloc* function, you must provide the declaration

```
extern char *malloc();
```

in your program. In addition, you must cast the result of every call to *malloc* to convert the result to the type that you need.

Some C library routines, the *printf* function for instance, are almost always used inconsistently. We may call *printf* with two arguments at one place, with four arguments at another, and so on. Furthermore, even if the numbers of parameters match in all calls, the data types of the parameters may not be the same. To avoid generating hundreds of lines of warning messages about *printf* and related functions, there is a way to tell *lint* not to complain. A special comment containing the word *VARARGS* can be placed immediately before the function definition. This has been done in the library where *printf* et al. are defined.

From the preceding discussion, you can see that you must not believe everything that *lint* reports. Every message should be treated as a warning only. However, it is worth the trouble to run *lint* and to read all of its messages carefully. Debugging C programs is so difficult that any time spent wading through the spurious *lint* messages to find the one or two that report genuine errors will be well-rewarded.

8.4. ACCESSING ENVIRONMENT VALUES

If you execute the UNIX command

```
printenv
```

you will see several lines of information printed at your terminal. A typical output would resemble

```
HOME=/u0/wendy
SHELL=/bin/csh
PATH=/usr/local/bin:/usr/ucb:/bin:/usr/bin:.
USER=wendy
TERM=vt100
EDITOR=/usr/ucb/vi
MORE=-c
```

The identifiers appearing on the left of the equals symbols are known as *environment variables*. The strings appearing to the right of the equals are their values. Environment variables are maintained by the UNIX system and by the command shell. Several of these environment variables, such as *USER*, are always provided. Others are present only if the shell executed commands supplied by the user to create them.

The shell always provides environment variables named *HOME*, *SHELL*, *PATH* and *USER*. It should be easy to guess their meanings. *HOME* is the name of the home directory for the user executing the current shell. *SHELL* is the default shell for the user (not necessarily the identity of the shell that is currently active). *PATH* is a list of directories containing executable programs. Whenever the user types a command name (without providing an explicit path to an executable file), the shell searches the directories listed for *PATH* to find the program to run. *USER* identifies the user executing the current shell.[2]

The values of environment variables can be accessed from within a C program. This ability allows the program to perform actions that are customized to a particular user or to a particular terminal type. For example, the *mail* program uses the value of *HOME* to locate the user's home directory and then attempts to read a file named ".mailrc" in this directory. Various other system programs, like the *vi* editor, perform similar actions. In addition to providing information about the execution environment, environment variables can be used to pass extra information to the program. For example, the environment variable *MORE* can be used to pass options to the *more* program. Although these options can be passed to *more* on the command line, it is often more convenient to the user to put them in the environment.

FIGURE 8.2. The printenv Program

```
#include <stdio.h>

/* This program simulates the printenv command */

void main( argc, argv, envp )
int argc;   char **argv, **envp;
{
    register char *cp;
    register int len;

    len = (argc > 1)? strlen(argv[1]) : 0;

    for( ; *envp != NULL; envp++ ) {
        cp = *envp;
        if (len > 0) {
            if (strncmp(cp,argv[1],len) != 0
                || cp[len] != '=')
                continue;
            cp += len+1;
        }
        puts( cp );
    }
    exit( 0 );     /* Set the status code */
}
```

---

[2] To be precise, *USER* shows the *effective* user identity.

There are two ways in which environment variables can be accessed from within a C program. The system passes an *environment pointer* to the program when it is invoked. This pointer is provided as the third argument of the *main* function of the C program. It is a pointer to an array of pointers to character strings. The end of the array is signalled by a NULL pointer. Each string has the form

NAME=*value*

where *NAME* represents the name of an environment variable and *value* its value. As an example of accessing the environment through the environment pointer argument, a sample program for printing either the entire environment or just one environment variable is reproduced in Figure 8.2. This program effectively reproduces the behaviour of the *printenv* shell command.

However, there is no need to include code like that in Figure 8.2 in a program that requires the value of an environment variable. The library function *getenv* may be used to look up the value of any variable in the environment. The argument to this function is a string that gives the name of the environment variable. The result from the function is the value of the variable. If no variable with the desired name exists in the environment, the result is the

FIGURE 8.3. Using the getenv Function

```
FILE *logfile;
char *logfilename = "/u0/wendy/.logfile";
         .
         .
         .
    logfile = fopen( logfilename, "a" );
    if (logfile == NULL) {
        fprintf(stderr, "Cannot write to %s\n",
            logfilename);
    } else {
        char *user;
        user = getenv( "USER" );
        if (user == NULL) user = "Unknown!";
        fprintf(logfile, "User = %s\n", user );
        fclose( logfile );
    }
         .
         .
         .
```

NULL pointer. Suppose that we would like to keep a record of who has been using a program. We could insert code like that shown in Figure 8.3 into the program so that it appends the value of *USER* to a log file. Note that the *getenv* function does not make use of the environment pointer passed to the program. There is a more direct means of access via an external variable named *environ*. Therefore, there is no need to declare three arguments to the *main* function when *getenv* is used. And, by the way, the code of Figure 8.3 is meant as an example of use only. It would be unsuitable for use in situations where security is important, since users can find ways to lie about who they are (they can create their own arrays of strings to pass as an environment) and would likely be able to destroy the log file.

QUESTIONS

1. Suppose that you create a C source file with the name "prog" (forgetting to append the ".c" suffix to the file name). If you attempt to compile the program with the command

    ```
    cc prog
    ```

    you will get the error message "bad magic number". What, exactly, does this message mean?

2. If you use *lint* on a program that contains even a single call to the *malloc* function, you will probably get the warning messages:

    ```
    malloc, arg. 1 used inconsistently
    malloc value used inconsistently
    ```

    What do these messages mean and how could you avoid getting them?

CHAPTER 9

DEVELOPING LARGE C
PROGRAMS

9.1. MULTI-FILE COMPILATION

Large C programs should be developed in several pieces. These different parts should be held in different files and may be compiled separately. All it takes is a little care to ensure that the different pieces fit together correctly. The way to make sure that the pieces match up properly requires the use of C *header* files. We will refer to these as *.h* files because that is the filename suffix required by the C compiler. However, to be certain that the general principles are understood first, we will forego their use in the following example.

A complete C program consists of a sequence of external declarations for variables and functions. Executable statements may only appear inside function declarations. The declarations can be split into two or more files and compiled separately, provided that some information gets repeated. Let us consider a trivial example. Suppose that we have three functions named *main*, *fn1* and *fn2*; and we have several global variables *x1*, *x2*, etc. We will assume that the functions need to access all of the global variables. A possible way of splitting the program into two files is shown in Figure 9.1.

The storage for the global variables, *x1*, *x2* and *x3*, is declared and initialized in the first file. These variables may, of course, be referenced from within the two functions, *fn1* and *fn2*. In addition, we have declared a variable *local-var* in the first file. The keyword **static** on the declaration causes the variable to be local to this file. It cannot be referenced from any other source file.

FIGURE 9.1. A Two File Program

File 1   (named 'prog1.c')

```
int x1 = 5;
char *x2[] = { "message 1", "message 2", "message 3" };
float x3 = 4.500;

static float localvar = 0.0;
static void fn2();

float fn1( a, b )
int a, b;
{
    /* body of fn1 appears here */
}

static void fn2( a )
char a;
{
    /* body of fn2 appears here */
}
```

File 2   (named 'prog2.c')

```
extern int x1;
extern char *x2[];
extern float x3;

extern float fn1();

static int localvar, anothervar;

void main( argc, argv )
int argc;  char **argv;
{
    /* body of main program appears here */
}
```

Similarly, the function *fn2* has been given the **static** attribute. This means that it can be called only from functions within the first file.

In the second file, we want the main program (the *main* function) to be able to access the variables, *x1*, *x2* and *x3*, declared in the first file as well as the function *f1*. Clearly, declarations for *x1*, *x2*, etc. are needed, even if only to provide type information to the C compiler. However, we do not want storage to be allocated and initialized for these external variables, because the storage allocation and initialization is taken care of in File 1. When the **extern** attribute is used in front of a declaration, it indicates that we are providing type information only for variables or functions defined in another file. The **extern** attribute need not be supplied for a function declaration because the compiler assumes this attribute as the default. However, it is probably good practice to include it in order to give a positive indication that this function is used or defined in other files. The second file contains a local variable named *localvar*. This is a distinct variable from the variable declared with the same name in the first file.

Our two files may be compiled separately. The first file can be compiled with the command

```
cc -c prog1.c
```

This command will create a relocatable object file named "prog1.o". Similarly, the second file can be compiled with

```
cc -c prog2.c
```

to create the file "prog2.o". Finally, the two object files can be merged and loaded into an executable program by executing

```
cc prog1.o prog2.o -o prog
```

where the executable program has been named "prog". This last step is relatively fast compared to the first two, because no compilation is performed. The *cc* command will invoke only the system loader (*ld*) to merge the object files and any library functions that they may reference into a complete, executable, program.[1]

The advantage of this approach is that the whole program need not be recompiled if, say, we later change the *fn1* function. We could make the changes to the first file, recompile just this file and then repeat the final merge step. Recompilation is particularly easy if the *make* utility is used. As we will see shortly, this versatile UNIX program can be set up to recompile automatically any files that have been changed since the executable program was last created.

---

[1] If you wish to compile and link both files in a single step, you may execute
```
cc prog1.c prog2.c -o prog
```

9.2. EFFECTIVE USE OF *.h* FILES

We have just seen one way in which a large program can be split into files for separate compilation. There is, however, an obvious danger in this approach. It is clearly necessary for the pieces of the program to interface correctly. And it would be very easy to make a change in one file but to forget to make a matching change in another file. Perhaps, the resulting mismatch might be quite obvious. For example, we may now be calling a function with three arguments whereas, in the definition for that function, only two parameters are declared. But, regardless of how obvious the mismatch is, the C compiler has no way of telling that the mismatch exists, precisely because the source files are compiled separately. Even if we compile two source files at the same time, as in the command

```
cc -c prog1.c prog2.c
```

the C compiler will not remember any information from the first file when it comes to compile the second file. Of course, the *lint* processor can find most such mismatches, but it is desirable that the C compiler be able to find the mismatches too. Through the use of *.h* files, we can assist the compiler in this task.

Let us consider an example. Suppose that we are developing a large program which makes use of queues of integers that obey a First-in, First-out (FIFO) queuing discipline. We will further suppose that the operations to be performed on these queues include

1) creating a new (empty) queue,

2) appending an integer to the end of a queue,

3) removing the first integer from a queue, and

4) finding the length of a queue.

Modern programming practice would consider the FIFO queue to be an *abstract data type* whose implementation details should be encapsulated in a separate file and kept secret from the remainder of the program. Regardless of whether you believe in the philosophy of abstract data types, it does make good sense to separate the functions that implement the abstract data type from the remainder of the program. You will find programs that follow this scheme to be easier to develop and debug.

For our example, we shall place the declarations for the various FIFO queue functions in a file named "intqueue.c", say. Our problem now is to make sure that the other source files use the FIFO queues correctly and without requiring any knowledge of how the queues are implemented. Thus, we should provide a header file, which we can name "intqueue.h", that defines the FIFO queue data type and its operations. Quite plausibly, the "intqueue.h" file could contain the definitions reproduced in Figure 9.2.

FIGURE 9.2. The intqueue.h Header File

```
/* These two structure definitions represent the
   queue implementation.  These definitions are
   used only in the functions which implement the
   FIFO queue operations.                        */

struct q_element { int   value;
                   struct q_element *link; };

struct q_header {  struct q_element *first, *last; };

/* Instances of FIFO queues are declared with the
   FIFO_Q type.  All operations on these queues
   are performed via the four access functions
   listed below.                                 */

typedef struct q_header *FIFO_Q;

extern FIFO_Q   make_new_q();
extern int      remove1(), q_length();
extern void     append1();
```

Our structure definitions indicate that the queue is to be implemented as a linked-list and that we will keep pointers to the first and last queue elements in a separate structure. Users of the queue manipulation package will work with pointers to the queue header structure, using the type name *FIFO_Q*. They will work with pointers to the structure rather than with the structure directly because some of the functions need to change the header structure. In other words, we are using pointers to achieve the effect of call-by-reference (or PASCAL **var**) parameter passing.

Users of the FIFO queue data type should neither directly reference any field names in the two structures nor should they use the structure tag identifiers. We note that, in C, it is nearly impossible to prevent users of the package from using these field names and structure tags and thus writing code that is dependent on the queue implementation. However, we will shortly see a couple of ways to discourage direct access to the queue implementation. (Some of the more modern programming languages, such as ADA, provide better support for abstract data types and can completely deny access to the internal details of the implementation.)

FIGURE 9.3. The intqueue.c File

```
#include <stdio.h>
#include "intqueue.h"

FIFO_Q make_new_q()
{
    FIFO_Q qh;

    qh = (FIFO_Q)malloc( sizeof(*qh) );
    qh->first = qh->last = NULL;
    return( qh );
}

int length_q( qh )
FIFO_Q qh;
{
    struct q_element *tp;   int length = 0;

    for( tp=qh->first; tp!=NULL; tp=tp->link )
        length++;
    return( length );
}

void append1( qh, new_element )
FIFO_Q qh;   int new_element;
{
    struct q_element *tp;
    extern char *malloc();

    tp = (struct q_element *)malloc( sizeof(*tp) );
    tp->value = new_element;
    tp->link  = NULL;
    (qh->last)->link = tp;
    qh->last = tp;
    if (qh->first == NULL) qh->first = tp;
}

            /* continued on next page ...   */
```

```
/*   ... continued from previous page */


int remove1( qh )
FIFO_Q qh;
{
    struct q_element *tp;   int result;

    tp = qh->first;
    if (tp == NULL) {
        error( "remove1 applied to empty queue" );
        abort();
    }
    qh->first = tp->link;
    if (qh->first == NULL) qh->last = NULL;
    result = tp->value;
    free(tp);
    return( result );
}
```

The "intqueue.c" file which implements the various queue manipulation operations might contain the code reproduced in Figure 9.3. This sample code has been deliberately written in a straightforward manner. The code can be considerably shortened through full use of C language features, but we leave that as an exercise to the reader.

It must be stressed that this file, which implements the queue operations, should be the only file where the structure tags *q_element* and *q_header* are used, and where field names *first, last, value* and *link* are used in association with FIFO queues.

One may object that including the *intqueue.h* in the *intqueue.c* file causes declarations for the various functions, *make_new_q* and the rest, to be seen twice by the C compiler. That is quite correct. However, the declarations in the *.h* file provide only data type information. When the compiler later reaches the full declarations, it will check that the data types in the full declarations match the data types provided in the *.h* file. The data type checking is important to us because it verifies that our function definitions are consistent with invocations of these functions contained in other files.

The other files that comprise the rest of our large program can create and use FIFO queues, as in the code fragment shown in Figure 9.4. This code fragment might conceivably appear as part of a discrete event simulation program.

Now, as mentioned earlier, there are ways to discourage users of the queue package from directly accessing internal details of the queue

FIGURE 9.4. Using the intqueue Package

```
#include "intqueue.h"
#define MAXINT 0x7fffffff   /* largest integer value */

FIFO_Q customer_queue;
int  time_now, next_arriv_time, finish_time;
          .
            .
              .
    customer_queue = make_new_q();
    finish_time = MAXINT;
    next_arriv_time = arrival_interval();

    do {
        if (finish_time < next_arriv_time) {
            time_now = finish_time;
            if (length_q(customer_queue) == 0)
                finish_time = MAXINT;
            else
                finish_time = remove1(customer_queue);
        } else {
            time_now = next_arriv_time;
            append1(customer_queue,service_time());
            next_arriv_time += arrival_interval();
        }
    } while( time_now < 10000 );
          .
            .
              .
```

implementation. A simple technique is to tell some white lies to the C compiler
and to users of the FIFO queue package. We can change the "intqueue.h" file
to contain the following definitions:

```
/* The FIFO_Q declaration, below, is a lie! */
typedef float *FIFO_Q;
FIFO_Q make_new_q();
int  length_q(), remove1();
void append1();
```

The choice of the (float *) type in these definitions is, more or less, arbitrary. Any pointer type will do. Other files which contain accesses to FIFO

queues will include this *.h* file, as before. The implementation file, "intqueue.c", must contain the actual structure definitions used for the queues. The code for the queue operation functions must also be modified so that there are explicit type casts from the fake `FIFO_Q` type to the `(struct q_header *)` type and vice versa, where appropriate. That is, the revised "intqueue.c" file could start off in the manner shown in Figure 9.5.

If some determined programmer in a big project insists on accessing an internal feature of the integer-queue type, this person must now know or deduce the structure declarations that appear only inside the "intqueue.c" file. The file could, of course, be protected against being read. Only its binary version, in the file "intqueue.o", need be made generally accessible.

9.3. THE make FACILITY

A really large C program might consist of scores of standard source files (files with the *.c* suffix) and dozens of include files (files with either a *.h* or *.i* suffix). If the program is under development or being debugged, there may be frequent changes to the source files. Every time that a *.c* file is changed, we must remember to perform a compilation and recreate the corresponding *.o* file. If an include file has been changed, all the *.c* files that include it usually need to be

FIGURE 9.5. A Revised Version of intqueue.c

```
#include <stdio.h>
#include "intqueue.h"

struct q_element { int  value;
          struct q_element *next; };

struct q_header {  struct q_element *first, *last; };

FIFO_Q make_new_q()
{
    struct q_header *qh;

    qh = (struct q_header *)malloc( sizeof(*qh) );
    qh->first = qh->last = NULL;
    return( (FIFO_Q)qh );
}


/* Remainder of queue implementation omitted */
```

recompiled. If a *.h* file includes a *.i* (or, as is quite legal, another *.h* file), the situation becomes a little unclear. Any change to the *.i* file requires that all *.c* files that include the original *.h* file need to be recompiled.

The fact of the matter is that it is altogether too easy to forget to recompile some source file. Then, when the different object code files are merged, we may end up with a program that does not work, and is hard to debug because it does not correspond to the current source code. A simple, but wasteful, way to avoid this kind of problem is to recompile every source file after a series of changes have been performed.

The *make* program is a software tool that can be used to keep track of which files need recompiling after any changes have been made and to actually issue the sequence of commands that performs all the necessary recompilations. Because *make* is a general tool, it can be used for much more than just keeping C programs properly up-to-date. However, we will not go into the full details here.

To know which files need recompiling after a change, we need to know how the files depend on each other. For example, if some file, "prog1a.c" say, contains the declaration

        extern int zflag;

and another file, "prog1b.c" say, contains the declaration

        int zflag=25;

then the two files are interdependent. We must not change the type of the variable from **int** to **short** in one file without making a matching change in the other file. It is actually rather poor practice to have files that are interdependent in this manner. The correct approach is to place the declaration

        extern int zflag;

in a *.h* file, "prog1ab.h" say. We will treat this particular declaration as being the only place in the program where the data type of *zflag* is determined. All other files will have to agree with this definition and we will force them to agree by having them include "prog1ab.h". File "prog1a.c" would have to contain the #include directive

        #include "prog1ab.h"

and file "prog1b.c" would have to contain the two lines

        #include "prog1ab.h"
        int zflag = 25;

This breaks the direct interdependence between the files "prog1a.c" and "prog1b.c". We can say that "prog1a.c" depends on data type information that is defined only in "prog1ab.h". Similarly, "prog1b.c" depends on information defined only in "prog1ab.h" too. Therefore, if the approach that we described earlier as *correct* is followed religiously, all file dependencies must be revealed by `#include` directives. We will now take the sanctimonious attitude that all dependencies do in fact correspond to uses of `#include` directives.

To illustrate the use of *make*, we will hypothesize a relatively small C program, which we will name "displayprog". That is, our executable version of the program will be held in a file with this name. The files comprising the program contain `#include` directives as below. We omit `#include` directives for *stdio.h* and any other header files contained in the standard library.

File "main.c":
```
        #include "treepack.h"
        #include "listpack.h"
```

File "treepack.c":
```
        #include "treepack.h"
        #include "graphpack.h"
```

File "listpack.c":
```
        #include "listpack.h"
        #include "graphpack.h"
```

File "graphpack.c":
```
        #include "graphpack.h"
```

File "graphpack.h":
```
        #include "tables.i"
```

The *make* utility has to be told the name of the target program, which is "displayprog", how this target program is to be built, how files used in the building process are themselves to be built, and what the dependencies are. All this information is kept in another file, called "Makefile" (or, optionally, "makefile"). If we were unsophisticated users of the *make* utility, we might set up our makefile to look like the one shown in Figure 9.6.

If you have all the source files and the *makefile* in the current directory, you need do no more than type the command

    make

and then sit back and wait for all the necessary compilations to be performed automatically. If you subsequently change one or two source files and, perhaps, delete an object file, you need only repeat the magic command

    make

to bring everything up-to-date. The *make* utility will recompile only those files that need to be recompiled and then recombine the object files to create the new version of "displayprog".

Before proceeding to explain how it all works, let us first run through the syntax of a makefile. Comments are introduced by a hash mark symbol (#) and continue up to the end of the line. An identifier that begins in the first column

FIGURE 9.6. A Simple Makefile For 'displayprog'

```
#         makefile to create 'displayprog'

displayprog: main.o treepack.o listpack.o
        cc main.o treepack.o listpack.o -o displayprog

main.o: main.c treepack.h listpack.h
        cc -c main.c

treepack.o: treepack.c treepack.h graphpack.h
        cc -c treepack.c

listpack.o: listpack.c listpack.h graphpack.h
        cc -c listpack.c

graphpack.h: tables.i
        touch graphpack.h
```

and is followed by a colon is called a *target*. It is usually, but not necessarily, the name of a program or file to be built. The identifiers that follow the target on the same line are called the *prerequisites*. These are usually the names of files which the target depends on. After the line defining a target and prerequisites, command lines may appear. These are commands which will be executed by the *sh* shell program when *make* needs to create the target or bring it up-to-date. Command lines must begin with a tab character.

Now we are ready to look at how it all works. Let us assume that none of the object files currently exists. The *make* program first discovers that its target is "displayprog". This is determined by the fact that "displayprog" is the first target to appear in the makefile. And *make* sees that the prerequisites for "displayprog" are the files "main.o", "treepack.o" and "listpack.o". If *make* had access to up-to-date versions of these files, it would be able to create "displayprog" from them by executing the commands that immediately follow in the makefile. However, *make* has to defer executing these commands until it it is sure that it has up-to-date versions of the named object files. Thus, *make* now has three sub-targets. It takes each sub-target in turn, starting with "main.o", the first file listed. *Make* now searches the makefile for a line that gives "main.o" as a target. When *make* finds it, *make* discovers that the prerequisites for "main.o" are the files "main.c", "treepack.h" and "listpack.h". On the line following is a command that tells *make* how to construct a new version of "main.o". But before it can execute this command, it must check the three new sub-targets. The first one is "main.c". Because *make* cannot find a line defining "main.c" as a target and because "main.c" is (or should be) an existing file, *make* assumes that "main.c" is up-to-date. Next, the process is repeated for "treepack.h" and then for "listpack.h". Having verified that these files all exist, *make* now returns to execute the command

```
cc -c main.c
```

which implicitly creates or re-creates the file "main.o". Having attained a sub-goal of providing an up-to-date version of "main.o", *make* proceeds to its next sub-target, which is "listpack.o". And so on. Eventually, *make* will achieve all its subtargets and perform the final command that links all the object files to create "displayprog". (We will defer explanation of the *touch* command, which appears in the makefile, until later.)

Having created the main target and all the object files that are subsidiary targets, let us suppose that we now change some file, say "treepack.h". What happens when we invoke *make* again? How does *make* avoid performing unnecessary re-compilations? The short answer is that *make* simply checks the times at which files were created (or last modified) to determine whether files are obsolete. In our example, "treepack.o" is shown as depending on "treepack.h". If the time of creation of "treepack.o" precedes the time of last modification of "treepack.h" then *make* knows it has to execute the commands that create an up-to-date version of "treepack.o". It should be noted that *make* still has to go through the process of checking targets, sub-targets, sub-sub-targets and so on. If *make* were to immediately compare the time of creation of "displayprog" against the times of creation for "main.o", "treepack.o" and "listpack.o", it would appear that "displayprog" is up-to-date. So, *make* does indeed follow the chains of dependencies making sure that all the files are up-to-date. *Make* does not check the creation time of "displayprog" against those of the three object files until after it has guaranteed that they are up-to-date. Thus, if a recompilation of "treepack.c" has been performed, *make* will now find "displayprog" to be out-of-date and will execute the command to link the object files.

The strange command

```
touch graphpack.h
```

which appears in one of the rules is there to force the files which use "graphpack.h" to become out-of-date. The *touch* command is a standard UNIX command, though normally used only in makefiles. This command does not alter a file, it just causes the time of last modification for that file to be reset to the current time. Thus if the file "tables.i" has been changed, we will fool *make* into thinking that "graphpack.h" has been changed too. And this is exactly the behaviour we desire, so that programs which include "graphpack.h" (and thus indirectly include "tables.i") will be recompiled.

Our makefile is, in fact, unnecessarily detailed. This is because *make* has some built-in rules for creating object files. Consider one of the sub-target files, say "treepack.o", and suppose that the makefile contains no rules for creating this file. In this situation, *make* will discover for itself that "treepack.c" exists and will automatically apply the C compiler to this file to create "treepack.o". (If "treepack.c" does not exist, but "treepack.p" exists, *make* would invoke the PASCAL compiler.) Also, *make* provides some simple macro facilities so that the makefile can be parameterized. Taking advantage of these more advanced features of *make*, we can improve our makefile to that shown in Figure 9.7.

FIGURE 9.7. An Improved Makefile For 'displayprog'

```
#        makefile to create 'displayprog'

CFLAGS= -g       ## so that we can use sdb or dbx

OBJS=       main.o treepack.o listpack.o

displayprog: $(OBJS)
         cc $(OBJS) -o $@

main.o: treepack.h listpack.h

treepack.o: treepack.h graphpack.h

listpack.o: listpack.h graphpack.h

graphpack.h: tables.i
         touch $@
```

The identifier *OBJS* is a macro which is assigned a list of names of the object files. The dollar symbol must be used when accessing the value of the macro, as in the two cases above. The identifier *CFLAGS* is a macro which *make* inserts as an extra argument to any implicit C compilation (that is, when no explicit rule has been given). Your makefile would normally contain the setting

        CFLAGS = -g

while a program is being developed[2] and, possibly, the setting

        CFLAGS = -O

after the program is working and fully debugged. The special macro invoked

---

[2] Note -g is needed for debugging with *dbx* or *sdb*; -gx is needed for *dbx* on the Pyramid computer.

by $@ yields the name of the current target. It can be used to shorten command lines, as above, and to reduce the amount of editing work if we ever decide to rename our files.

There are some more details about *make* that are worth knowing. First, it may be helpful to know how to avoid having *make* perform unnecessary recompilations. Suppose that you simply change a comment in a *.h* file. This innocuous change could easily result in several wasted compilations the next time you use *make*. You could prevent the re-compilations by manually typing a *touch* command for all the object files involved. However, *make* has an option that will cause it to perform the touching actions. Executing the command

    make -t

will cause *make* to touch whatever files are necessary to make all of them appear to be up-to-date. No re-compilations whatsoever will be performed. Obviously, this command must be used very carefully.

Second, we should consider the problem of debugging makefiles. If you construct a fairly complicated makefile, you may have some difficulty understanding the behaviour of *make*. A useful aid for setting up the makefile initially is the −n flag. If the command

    make -n

is executed, *make* will simply report all the actions that it would perform if it were to be invoked normally. That is, *make* simply prints the shell commands without actually executing them. A second flag, −d, is available for tracing through the interpretation of a makefile. When the command

    make -d

is executed, *make* performs all the actions that bring the program up-to-date, but it also explains why it is performing each action. That is, *make* prints out exactly which rules it is using and prints modification and creation times for all the files involved. The output is lengthy, but reasonably easy to follow.

QUESTIONS

1. Why is it incorrect to begin the definition of the function *main* in a program with the line:

    ```
    static void main(argc,argv)
    ```

2. Why should every declaration of a variable in a *.h* file have the **extern** attribute?

3. There is a software tool called *mkmf* which inspects all the source files that form a program and automatically constructs an appropriate makefile. This makefile contains the commands needed to create the program. The makefile even includes all the dependency rules. How do you think *mkmf* works?

4.   In view of the close connection between arrays and pointers, it might seem reasonable to replace a declaration like

```
extern int table[];
```

with

```
extern int *table;
```

However, this is not correct. Why not?

CHAPTER 10

DEBUGGING, FORMATTING AND PROFILING C PROGRAMS

10.1. INCLUSION OF DEBUGGING CODE

Only a naive programmer assumes that his or her program will execute correctly on the first attempt. Even after the typographical errors and other errors detected at compilation time have been removed, it is quite likely that the program will contain logic errors. A wise programmer plans ahead for execution errors and includes extra statements that would help him or her locate the source of the problem. These extra statements would normally perform tests on the validity of data, check whether assertions hold, or simply output the values of variables at critical points in the program's execution.

You can use the C preprocessor to good advantage. It can expand macros into debugging statements that would otherwise be too repetitive to keep typing into the program. It can also conditionally include debugging statements depending on the states of one or more debugging flags. Some useful macros are defined in Figure 10.1, below.

These macros and functions will be effective only if the *DEBUG* preprocessor variable is defined. That is, the compilation flag −DDEBUG is supplied if checking is desired and omitted otherwise. Now how do these macros and functions work and how are they used?

The *ASSERT* macro is for testing assertions. If, at some point in the program, you believe that the pointer variable *chptr* should have the value *NULL*, you can insert the line

FIGURE 10.1 Useful Debugging Macros/Functions

```
#ifdef DEBUG

#    define ASSERT(p)   if ( !(p) ) { \
         fprintf(stderr, "Assertion p failed.\n"); \
         abort(); }

     void PCHK( p )   int *p; {
         extern int end, *sbrk();
         if (p < &end || p >= sbrk(0)) {
             fprintf(stderr, "Bad Pointer (%X)\n", p);
             abort();
         }
     }

     int XCHK( ix, size ) int ix, size; {
         if (ix < 0 || ix >= size) {
             fprintf(stderr, "Bad Index: %d not in \
range 0 to %d\n", ix, size-1);  abort();
         }
     }

#else  /* provide dummy definitions */

#    define ASSERT( p )    { }
#    define PCHK( p )      { }
#    define XCHK( a, b )   ( a )

#endif
```

```
        ASSERT( chptr == NULL );
```

into the program at this point. If you compile the program with the *DEBUG* variable set, and if your belief turns out to be wrong, your program will output the lines:

```
        Assertion  chptr == NULL  failed.
        Illegal instruction (core dumped)
```

The second line is a result of the call to *abort*. This call and the creation of a core file are deliberate – they give you the option of using *adb* or another debugger to analyze the error symptoms further. (The *adb* debugger is explained later in this chapter.) Incidentally, the *ASSERT* macro illustrates that the C preprocessor in Berkeley UNIX expands macro parameters that are referenced inside character strings.[1]

The *PCHK* function is intended to test whether a pointer variable is not *NULL* and refers to storage that was dynamically allocated (via *malloc* or *calloc*). If you want to check the validity of a pointer *cp* in the program before you dereference it, you can insert the line:

```
PCHK( cp );
```

The tests performed by the function assume that dynamically allocated storage begins at a data address with the label *end* (this label is defined by the system loader, the *ld* program, which is invoked as the last stage of a C compilation). The address of the end of dynamically allocated storage increases as the program executes (as a result of calls to *malloc* or *calloc*). The function call `sbrk(0)` returns the address of the next byte of memory after the area that has been dynamically allocated. Before you use *PCHK* in your program, you should note that an assignment like

```
cp = &xyz;
```

assigns a perfectly valid pointer value to *cp*, but this pointer value fails the check implemented by *PCHK*. The function checks *only* if the pointer value refers to storage allocated by *malloc* or *calloc*.

If you have already run some C programs, you will probably have discovered that C does *not* check array indexes to see that they are in range. If you want such a check, you have to do it yourself and the *XCHK* function is designed to make this check easy. If, say, an array *buff* is declared in the program as

```
char buff[80];
```

then a use of the array, as in

```
buff[i++] = '*';
```

can be replaced by

```
buff[ XCHK(i++,80) ] = '*';
```

Assuming that the program is compiled with *DEBUG* defined, the subscript expression in this use of the array will now be checked to see if it is in range. If you want all references to the *buff* array to have index checking, you can reduce the amount of typing by defining another macro

```
#define BUFF(ix)    buff[ XCHK(ix,80) ]
```

and use this new macro to access the array. That is, the use of the array given above can be coded as

---

[1] The C Preprocessor may not behave this way in other versions of UNIX.

```
BUFF( i++ ) = '*'
```

Similar macros can be defined for other arrays in your program.

As stated earlier, all these debugging macros and functions may be left in the program source code. If you ever think the tests are no longer needed, simply re-compile the program without setting the *DEBUG* preprocessor variable. It would be unwise to delete the debugging statements from the source code file. You never know when you may need them again.

10.2. THE adb, sdb AND dbx DEBUGGERS

When a C program goes wrong at execution time, the sole error message is likely to be something similar to

Bus error (core dumped)

The last part of this message message means that the UNIX system has created a file named "core" which contains a memory image of the data area of the program at the moment of error. This *core* file can always be analyzed to some extent with the *adb* debugger. If you had some forethought and had compiled your C program with the "-g" compilation flag in effect[2], you would also be able to use the *sdb* or *dbx* debuggers, which are a little more user-friendly. The *adb* and *sdb* debuggers are provided with the Berkeley 4.1bsd system and later versions; *dbx* is a newer product provided with 4.2 and later versions.

These debuggers are fairly complicated processors, with many advanced features for program checkout and program patching. However, it is simple to discover the approximate place in the program where the execution error occurred, and to discover some information about program variables.

Assuming that the "-g" (or "-gx") option was not in effect for compilation, we would be forced to use *adb*. Therefore we will look at this debugging tool first.

10.2.1. The adb Debugger

Imagine that your program has just crashed and created a core file. (This should not be too difficult to imagine!) If the executable program was named "prog", we can type the command:

adb prog

The *adb* processor will read the executable file *prog* to obtain a copy of the instruction area of the program and to obtain symbol table information. Provided that a file named "core" exists, *adb* reads it too to obtain a copy of the data area of the program and of the machine registers at the time of the crash.

---

[2] The 4.2 system on the Pyramid computer requires use of the "-gx" compilation flag with the *dbx* debugger.

TABLE 10.1 Useful adb Commands

`$q`	terminates *adb*.
`$r`	prints the contents of the registers and the current instruction at the time the program stopped.
`$e`	prints the names and values of all external variables.
`$c`	prints a stack trace, showing all active functions at the time that the program stopped.
address/format	prints data locations, starting at the given address and according to the specified format. An address may be given as an external name, or as an absolute address, or as an address expression. Examples of each are `_counter  0de558a _array1+4c`

Now, *adb* has a large repertoire of commands for printing out parts of the program, from both the instruction and data areas. Some of the more useful commands are listed in Table 10.1. The first *adb* command you should try is `$C`. Typing this command will produce the sequence of function calls that took place for control to reach the point of error. The first function name printed is the function that was being executed when the program crashed. The last function name printed should be *main* because this is the function that was initially invoked in your program. You will see that all the function names are printed with an underscore character at the beginning. For example, you see _*main* printed instead of *main*. This is because the C compiler prefixes an underscore character to C identifiers when creating external names used by the loader program. The function call sequence also includes the values of parameters for the functions as they were at the moment of the crash.

It is also easy to print out the current values of global variables. If you have a global variable *x1* of type **int**, you can print its value in decimal by typing

    `_x1/D`

(The letter *D* is a format code that means decimal output of a 4-byte longword.) If *x2* is an array of 10 integers, we can print the entire array either by typing

    `_x2/10D`

or

        _x2,10/D

If *x3* is a character array, we can print its contents with a command like

        _x3/20c

If *x4* is a pointer type, we can obtain the value of that pointer in hexadecimal with

        _x4/X

If the result prints as `eed4` say, it means that *x4* is pointing at a data object located at address `0x0eed4`. We can print the value of that data object by typing, for example,

        0eed4/10D

(The leading zero is required to differentiate the address from the name of a function or variable.) Finally, to exit from *adb*, the command

        $q

should be typed.

There is no easy way to determine the values of local variables from *adb* if you are using the VAX or Pyramid implementations of UNIX. Storage for local variables with the *automatic* storage class is allocated on a system stack. This stack can be inspected with *adb*, but it is not easy to work out which words of storage in the stack correspond to which variables.

On the SUN computer, *adb* has the capability of printing the values of local variables. But to obtain this capability (and additional features normally found in the *sdb* debugger), the program must have been compiled with the −go option in effect.

10.2.2. The sdb Debugger

The *sdb* debugger is invoked in a similar way to *adb*. Some of the basic *sdb* commands are listed in Table 10.2. The main advantage of *sdb* over *adb* is that it will print the values of local variables in functions. This is why you can optionally prefix a variable name with a function name. If the variable is local to some function, there may be other variables with the same name elsewhere in the program and therefore the function name is necessary information.

Since *sdb* has been made obsolete by the introduction of *dbx* in Berkeley 4.2bsd UNIX, we will not examine it any further. On the SUN computer, *sdb* is not even provided (much of its functionality is incorporated into *adb* anyway).

TABLE 10.2. Useful sdb Commands

t	prints the list of currently active functions.
q	exits from *sdb*.

func: *var*/*format*	prints the value of a specified variable, *var*, in a given function, *func*. If the variable is global, the function name prefix is omitted. The format codes are **c** for **char** type, **d** for decimal output of an integer type, **x** for hexadecimal output of an integer type, and **s** for output of a character pointer (the referenced string up to a null terminator is printed). The *var* part of the command may be written in one of the forms
	    variable[*number*]
	    variable->*field*
	    variable. *field*
	according to whether the variable in question is an array, a pointer to a structure or a structure, respectively.

10.2.3. The dbx Debugger

The *dbx* debugger is invoked similarly to *adb* and *sdb*. That is, it can be invoked by the command

        dbx prog

where "prog" is the name of the executable program that has crashed. All compilation stages in the construction of "prog" must have had the −g flag in effect.[3] Some of the simpler *dbx* commands are listed in Table 10.3.

The *dbx* debugger is relatively intelligent because it automatically prints variables in formats that suit their declarations. For example, if a variable is declared in the program to have the type (char *), then the storage that the variable references is printed as an ASCII character string up to the terminating null byte.

If there are several variables with the same name, print will print the instance of the variable that belongs to the current function. To print the value of a different instance, it is either necessary to qualify the name or to change the current function. A full qualification for a variable name includes

---

[3] To be able to use *dbx* on the Pyramid computer, your program must have been compiled with the −gx flag in effect.

TABLE 10.3. Useful dbx Commands

`where`	prints a list of the active procedures and functions.
`dump`	prints out the values of all active variables.
`print` *expr-list*	prints the values of particular values or expressions. For example, the command `print arr1[5], strct5.fieldz` would print the values of element 5 of the array *arr1* and of the field named *fieldz* in a structure named *strct5*. The expected answer is also printed if *strct5* is a pointer to a structure rather than being the structure itself. By default, the variables printed are those belonging to the current function (see the next command).
`func` *func-name*	changes the current function to the one specified.
`list` *func-name*	lists the first 10 lines of the source code for the named function in the current file. If no argument is provided, the next 10 lines are printed.
`file` *file-name*	changes the current file to the one specified. (If no argument is provided, the name of the current file is printed.)
`which` *vrbl-name*	prints the fully qualified names for all visible occurrences of the named variable.
`help`	gives a summary of available *dbx* commands.
`quit`	exits from *dbx*.

both the name of a source code file and a function name. For example:

        `print prog3.foo.x`

will print the variable *x* inside function *foo* which is defined in the C source file "prog3.c". The *which* command is useful for finding out what *dbx* expects as the full qualification for a variable.

  While inspecting the values of variables in a program, it is desirable to have access to a listing of the program source code. Of course, one could make a listing of the program before invoking *dbx*. Alternatively, *dbx* provides a convenient way of inspecting source code. If your source code is entirely contained in one file, you can just type a command similar to

> list 35,54

to list lines numbered 35 through 54. More conveniently, perhaps, you can type a command like

> list foo

which lists the first few lines at the beginning of the function named *foo* in your source file. If you type

> list

with no argument, the next ten lines in the source file are listed. This command is handy for continuing the printout of a function definition.

If the source code for your program is contained in several files, you may have to tell *dbx* when to change files. *Dbx* has a notion of a *current file*. You can find out which is the current file by executing

> file

The list command will print functions only from the current file. When you need to print from another file, you must execute either the func command or a command similar to

> file prog2.c

which changes the current file to "prog2.c". The func command changes the current function to the named function and also changes the current file to the one containing the source code of this function.

If you use *dbx* a lot, you will probably grow tired of typing out the full command names. The solution is to define some suitable abbreviations. You should create, in your home directory, a file named ".dbxinit". Into this file, you should place lines similar to

> alias p print
> alias l list
> alias f func

>> etc.

When you next use *dbx*, you may then use p as a synonym for print, and so on.

10.3. TRACING PROGRAM EXECUTION WITH dbx

Perhaps every programmer has encountered bugs that elude detection for a long time. After re-reading the source code many times and after puzzling for hours over the values of variables at the time of failure, the only recourse might be to monitor the program's execution. The programmer can easily insert debugging output statements into the program in the way suggested at the start of this chapter. This practice is recommended for any large program. It is quite possible, however, that the debugging output will not reveal the source of the error (perhaps the wrong variables are being printed or the wrong conditions are being tested). It is even possible that the error symptoms will go away when the debugging statements are included and re-appear when the statements are removed!

The ultimate resort is to use one of the debuggers to trace the program's execution. All three of the debuggers mentioned in this chapter have the capability of tracing, but we will only describe the use of *dbx* here. Several *dbx* commands useful for tracing execution are summarized in Table 10.4. We will now explain how they are used.

First, any "core" file should be removed from the current directory. Next, *dbx* is invoked with the same kind of command as before, namely

```
dbx prog
```

where *prog* is the name of the troublesome program.

TABLE 10.4 dbx Commands For Tracing Execution

trace *func*	causes a line showing the function name and argument values to be printed whenever the function is entered.
trace *vrbl*	prints information about every assignment to the named variable.
stop in *func*	causes *dbx* to halt execution when control enters the named function.
stop *vrbl*	causes *dbx* to halt execution when the named variable is about to be changed.
run *args*	causes execution of the program to begin, passing in the command line arguments (if any). If the program reads from standard input, the input can be taken from a file by adding <*filename* to the command. If the program writes to standard output, that output can be sent to a file by adding >*filename* to the command.
cont	causes execution to resume after it has halted as a result of the *stop* command or as a result of an interrupt.

Using your knowledge of the problem symptoms exhibited by the program, you must have some idea of which functions are performing incorrect actions or which variables are being assigned the wrong values. You should now type *trace* or *stop* commands for such functions and variables. You would use a *trace* command if knowledge about the function argument values or about the value being assigned to a variable (and where the call or assignment is taking place) is sufficient for your purposes. You would use a *stop* command if you want to retain the freedom to inspect any variable in the program when the call or assignment has taken place.

Now you can start execution of the program using the *run* command. If the program normally has no arguments, the command

        run

will suffice. If you would normally invoke the program with arguments, as in

        prog -x bananas

you would type

        run -x bananas

If your program normally reads from its standard input, the running program will, by default, read from the keyboard. If you have input data in some file, "indata" say, you can type the *run* command as

        run -x bananas < indata

If your program writes to its standard output, that output will, by default, appear on the screen. If there is much output, or if it contains non-ASCII characters, this output will interfere with the information displayed by *dbx*. In this case, you would want to redirect the output into a file. An example of a redirection is

        run -x bananas > output

After the *run* command has been entered, the program is executing. If you had previously entered any trace commands, *dbx* will automatically display tracing information on the screen. If you had entered any *stop* commands, execution will halt when control reaches the specified function or when an assignment to a specified variable occurs. When execution halts like this, *dbx* informs you of where and why execution was halted and then gives you a prompt for a new command. You can enter any *dbx* commands at this point. You may print the values of variables, specify new functions to be traced, do anything. If you subsequently wish to resume execution from the point where the program was halted, the cont command should be used.

If your program appears to be stuck in an infinite loop at any point, the *break* key or *Control-C* character combination will generate an interrupt that causes execution to halt. Then *dbx* will report the current program location and prompt for a command.

The description of *dbx* in this chapter does not, by any means, exhaust all its capabilities. For more details, there is no better source of information than the on-line manual entry.

10.4. FORMATTING C PROGRAMS

On all standard UNIX systems, there is a program *cb* which improves the appearance of C source code. (*Cb* is an abbreviation of "C Beautifier".) The output from the program is source code where indentation has been consistently used. To produce a pretty printout of a C source file *prog1.c*, a command line similar to the following might be used:

```
cb < prog1.c | pr -h 'Phase 1: prog1.c' | lpr
```

The *cb* program uses a tab character for each level of indentation. By default, most UNIX utilities assume that tab stops occur in every eigth column. This means that listings of beautified C source code on 80-column terminals or printers tend not to be so beautiful. The listing is likely to contain many lines that are truncated or lines that overflow onto following lines, depending on how the printer software handles the situation. However, a listing on a 132-column printer or a display terminal in 132-column mode is usually satisfactory.

On the Berkeley 4.2bsd and 4.3bsd UNIX systems, there is an alternative formatting program called *indent*. If you execute the command:

```
indent cprog.c
```

the C source file "cprog.c" will be changed in order to make the indentation of statements follow consistent rules. By default, *indent* uses 4 spaces for each level of indentation. Unless your program logic is very convoluted and involves deeply nested control constructs, statements should rarely reach the 80 column barrier.

Finally, if you have access to a laser printer or some other printer that can be driven by the *troff* program, you should know about a special program, *vgrind*, for printing C source code. It takes full advantage of different character fonts and character sizes to generate a source listing that looks as though it was professionally typeset. However, *vgrind* (as its name suggests) and *troff* are extremely costly in computation time. *Vgrind* is quite unsuitable for running off listings, but can be used to good advantage if you wish to include some C source code in a book or report.

10.5. IMPROVING EXECUTION EFFICIENCY

If a program is likely to be executed a large number of times or if the program executes for a very long time, it is worthwhile improving the program to make it efficient. A certain amount of speed-up, perhaps 10%, can be achieved by compiling the program with the optimize flag, −O, in effect. However, much larger speed improvements can usually be obtained by tuning the program.

Some relatively easy ways of making a C program execute more efficiently are listed below. As we will argue in the next section of this chapter, it is not worth the effort of following these suggestions throughout the entire program. They need only be adopted in those regions of the program where the most execution time is spent.

- Use the **register** attribute

  Variables which are used as loop indexes and other variables which receive heavy use inside loops should be given the **register** attribute. Any simple variable which is declared locally inside a function and which has the **int** or **float** type may be given the **register** attribute. On the VAX implementation, there are only 7 registers free for use, so you should not supply the **register** attribute for more variables than that. On the other hand, the Pyramid computer has a large number of registers available. The first 20 or so local variables of a function are implemented as registers automatically. Therefore, the **register** attribute is usually redundant.

- Use macros instead of functions

  Simple functions that contain only one or two statements can usually be replaced by equivalent macros. This reduces the number of instructions executed because function arguments to do not have to be pushed onto the stack and accessed from stack locations. However, the use of macros can make it harder to debug the program. It is a good idea to defer replacement of functions with macros until the program is working and, even then, replace only functions that are called a large number of times.

- Move code out of loops

  You should attempt to minimize the number of statements and the complexity of those statements inside loops.

- Avoid repeating calculations

  You should not repeat calculations that are much more complicated than a simple addition or subtraction. Instead, save the result of the calculation in a temporary variable and use that variable rather than recalculate the value. Temporaries can be implemented as local automatic variables, as in

  ```
  { float temp = f(a);
      printf( "%.2f, %.2f\n", temp, a*temp );
  }
  ```

- Avoid floating-point calculations

  If you can, you should calculate quantities using only integers. Integer arithmetic is normally much faster than floating-point arithmetic. If you need to manipulate values that are not integers, you can probably scale the values by a convenient power of 2 or a power of 10.

- Use pointers instead of array indexing

  When you are making a pass through an array, perhaps searching for a particular element, the normal coding approach is to use an index variable that ranges from zero up to the greatest index. However, a C program will normally execute faster if you use a pointer to the first array element and increment that pointer on each loop iteration. For best results, the pointer variable should have the **register** attribute.

The execution speed improvements achieved by using the preceding suggestions are not the end of the story by any means. The greatest speed improvements will normally come from careful algorithm design and making appropriate choices of data structures. The importance of algorithm design is often illustrated in computer science books with the problem of sorting an array. To be slightly different, let us look at the problem of maintaining a list of English words. (Actually our program will work with arbitrary character

FIGURE 10.2. Version 1 Of check_word

```c
#define MAXWORDS 4096
char   *wordlist[MAXWORDS];
int    wordcnt = 0;

int check_word( word )
register char *word;
{
    register int i;
    char *newstring;

    for( i=0; i<wordcnt; i++ ) {
        if (strcmp(word,wordlist[i]) == 0)
            return 1;
    }

    if (wordcnt>=MAXWORDS) {
        fputs("Word table is full!\n",stderr);
        exit( -1 );
    }
    newstring = (char *)malloc( strlen(word)+1 );
    strcpy( newstring, word );
    wordlist[wordcnt++] = newstring;
    return 0;
}
```

strings, so there is nothing that intrinsically restricts it to English words.) We will provide just one operation on the list. This operation, *check_word*, will search the list to see if its argument is a member of the list. If it is a member, the function returns a true result (one). If it is not a member, the word is inserted into the list and the function returns a false result (zero). If we are bold enough to place a limit on the number of words in the list, we might quickly rattle off C code similar to that shown in Figure 10.2.

Our first version of the code searches through the list relatively slowly. If the word we are seeking is actually in the list, we would have to search half way through the list on average. And if the word is not present in the list, we have to search the entire list. We could speed the search loop up a little by using a pointer to the array elements rather than an index into the array, as suggested above. But the improvement in speed would be minimal compared to what can be achieved by changing the search algorithm. If we realize that the searches are going to be too slow, we might consult a book on algorithms and discover the binary search technique. (The book cited at the end of the chapter might be consulted.) At the cost of making insertions of new words much more expensive, we can reduce the number of loop iterations involved in searching to about the logarithm (to base 2) of the number of words in the list. Our new version of the functions would look similar to that given in Figure 10.3. Binary search requires that the list of words be maintained in sorted, lexicographic order. This is why the word insertion code has become much more complicated. The words already in the list have to be moved down to make a space for the new word to be inserted at its correct position.

However, we might find that a word search function is still too slow. For one thing, comparisons between words require the *strcmp* function to be called and that is relatively expensive. Our third and final version of the program appears in Figure 10.4.

The third version uses a data structure called a *hash table*. To be technical, it is called an open hash table. More information about open hashing and alternative hashing methods can be found in the book cited at the end of the chapter. Our words are held in linked lists, known as *buckets*. The hash function, called *hash* in the code, selects which of the 64 buckets our word will be kept in. When we want to find out if the word is in our table, we first determine which bucket to search. Then we perform a linear search through all the words contained in the bucket. If the word is not found, we insert it at the front of the bucket.

To help you visualize the hash table and the linked lists, Figure 10.5 shows a small scale version of a hash table. "It was nice to have had." In this diagram, the table is scaled down to have only eight buckets and it is shown containing the words from the fragment of English text "It was nice to have had." To make the diagram more interesting, we have assumed that the hash function returned the same value, one, for the words 'had' and 'was'. Similarly,

FIGURE 10.3. Version 2 Of check_word

```
#define MAXWORDS 4096
char   *wordlist[MAXWORDS];
int    wordcnt = 0;

int check_word( word )
register char *word;
{
    register int first, last, middle, t;
    register char *newstring;

    first = 0;  last = wordcnt;
    while( first < last ) {
        middle = (first + last) >> 1;
        t = strcmp(word,wordlist[middle]);
        if (t == 0) return( 1 );
        if (t < 0)
            last = middle;
        else
            first = middle+1;
    }

    if (wordcnt++ >= MAXWORDS) {
        fputs("Word table is full!\n",stderr);
        exit( -1 );
    }
    newstring = (char *)malloc( strlen(word)+1 );
    strcpy( newstring, word );

    if (t < 0) first = middle;
    /* 'first' indicates where new word must go */
    for( last=wordcnt; last >= first; last-- ) {
        wordlist[last+1] = wordlist[last];
    }
    wordlist[first] = newstring;
    return 0;
}
```

FIGURE 10.4. Version 3 Of check_word

```
#define NBUCKETS 64   /* must be a power of 2 */

typedef struct listitem {
          char *word;
          struct listitem *next_item;
        } *itemptr;

itemptr  bucket[NBUCKETS];

int hash( word )
register char *word;
{
    register int len = strlen( word );
    return( (word[0]*379 + word[len-1]*73 + len)
            & (NBUCKETS - 1) );
}

int check_word( word )
register char *word;
{
    register itemptr bp;
    register int ix;
    char *newstring;

    ix = hash(word);
    for( bp=bucket[ix]; bp!=NULL; bp=bp->next_item ) {
        if ( strcmp(bp->word,word) == 0 ) return 1;
    }
    newstring = (char *)malloc( strlen(word)+1 );
    strcpy( newstring, word );
    bp = (itemptr)malloc( sizeof( *bp ) );
    bp->word = newstring;
    bp->next_item = bucket[ix];
    bucket[ix] = bp;
    return 0;
}
```

FIGURE 10.5. Hash Table Organization

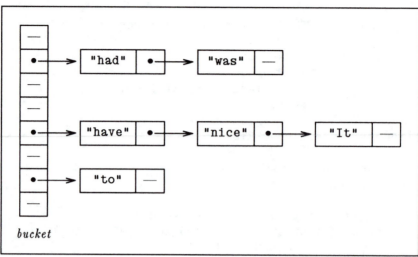

the hash function returned four for each of the words in the second linked list and six for the word in the third list. In practice, we would expect to find the words distributed more evenly between the different hash buckets than this.

Now a linear search through a linked list is, in itself, no more efficient than the linear search through an array that was performed in the first version of the program. The advantage of the hash table method is that the number of words in one of our buckets is, on average, one sixty-fourth of the number of words that would have been in the array. Therefore the search should proceed about 64 times faster. And if the speed-up factor of 64 is insufficient, we simply have to change the constant 64 in the program. It could be increased to any suitable power of 2. As an added bonus, our code does not place any prior limit on the number of words that can be entered into the table.

10.6. EXECUTION PROFILING WITH prof AND gprof

The previous section attempted to stress the importance of choosing an efficient algorithm and of choosing suitable data structures. Should we write a large program using the most efficient algorithms and the most suitable data structures throughout? The answer is almost certainly no. The fastest algorithms are usually longer, more complicated and more difficult to debug than equivalent simple-minded algorithms. Furthermore, data structures that promote execution speed are likely to require more memory than simpler data structures.

The best approach is to use the fastest algorithms, with their corresponding data structures, where it matters the most. That is, we should be extra careful only in those parts of the program where the most execution time is spent. An often quoted observation is that 90% of the execution time of a program is spent in only 10% of the code. If you know which statements comprise the important 10% of the program, you will know where to concentrate your effort.

There are two tools to help you identify those regions of a program where the most time is spent. One tool, available on most versions of the UNIX system, is called *prof* (short for *Program Profiler*). The other tool, special to the Berkeley UNIX system, is called *gprof* (a contraction of *Graph Profiler*).

10.6.1. The *prof* Profiler

To illustrate the use of *prof*, we will run through its use on an actual program. Suppose that we want a program to count the number of distinct words that appear in a document. By an amazing coincidence, this program will need the *check_word* function that we designed in the previous section of this chapter.

FIGURE 10.6. A Program to Count Words

```
#include <stdio.h>
#include <ctype.h>

void main() {
    char wordbuff[128], *wp;
    int  ch;
    int  word_cnt = 0;

    while( (ch = getchar()) != EOF ) {
        if ( isspace(ch) || ispunct(ch) ) continue;
        wp = wordbuff;
        do {
            *wp++ = ch;
            ch = getchar();
        } while( ! isspace(ch) && ! ispunct(ch) );
        *wp = '\0';
        if ( check_word( wordbuff ) == 0 )
            word_cnt++;
    }
    printf( "The file contained %d distinct words\n",
        word_cnt );
}
```

The main program to count distinct words that calls *check_word* is listed in Figure 10.6. We started by combining the code of Figure 10.6 with the implementation of *check_word* given in Figure 10.2 to create a file named "count1.c". Next, we compiled the program with the command

```
cc -p count1.c -o count1
```

The −p flag tells the C compiler to insert extra instructions in the program to count and to time all function calls. Then we performed a sample execution of the program, using the command

```
count1 < /usr/man/man1/stty.1
```

This command uses the on-line documentation for the *stty* command as the sample input file.[4] After whirring away for a surprising long time, the program prints a message that the file contains 429 distinct words and then halts. This is exactly the behaviour that we would expect. However, the −p flag has had an important side effect. While the program was executing, all function calls were being timed. And when the program finished, it created a file named "mon.out" which contains the results of the timing measurements. This file does not contain ASCII characters. A readable printout of the file is created by the *prof* program. If we now execute the command

```
prof count1
```

we obtain output like that shown in Figure 10.7.

In this tabular output, there is one line for each function in the program. Several functions are not immediately recognizable as belonging to the program. Most of these functions are automatically included in the program from the C library to perform input-output handling (included because of our use of the *getchar* macro and the *printf* function). One more function, *sbrk*, is included because it is called by *malloc*. And a couple more are included because they take care of timing the function calls and of creating the "mon.out" file.

The first column of the table shows how much execution time, in total, each function consumes. We see that 42.9% of all execution time is spent in the *strcmp* function. The next most important function is *check_word*, which accounts for 27.9% of the time. Since it is *check_word* which calls *strcmp* (and *malloc* and *strcpy* too), the total percentage of time spent in *check_word* is really 27.9% + 42.9% + 0.3%, or 71.1%. (The third line in the table is for *mcount*, which is the function timing our function calls.) Using the information in the second column of the table, we can see that *strcmp* and *check_word*, between them, account for 25.2 seconds of execution time (out of a total of 35.6 seconds).

---

[4] To count words properly, we should first pipe the program input through *deroff* to remove all the embedded formatting commands. (This hardly seems necessary in a timing experiment.)

FIGURE 10.7. Output Of prof For count1

%time	cumsecs	#call	ms/call	name
42.9	15.26	194810	0.08	_strcmp
27.9	25.18	1490	6.66	_check_word
22.8	33.30			mcount
3.7	34.60			_monstartup
2.2	35.38	1	783.62	_main
0.3	35.50	429	0.27	_malloc
0.1	35.55	3	16.67	_read
0.1	35.60	429	0.12	_strlen
0.0	35.61	1	16.67	__doprnt
0.0	35.61	3	0.00	__filbuf
0.0	35.61	38	0.00	__flsbuf
0.0	35.61	2	0.00	_fstat
0.0	35.61	1	0.00	_gtty
0.0	35.61	1	0.00	_ioctl
0.0	35.61	1	0.00	_isatty
0.0	35.61	1	0.00	_printf
0.0	35.61	1	0.00	_profil
0.0	35.61	11	0.00	_sbrk
0.0	35.61	429	0.00	_strcpy
0.0	35.61	1	0.00	_write

If we repeat the execution profiling experiment using the code of Figure 10.3, we obtain the profile output shown in Figure 10.8. Only the first few lines of the table are reproduced here. Although *check_word* and *strcmp* still account for 67.3% of all execution time, the total time spent in these two functions has been considerably reduced. Together, they now consume only 4.65 seconds of time.

If we were striving for a very efficient program, we would see from Figure 10.8 that the best place to concentrate our efforts is still the *check_word* function. This should encourage us to completely change our strategy and, for example, use a hash table implementation. Substituting the code of Figure 10.4 to create program "count3", and repeating the program profile leads to the results shown in Figure 10.9. (If these timings do not convince you about the virtues of hashing, probably nothing will!) At this point, there is not much more that we can do other than to make some very minor improvements to the main program. And, if we intended to run the program on larger files, we should probably increase the number of buckets.

FIGURE 10.8. Output Of prof For count2

%time	cumsecs	#call	ms/call	name
45.8	1.88	1490	1.26	_check_word
21.5	2.77	10550	0.08	_strcmp
10.5	3.20	1	433.49	_main
10.5	3.63			mcount
4.9	3.83	429	0.47	_malloc
2.0	3.92			_monstartup
1.2	3.97	429	0.12	_strcpy

etc.

FIGURE 10.9. Output Of prof For count3

%time	cumsecs	#call	ms/call	name
22.1	0.57	1	566.87	_main
18.8	1.05	1490	0.32	_check_word
16.9	1.48			mcount
10.4	1.75	858	0.31	_malloc
7.8	1.95	5213	0.04	_strcmp
6.5	2.12	1490	0.11	_hash
6.5	2.28	1919	0.09	_strlen

etc.

10.6.2. The *gprof* Profiler

Our sample program was a little too simple to illustrate any deficiencies in *prof*, but it is not difficult to understand without an example. In our sample program (it does not matter which version), the *strcmp*, *strcpy* and *malloc* functions were called only by the *check_word* function and these were the only functions that *check_word* called. Therefore, if we wanted to know how much time is spent executing *check_word*, including all functions called by *check_word*, we just have to add the times for the four functions together. If some other function in the program had also contained a call to *strcmp*, say, we would no longer be able to compute total execution times at all accurately. The *gprof* profiler is designed to overcome the deficiency.[5] As well as producing a table of function

---

[5] *gprof* is not currently available on the Pyramid implementation of Berkeley UNIX.

times similar to that produced by *prof*, it also shows figures for functions depending on the caller.

To use *gprof*, it is necessary to supply the −pg compilation flag to *cc*. For example, the command might be

```
cc -pg -O count3.c -o count3
```

When we execute the program, it creates a file named "gmon.out", which contains the timing information. Finally, executing the command

```
gprof count3
```

will output a rather voluminous amount of timing information (along with an explanation of how to interpret the information). Too much, unfortunately, to reproduce here.

FURTHER READING

- A.V. Aho, J.E. Hopcroft and J.D. Ullman. *Data Structures and Algorithms.* Reading, Mass.: Addison-Wesley, 1983. This authoritative, yet readable, book contains more information about the binary search and hashing techniques used for the word counting problem in the chapter.

QUESTIONS

1. Can you design index range checking functions and/or macros that will print the name of the array (as well as the bad subscript value) when the check fails?

2. If we really needed to speed up the final version of *check_word* shown in Figure 10.4, we could considerably reduce the amount of time expended in *malloc*. How?

3. Without making any *major* changes to the code in Figure 10.4, there are at least two ways to reduce the number of calls to *strcmp*. What are they?

4. When final versions of programs are produced, they should not include any object files that were created with the −p (or −pg) options. Why not?

CHAPTER 11

SYSTEMS PROGRAMMING –
PROCESSES AND SIGNALS

11.1. PARALLEL PROCESSING

Most computers, probably including the one you use, can only execute one machine instruction at a time. Yet, if your computer is under the control of the Berkeley UNIX operating system, several people could be using the computer at the same time. It appears to each user that the computer is executing instructions solely on his or her behalf. The ability of a single computer with a single processing unit (CPU) to execute several programs simultaneously is known as *multiprogramming*. The computer system executes, perhaps, several thousand instructions of one user's program, then suspends execution of that program and switches to another user's program. By regularly switching from one user to another (a scheme called *time-slicing*), each user has the illusion that his or her program is continuously executing. As more users sign on to the system, programs receive time slices less often and the illusion of continuous execution may begin to break down.

So far we have considered situations in which each user has only one program executing at a time, but the UNIX system allows each user to have several simultaneously executing programs. All one need do to have two programs running is to start up the first program as a background job. We could, for example, type the commands

```
cc giantprog.c -o giantprog &
vi anotherprog.c
```

which initiate a long-running C compilation and then, while that compilation is running, edit a file using the *vi* editor. Having two or more programs running simultaneously does not represent any great problem to the UNIX system. The operating system just has to share the CPU among a few more programs using the time-slicing mechanism.

We do not need the shell command language to create two simultaneously executing programs. The same effect may be achieved by including the appropriate function calls inside a C program. But, before we can examine these functions, we have to become more precise in our use of terminology. In particular, we have to introduce the concept of a *process*. A process is a program, consisting of instructions and data and machine register contents, with an environment and an instruction pointer that indicates the next instruction that is to be executed in the program. The process environment is information maintained by the system about the process. It includes the file descriptor table, accounting information, a unique identification number for the process, and a few other details.

At first sight, it might seem that our definition for a process also seems to describe a program. That is correct: a process is just a special case of a program. In general, however, a program may split itself into two or more separate pieces, each of which execute independently. These pieces are called *processes*. Initially, a program begins execution as a single process. This process executes by receiving regular time slices from the operating system. In the course of its execution, the process may call a function that causes the operating system to create a new process. Both the original process and the new process receive time slices from the operating system and, therefore, appear to execute simultaneously. After the new process has been created, we would say that the program consists of two processes. Possibly the two processes execute the same sequence of machine instructions, but this is not necessarily the case. Possibly the two processes share the same data area in memory, but this too is not necessarily the case. The only thing that we can say with certainty is that the program has two threads of control. In other words, there are two separate instruction pointers indicating two, independent, next instructions to be executed.

Any C program can fork into two instances of itself by making a call to the *fork* system function. A simple program that does exactly that is shown in Figure 11.1. The new process that is created by the call to *fork* is an exact duplicate of the process that makes the call. The duplicate process is provided with a copy of the data area of the original process, but in a different region of main memory, and it is provided with a copy of the original process' environment. Since the new process has the same data and environment as the original process, it has access to exactly the same open files. The only easily discernible

FIGURE 11.1. An Experiment in Forking (#1)

```
#include <stdio.h>

void main() {
    int pid;

    fork();

    pid = getpid();
    for( ; ; ) {
        printf( "Hello, my name is %d!\n", pid );
    }
}
```

differences in the environment are that the accounting information shows that the new process has consumed no CPU time, the new process has a different identification number and the identity of its parent process is different. Every active process in the system has a unique identification number, which is called the *process id*. A process can find out its process id by calling the *getpid* function.

The program of Figure 11.1 clones itself into two separate processes and then each process repeatedly outputs its process id. If you care to execute this program, you will see output similar to

```
Hello, my name is 7050!
Hello, my name is 7050!
Hello, my name is 7050!
Hello, my name is 7051!
Hello, my name is 7051!
Hello, my name is 7050!
    etc.
```

You see several output lines with one process id, then several with another process id, then several more with the first process id, and so on. The number of consecutive lines with the same process id corresponds to how many lines can be output in a single time slice. You will not see individual output lines broken up, interrupted by a line from the other process, because the standard output functions normally use line buffering.

It is important to be clear that each process has its own data area. If one of the processes writes to a global variable, that assignment can have no effect on any other processes. This behaviour is exemplified to some extent by the program in Figure 11.1 because there is apparently only one variable named *pid* in the program, yet two different process ids are printed. Figure 11.2 should help to make the situation even clearer. In this next example, we can see that the *fork* function returns a result, or in fact, two results – one result for the original process that invoked *fork* and a different result for the new process. The result returned to the original process, called the *parent* process, is the process id of the new process. The result returned to the other process, the *child* process, is zero. If you care to run the second program, you will see forty numbered lines from the child process interwoven with forty numbered lines from the parent process. The fact that you see forty correctly numbered lines from each should prove to you that there are two copies of variable *i* after the forking operation.

A new function, *wait*, is used in the example. This function causes the process that calls it to be suspended until a child process has completed execution.[1] The parameter to *wait* is a pointer to a word in memory. When control returns from the call to *wait*, this word holds flags that indicate the completion status of the child process. The *wait* function also returns the process number of the child process that completed as its result. Our program needs to check

FIGURE 11.2. An Experiment in Forking (#2)

```
#include <stdio.h>
#define NLINES 40

int i, pid, status;

void main() {
        pid = fork();

        if (pid == 0) {          /* child process */
            for( i=1; i<=NLINES; i++ )
                printf( "%d.  I am the child!\n", i );
        } else {  /* parent process */
            for( i=NLINES; i>0; i-- )
                printf( "%d.  I am the parent!\n", i );
            wait( &status );
        }
}
```

---

[1] Or until the calling process receives some signal. Signals are discussed later in this chapter.

the process number only if it is possible that there is more than one child process running (or perhaps no child process running).

If necessary, our program could test the flags to see whether the child process terminated abnormally. A suitable definition for the layout of flags in the status word can be found in the include file "sys/wait.h". Since completion status is unimportant to us in the sample program, we will not go into the details until later.

There is no requirement that the parent process wait for its child processes to finish before exiting itself. If the parent process terminates first, all its child processes become so-called orphaned processes, but carry on executing normally. It is almost always poor programming practice to create orphaned processes, because there may be no indication to the user that there are still processes running. If one of the orphaned processes gets into an infinite loop, the user may be completely unaware of this, and the orphaned process may continue execution even after the user has logged out. By having the parent process wait for its children, the user will have a more explicit indication that there is a running program. (If the program is run as a foreground job, no command prompt will appear until the parent process completes.)

What use is the *fork* function in a program? To a certain extent, the creation of a new process may let you get more computational work done because you would have two processes receiving time slices from the system rather than one. However, exploiting this fact could make you unpopular with other users, who might notice a degradation in their service. There are two real reasons why a new process might be needed. The first reason is that we may want the new process to watch for some external event that is logically unrelated to the task being performed by the parent process. Possible external events include timer interrupts or inputs received from a communications line. The second reason is that we may want the new process to execute some other program in the system. Possibly the parent process and the new process will communicate via standard input-output in the same manner as pipes. Whatever the reason for creating the new process, there would usually need to be some means for the processes to communicate with each other. But to simplify matters, let us begin with an example where there is no need to communicate.

Our example will emulate the *system* function, which was mentioned in an earlier chapter. If you insert the statement

```
system( "date >> logfile" );
```

into a C program, the string argument will be passed to an instance of the *sh* shell command processor for execution. Our program example will be code that imitates the effect of the *system* function, but where we will invoke the *csh* shell instead. The few lines of C code needed to achieve this effect are given in Figure 11.3.

FIGURE 11.3. Execution of a csh Command

```
#include <signal.h>
int pid, status, wait_result;
char *command;  /* the csh command */
void (*old_INT_handler)(), (*old_QUIT_handler)();
    . . .
    command = "date >> logfile" ;
    . . .
    pid = fork();
    if (pid == 0) {  /* child process */
        execl( "/bin/csh", "csh", "-c", command, 0 );
        fprintf(stderr,"unable to invoke csh!\n");
        exit( 127 );
    }
    old_INT_handler  = signal( SIGINT, SIG_IGN );
    old_QUIT_handler = signal( SIGQUIT, SIG_IGN );
    do {
        wait_result = wait( &status );
    } while(wait_result != pid && wait_result != -1);
    signal( SIGINT,  old_INT_handler );
    signal( SIGQUIT, old_QUIT_handler );
    . . .
```

To be more generally useful, we should, of course, package our code as a function that is used in the same way as *system*. In the example, we clone a child process as in the earlier examples. A second copy of the original program is of no use to us, so we have the child process immediately transfer control to the *csh* program. The transfer is achieved with the *execl* function. This function makes a request to the UNIX system to replace the current process (the one calling *execl*) with a new process. The new process is an executable program whose pathname is given by the first argument. The second and subsequent arguments are the parameters that will be supplied to the program and may be accessed by that program via its *argv* argument. The end of this list of parameters is indicated by a zero. In our example, we are asking the UNIX system to execute the program "/bin/csh" and for this program to see the argument values:

$$
\begin{array}{lll}
\text{argv}[0] & = & \text{"csh"} \\
\text{argv}[1] & = & \text{"-c"} \\
\text{argv}[2] & = & \textit{the csh command}
\end{array}
$$

The -c flag indicates that a shell command is provided as the next argument (instead of having the shell read a command from the standard input). Control does not normally return from the call to *execl*. If it does, it means that the UNIX system was unable to execute the program named in the first argument.

Before continuing with the explanation of the sample program, we should note that *execl* is but one function in a family of seven similar functions for overlaying the current process with a new program. The most general of these functions is *execve*, which is used if the number of arguments to be passed to the program is not known in advance and if the program is to be supplied with a new set of environment variables. Further details can be obtained from the on-line manual entries for *execve* and *execl*.

While the child process in our sample program is using the *csh* shell to execute the command, the parent process waits for the child to complete. The calls to the *signal* function should be ignored for the moment; they will be explained later in this chapter. The parent process in this program uses a more general, and more reliable, method of waiting for a child to complete than in the program of Figure 11.2. The code checks that it is really the child process that has completed when control returns from the call to *wait*. If control returns because some other child has completed (or for some other reason), we repeat the wait request. One more detail is taken care of too. If there are no children processes when the call to *wait* is made, the result returned by *wait* is −1. In our sample program, it would be possible to obtain this −1 result only if the earlier call to *fork* fails. Although such a failure is unlikely,[2] it is desirable to code the wait loop in such a way that it is guaranteed to terminate.

To conclude the discussion of *fork*, we should note that the 4.2bsd and 4.3bsd versions of Berkeley UNIX provide a function named *vfork*. In our example of Figure 11.3, the system creates a duplicate copy of the program and then immediately discards this program copy, replacing it with the *csh* program. It is clearly inefficient to create a new process whose first action is to call *execl*, especially if this process was occupying a large region of memory. (Recall that the data space of the process is completely duplicated by the call to *fork*.) If you have code similar to that shown in the figure, you may substitute *vfork* for *fork* and _*exit* for *exit* (in the child process only) and thereby avoid the inefficiency. The child process should not make any assignments to global variables before calling *execl* or else there may be some surprising results. This is because *vfork* suppresses the duplication of the parent process' data space. The manual entry warns that *vfork* represents only a temporary solution to the efficiency problem; so it is probably not worthwhile using *vfork* in your own programs.

---

[2] The *fork* function will fail create a new process if you already have the maximum allowed number of processes.

11.2. SIGNALS

When a program forks into two or more processes, rarely do these processes execute independently of each other. The processes usually require some form of synchronization or some method of passing data between them. Data has to be passed using input-output functions and we will be looking at the mechanisms for doing this in the next section of this chapter. The UNIX method of synchronizing processes is based on the *signal* mechanism. To keep explanations simple, we will start by considering signals in situations where there is only a single process running.

11.2.1. Introduction to UNIX Signals

A signal is very similar in concept to a machine interrupt. When a computer detects an unusual event, it stops executing the current program and transfers control to an interrupt routine that is located somewhere in the code of the operating system. When a C program receives a signal, control is immediately passed to a function called a signal handler. The signal handler function can execute some C statements and exit. It can exit in three different ways: it can return control to the place in the program which was executing when the signal occurred; it can return control to some other point in the program; or, finally, the signal handler can terminate the program by calling the *exit* or _ *exit* functions.

There are many kinds of signal supported in the Berkeley UNIX system. The different signal types have numbers which range from one upwards. However, for readability and portability reasons, programs should not use these numbers directly. Preprocessor names for the signal types are defined in the include file "signal.h". A list of signal types appears in Table 11.1. The list may not be complete for your implementation of the Berkeley UNIX system. In particular, the SUN implementation has additional signals used for managing windows.

Several signals, such as the SIGFPE signal (floating point exception), correspond to machine interrupts. If your C program attempts to divide by 0.0, say, a machine interrupt is generated. An interrupt routine in the operating system will trap the interrupt and pass control to the signal handler function in your program that is currently responsible for the SIGFPE signal. Other signals are directly generated by your program or by other programs within the UNIX system or by typing certain characters on the keyboard. The characters that generate interrupts are normally chosen to be control characters (two key combinations that include the *Control* key). The default choices for these characters can be changed with the *stty* command. But, assuming that you have not changed the defaults, the keyboard-generated signals used most often are as follows: typing the *Control-Z* key combination while a program is running generates a SIGTSTP signal and this would normally cause the program to be temporarily suspended; hitting the *break* key or *Control-C*

TABLE 11.1. List of Signal Types

Name	Description	Default Action
SIGHUP	hangup	T
SIGINT	interrupt	T
SIGQUIT	quit signal	TC
SIGILL	illegal instruction	TC
SIGTRAP	trace trap	TC
SIGIOT	IOT instruction	TC
SIGEMT	EMT instruction	TC
SIGFPE	floating point exception	TC
SIGKILL	kill signal	T
SIGBUS	bus error	TC
SIGSEGV	segmentation fault	TC
SIGSYS	bad argument to system call	TC
SIGPIPE	write to a closed pipe	T
SIGALRM	timer alarm	T
SIGTERM	termination signal	T
SIGURG	urgent socket message	I
SIGSTOP	unignorable stop signal	S
SIGTSTP	keyboard stop signal	S
SIGCONT	continue after stop	I
SIGCHLD	change in child status	I
SIGTTIN	background terminal input	S
SIGTTOU	background terminal output	S
SIGIO	I/O has become possible	I
SIGXCPU	CPU time limit exceeded	T
SIGXFSZ	file size limit exceeded	T
SIGVTALRM	virtual time alarm	T
SIGPROF	profiling time alarm	T

where: **T** = terminate; **TC** = terminate with core dump; **I** = ignore; **S** = stop.

combination generates a SIGINT signal and this normally causes the program to be terminated; hitting the *Control-* key combination generates a SIGQUIT signal and this normally causes the program to be terminated and a core dump file to be generated.

Initially, a default action is provided for each kind of signal. The default action for several signals is to terminate the program. For another group of signals, including SIGFPE, the action is to terminate the program and generate a file named "core". This file contains a memory image of the program for use by the *adb*, *sdb* or *dbx* debuggers. For another group of signals, including SIGTSTP, the default action is to suspend execution of the program. Finally, there are a few signals where the default action is to do nothing. That is, the signal is ignored.

For nearly all signal types, the default action can be changed. The two signal types where the default action cannot be overridden are named SIGKILL and SIGSTOP. The inescapable action for a SIGKILL signal is to terminate the process. The existence of SIGKILL means that there is always a guaranteed method of terminating a process (short of the drastic step of shutting the computer system down). The action for SIGSTOP is to stop the process and this provides a guaranteed method of temporarily halting a process. Changing the action to be performed when a signal is received is accomplished through the *signal* or *sigvec* functions. The former function has a simpler interface and is standard in all versions of the UNIX system so we will consider it exclusively.

A simple example involving signals appears in Figure 11.4. What happens if we enter this program, compile it and run it? The computational part of this program is uninteresting, to say the least. Every several seconds, the program outputs a dot on the screen. When you get tired of this behaviour, you can interrupt the program. Hitting the break key on your terminal should generate the SIGINT signal and cause the signal handler function to be executed. You can send the program some different signals by typing various control character combinations. You can see which control characters have special purposes by executing the command

    stty all

The character appearing under the heading *intr* is an alternative to *break* for generating the SIGINT signal, while the character under the *quit* heading generates the SIGQUIT signal. (If the notation ^\ appears under *quit* this means that the *control-* key combination generates the signal.)

If you run the program as a background job, you can try sending an even greater variety of signals to the program. Assuming that you are using the *csh* command shell and that you have just started this program, you can send it the SIGTERM signal by executing the command

    kill %+

You can send it any signal you like by including another argument in the command. For example,

    kill -9 %+

will send it the SIGKILL signal, and this will terminate the program

FIGURE 11.4. An Experiment with Signals (#1)

```
#include <stdio.h>
#include <signal.h>

int i = 0;

void quit( code )
int code;
{
    fprintf( stderr,
        "\nInterrupt (code = %d, i = %d)\n", code, i );
    exit( -1 );  /* abnormal termination */
}

void main() {

    /* intercept various termination signals */
    signal( SIGINT,  quit );
    signal( SIGTERM, quit );
    signal( SIGQUIT, quit );

    /* show the passage of time */
    do {
        i++;
        if (i % 100000 == 0) putc('.',stderr);
    } while( i != 0 );

    /* terminate successfully (after a few hours) */
    exit(0);
}
```

immediately. Either signal names (without the *SIG* prefix) or signal numbers may be used in the *kill* command; so

```
    kill -KILL %+
```

is an alternative method of giving the same command. In addition to the *kill* command, a C process can send a signal to itself or to any other process by calling the library function named *kill*. The *kill* function is discussed later in the chapter.

11.2.2. Proper Use of the *signal* Function

Before proceeding to more difficult examples, we should be clear about what the *signal* function is doing and how it works. For each process, the UNIX system maintains a table of the action that should be performed for each kind of signal. When the process calls the *signal* function, the table entry for the signal type named as the first argument is changed to the value provided as the second argument. There are three possibilities for the second argument. It may be: SIG_IGN (ignore the signal), SIG_DFL (perform the default action), or a pointer to a signal handler function. (SIG_IGN and SIG_DFL are names defined in the "signal.h" header file.) The *signal* function returns the old table entry as its result. If you eventually wish to restore the original signal handling action, you should save this result. The data type of the result is *pointer to function returning* **void**. The variable used to hold the result should therefore be declared in a manner similar to

```
void (*signal_result)();
```

The result returned by *signal* explains the signal handling code that was included in Figure 11.3 earlier. In that code, the parent process disabled the SIGINT and SIGQUIT signals while it was waiting for the child process to finish. Later, when the child has terminated, the original signal handling actions are restored. Why should the parent process not respond to these signals? It should not in case the child process installs handlers for either kind of signal. If it does, the parent process may be killed by the signal while the child continues – and this orphaned process can become a nuisance. (It may, for example, try to read from the keyboard and so interfere with your shell commands.)

This is, perhaps, an appropriate point to consider another problem with signal handling. It is often the case that a parent process wishes to ignore a certain kind of signal and so executes a call like

```
oldhandler = signal( SIGHUP, SIG_IGN );
```

in which we use SIGHUP as a plausible example of a signal that might be ignored. But if the parent process spawns a child that performs an *execl* call to execute a self-contained program, it is quite possible that this program will contain a call like

```
oldh = signal( SIGHUP, myhandler );
```

This call has the effect of causing the child process to accept signals that are being ignored by the parent. There are undoubtedly some situations where this behaviour is desirable. But it is more likely to be the case that the child process should not start intercepting signals whose default action has previously been changed (by the parent) to SIG_IGN. Therefore, the *normal* method of installing a new signal handler is to use a code sequence like the following:

```
oldhandler = signal( SIGHUP, SIG_IGN );
if (oldhandler != SIG_IGN)
        signal( SIGHUP, newhandler );
```

That is, before installing our new signal handler, we should check to see that the current action for this signal is not SIG_IGN.

Now that we have been through all the details of installing a signal handler, let us consider the actions that take place when a signal handler is called. If a signal occurs and control is transferred to a signal handler function, further occurrences of this kind of signal are temporarily inhibited. This signal type is said to be *blocked*. If and when control is returned from the signal handler, this signal type will automatically be unblocked. But only this one kind of signal is blocked while the signal handler is executing. It is quite possible for a different kind of signal to interrupt the signal handler.

When a signal handler function is invoked, it is passed three arguments. The first argument is the number of the signal. The second argument is an integer code that, for some signal types, refines the reason for the signal occurring. For example, the SIGFPE signal is generated for almost any kind of arithmetic error that includes integer divide by zero, floating point divide by zero, and floating point overflow. The third argument provides information on where the program was interrupted.

11.2.3. Returning Control from Signal Handlers

The previous example simply terminated the program when the signal was received. But what if we want to resume the interrupted code? Or, what if we would like to continue execution at a different place in the program? Figure 11.5 illustrates both of these possibilities.

In this short program, the signal handler for the SIGQUIT signal prints the current value of the variable i and then returns control to the point in the main program that was interrupted. If you run this program, you can generate the signals (normally with the *Control-* key combination) and see that variable i is continually increasing in value. If, however, you generate the SIGINT signal (with the *break* key or your interrupt control character), you will be prompted for input from the keyboard. Typing a letter "y" (or "Y") causes the computation loop in the main program to be restarted. Typing anything else causes the program to be terminated.

Restarting the main loop requires a control transfer to a point in the program different from the point of interruption. The *setjmp* and *longjmp* functions are useful in this case. When a call to *setjmp* is executed, the return point of this function is remembered in the buffer supplied as the function argument. The function returns zero as its result. Subsequently, if we execute a call to *longjmp* and supply this buffer as the first argument, control will be transferred to the position remembered in the buffer. This point in the code is at the return

FIGURE 11.5. An Experiment with Signals (#2)

```
#include <stdio.h>
#include <signal.h>
#include <setjmp.h>

jmp_buf return_pt;

int i;

void trap_int() {
    char answer[80];
    fputs( "\nDo you wish to restart? ", stdout );
    gets( answer );
    if (*answer != 'y' &&
        *answer != 'Y') exit( -1 );
    longjmp( return_pt, 1 );
}


void trap_quit() {
    printf( "\ni = %d\n", i );
}


void main() {
    signal( SIGQUIT, trap_quit );

    if (setjmp(return_pt) == 0)
        signal( SIGINT, trap_int );

    for( i=1; i!=0; i++ ) {
        if ( i%100000 == 0 ) {
            putchar('.');
            fflush(stdout);
        }
    }
    puts( "\nFinished!" );
}
```

from *setjmp*. Thus it might seem to the user of *setjmp* that control returns from the call more than once. It may be important to your program to distinguish the original return from *setjmp* from apparent returns generated by *longjmp*. Therefore, you can supply a value to *longjmp* (as its second argument) that will be used as the return value of *setjmp*. Any non-zero value is sufficient to distinguish the two kinds of return.

Notice that our program is careful not to set the SIGINT signal handler until after we have initialized the *return_pt* buffer with *setjmp*. (Otherwise the occurrence of a SIGINT signal between setting the signal handler and initializing the buffer could cause a wild jump of control.) We only need to set the signal handler if the result from *setjmp* is zero.

There is one important point to note with the use of *setjmp* and *longjmp*. When *longjmp* is executed, the function that contained the call to *setjmp* which set the buffer must still be active. If this function has returned or even if it has returned and been re-entered, execution of the *longjmp* can cause chaos. The local variables of the function to which *longjmp* returns may contain garbage and when this function attempts to return to its caller, a wild jump may occur. This happens because the local variables and return address for active procedures are held on a data stack. When *longjmp* is executed, the stack is popped so that it has the same height that it had had when the *setjmp* was executed. If this fails to restore the stack to its earlier configuration, there will almost certainly be chaos.

11.2.4. Signalling Between Processes

One process may send a signal to another process, provided that this other process also belongs to you.[3] The signal mechanism may be used for various purposes. It may be used to kill errant processes, to temporarily suspend execution of processes, to make processes aware of the passage of time, or to synchronize the actions of processes.

To send a signal to a process, you will usually need to know the number of that process (its *process id*). The only exception occurs when you need to send the same signal to all processes in a *process group*. (If your program has been forking and has created several processes, all these processes should belong to the same group.) A parent process can always know the numbers for its child processes, because the *fork* function returns the number of the new child process to the parent. A child process can always determine the number of its parent because there is a system function *getppid* that returns this number. And, a process can always determine its own number with the *getpid* function. The function call that sends a signal is *kill*. Its name is, perhaps, misleading because it does not necessarily kill the process that receives the signal. A possible call is

---

[3] To be precise, the two processes must have the same effective user id.

```
kill( getppid(), SIGINT );
```

which sends the SIGINT signal to the parent of the current process.

The necessity of knowing process numbers and the requirement that the processes have the same effective user id will, in practice, restrict the signal mechanism to processes that have a common parent. If you use it only for processes that belong to the same program, you should not encounter any difficulties.

11.2.5. Use of Timer Signals

There are many situations in which a program needs to be aware of the passage of time. Perhaps we would like to terminate a process that is taking too long, perhaps there is some action that needs to be performed periodically, such as writing checkpoint information to a file.

The Berkeley UNIX system maintains three interval timers for each process. These timers are counters which are being continuously decremented. When a timer reaches zero, a signal is sent to the process. One timer is used for measuring real time. Real time is time as it is measured by a clock on the wall; the rate of passage of real time is completely independent of what the computer is doing. For example, if you set the real interval timer to hold 10 seconds, then 10 seconds later, a SIGALRM signal is delivered to the process. A second timer measures virtual time. This timer is like a stopwatch that runs during time slices received by the process and is stopped at other times. In other words, the virtual timer measures the amount of CPU time that the process is consuming. When the virtual interval timer expires, a SIGVTALRM signal is delivered. The third timer measures virtual time plus system time. That is, the timer is being decremented while the process is executing and while the UNIX system is executing a request on behalf of the process. When this timer trips, a SIG-PROF signal is delivered. As the signal name suggests, this timer is intended to be useful to program profilers (such as those described in Chapter 10).

An interval timer is set with the *setitimer* function. This function both sets the timer to hold a new value and returns the old value of the timer. To simply inspect the value held in an interval timer, the *getitimer* function can be used. As a short example of the use of the virtual timer, Figure 11.6 shows the use of a function that prints regular progress reports on how much CPU time has been consumed. As the code illustrates, timer values are split into two separate words. One word (the structure field named *tv_sec*) holds seconds. The other word (field *tv_usec*) holds microseconds. The fact that intervals can be expressed to microsecond accuracy should not be understood to imply that operating system can time processes to that degree of accuracy. Some room for improvement in timing accuracy has been left to accommodate faster computers. On the VAX/780 implementation of the Berkeley UNIX system, timing resolution is only 10 milliseconds.

FIGURE 11.6. A CPU Time Meter Function

```c
#include <stdio.h>
#include <signal.h>

int interval=10;   /* report every 10 seconds */

void vt_tick()
{
    static int total_time = 0;

    fprintf(stderr,"\nCPU Usage = %d secs.\n",
        (total_time += interval) );
}


void start_cpu_meter() {
#    include <sys/time.h>
    struct itimerval vt_val;

    if (interval <= 0) return;

    signal( SIGVTALRM, vt_tick );

    vt_val.it_value.tv_sec     = interval;
    vt_val.it_value.tv_usec    = 0;
    vt_val.it_interval.tv_sec  = interval;
    vt_val.it_interval.tv_usec = 0;
    setitimer( ITIMER_VIRTUAL, &vt_val, NULL );
}


void main() {
    int i = 0;

    start_cpu_meter();
    for( ; ; )   /* consume some CPU time */
        i++;
}
```

Which of the three interval timers to use is specified in the first parameter of *setitimer*. A pointer to a structure containing the new timer value is passed as the second parameter. A pointer to a structure that would receive a copy of the old timer value could be passed as the third parameter. The old value is not returned if *NULL* is passed.

The structure passed to *setitimer* actually contains two timer values. One value, the *it_value* field, specifies the time until the next signal is generated. The other value, the *it_interval* field, can be used to obtain repeated signals at regular intervals. For example, if we set *it_value* to 5 seconds and *it_interval* to 3 seconds, we would receive signals after 5 seconds, 8 seconds, 11 seconds, and so on.

A simpler version of *setitimer* is available. It is called *alarm* and is available on all versions of the UNIX system, whereas *setitimer* is available only on the Berkeley UNIX system. The call `alarm(n )` generates a single SIGALRM signal after a delay of *n* seconds. Other functions useful for timing purposes include *sleep* and *pause*. The *sleep* function causes the calling process to be suspended for the period of time specified by its argument. The *pause* function suspends the calling process until after the next timer signal has arrived and the signal handler function returns from handling that signal.

11.2.6. Handling the SIGTSTP Signal

A program executing as the foreground job can normally be suspended by hitting the *Control-Z* key combination. This control character causes a SIGTSTP signal to be sent to every process in the job[4] and the default action for the SIGTSTP signal is to suspend the process. A suspended process can later be restarted by sending it the SIGCONT signal. The *csh* commands that restart a stopped job send this signal to every stopped process in the job (process group).

Some programs must intercept the SIGTSTP signal to perform some special actions. The *vi* editor, for example, normally operates with the terminal in the *raw* and *noecho* modes.[5] (Raw mode implies that none of the special characters such as *Control-U* to erase a line, etc., will work.) If *vi* is simply stopped in its tracks, the terminal will be left in a strange state in which no characters echo on the screen, backspacing will not erase mistakes, and so on. Consequently, *vi* and programs like it must intercept SIGTSTP to restore the terminal to its usual mode. Later, when *vi* is restarted, it must set the terminal modes again and redraw the screen. The signal handler for SIGTSTP in a program like *vi* should have the structure shown in Figure 11.7. Assuming that the

---

[4] To be more accurate, the signal is sent to every process in the *process group*. All processes in the Berkeley UNIX system belong to some group, each group being identified by a process group number. The *csh* command shell creates a separate process group for execution of each job.

[5] We will be looking at terminal modes and how to change them in the next chapter.

FIGURE 11.7. A SIGTSTP Signal Handler

```
#include <signal.h>

void suspend() {
            .         /* restore terminal to normal
            .            operating mode, and move
            .            the cursor to last line        */
            .
    fflush(stdout);   /* flush pending output */
    sigsetmask( 0 );
    signal( SIGTSTP, SIG_DFL );
    kill( 0, SIGTSTP );

    /* control returns here after
       the process is restarted    */
    signal( SIGTSTP, suspend );
            .         /* set the terminal modes
            .            and redraw the screen        */
            .
}
```

main program installs this signal handler by executing

> `signal( SIGTSTP, suspend );`

a *Control-Z* character will cause control to enter our *suspend* function. This function should begin by restoring the terminal modes, and flushing output that is pending for the terminal and for any open files. In general, the function should ensure that the program environment is returned to the state that the user expects. The user of the program is likely to be unhappy if, for example, subsequent commands typed on the keyboard do not echo on the screen. Next, the function unblocks SIGTSTP signals with a call to the *sigsetmask* function (recall that further deliveries of a signal are automatically blocked while control is in the handler for that signal). It then restores the default processing action for the SIGTSTP signal. Now that we are ready for the process to be stopped, we send the SIGTSTP signal to ourself with the *kill* function, and our process is stopped because that is the default action for the signal.

Later, when the program is restarted, control resumes at the statement following the call to *kill*. We immediately reinstall the signal handler and then we can go about setting terminal modes to whatever the program requires, redrawing the screen, and doing anything necessary to put the program back in a suitable state for resuming execution. Finally, control can return from the signal handler to where we were when the *Control-Z* character took effect.

QUESTIONS

1. What will happen if you put the following line of code in a program?

    ```
    for( ; ; ) fork();
    ```

2. What would happen if we forgot to include the call to *sigsetmask* in the *suspend* signal handler of Figure 11.7?

3. There may be occasions when you want a program to terminate itself and simultaneously generate a "core" file. What statements could you include in your program to force this kind of termination?

4. Can you use the *setjmp, longjmp* facility to simulate coroutines? That is, can you use these system functions to transfer control backwards and forwards between, say, the middle of function A and the middle of function B?

5. Suppose that you have a program that calls *vfork* to create a child process and that this process immediately calls *execl* to pass control to another program. Normally, control will never return from the call to *execl*. However, if the program named in the call to *execl* cannot be found or if there is some other error, control does return. If control returns, the child process must terminate by calling the _ *exit* function, not the *exit* function. Why?

CHAPTER 12

SYSTEMS PROGRAMMING –
COMMUNICATIONS

12.1. PIPES

In the shell command language, output from one command can be piped to the
input of another command. For example, to print a formatted listing of a C
source file, we might execute

```
cb program.c | lpr
```

Since the shell command processor is just another C program, a method of
starting up processes and connecting the standard output of one process to the
standard input of another process is needed. But before we get to the actual
procedure of making these connections, we should take a look at how input-
output and multiprocessing coexist.

When a new process is created, it inherits exactly the same set of open
files as its parent possessed when it executed *fork*. This means that if both the
parent and the child continue execution and both write to their standard outputs, the output will be interleaved. Indeed, if output is being buffered, any
output that was in the buffer when *fork* was executed can be output twice.
Similarly, if both processes read from their standard inputs, they will both read
characters that were in the buffer at the time of the fork. After this, the two
processes are in competition for input characters. The input will sometimes go
to one process and sometimes to the other, but never to both processes.

To avoid such chaos, it is advisable for the parent process to wait for the
child to finish before performing any more input or output. It is also a good
idea for the parent process to execute **fflush(stdout)** before calling *fork*. If
input is line-buffered, as *stdin* from the keyboard is by default, the parent process need only make sure that it has read a complete line of input before executing the *fork*.

At the low-level input-output interface to the system, it is easy to rearrange file descriptors. If you recall from Chapter 7, open files correspond to
slots in an object description table. When the shell invokes a program, it opens
files as necessary so that standard input for the program corresponds to slot 0,
standard output to slot 1 and standard error output to slot 2. The index position of an open file in this table is called its *file descriptor*, so standard input
has the file descriptor 0. When a new file is opened, the system uses the lowest
numbered empty slot in the table. Therefore, if you want your program to read
from the file "/tmp/junk" when it reads from the standard input, you need
only include the following lines of code in your program:

```
close( 0 );         /* close standard input */
if (open("/tmp/junk", O_RDONLY, 0) != 0)
    fprintf(stderr,"oops!\n");
```

Yes, you are allowed to close the standard input or output files! Closing the
standard input frees slot 0 in the object descriptor table, so that the next file we
open will be given this slot. This change affects stream input-output too.
When *stdin* is supplied as a parameter to the stream-oriented functions, these
functions use file descriptor 0 to read more input. Thus, next time that they
read new data into the buffer, they would read from the file.

Since it is possible to replace the open file in a particular slot in the table,
is it also possible to exchange two entries? If we close and reopen the two files,
we could achieve such an exchange. But closing and reopening a file is undesirable. Not only is it inefficient, it would also lose the current position in the file.
To do the job properly, we need the help of either the *dup* or *dup2* system functions. If we make a call like

```
newfd = dup( oldfd );
```

where *oldfd* is a descriptor for an open file, the function creates a duplicate file
descriptor and returns this descriptor as the result. Afterwards, output to the
file can be performed by calling the *write* function with either file descriptor.
Similarly, input operations on the file could use either descriptor. When *dup*
creates the new entry in the object descriptor table, it uses the slot with the
lowest numbered position. The *dup2* function is used if we want to force the
new descriptor to have a specific number. (The name *dup2* appears to be an
abbreviation for *duplicate to*.) If we make the call

```
dup2( oldfd, newfd );
```

then the table slot at position *newfd* is forced to contain a duplicate of the slot at position *oldfd*. Any open file already occupying position *newfd* is automatically closed by *dup2*. To clarify, here is how we could use *dup2* to replace standard input with input from "/tmp/junk" again:

```
fd = open( "/tmp/junk", O_RDONLY, 0 );
dup2( fd, 0 );
close( fd );
```

The close of the *fd* entry still leaves slot 0 open for input from the file. This code, used for replacing the standard input with another input source, should be preferred over the code given previously. The *dup2* call explicitly specifies which file descriptor number to use and automatically takes care of any previous uses for that file descriptor.

After all this preamble dealing with file descriptors, we can now get back to the subject of pipelining. We can create a pipe with the system call *pipe* (what else?). The call creates an internal system buffer and two file descriptors. One file descriptor is used for writing and the other for reading. Writing causes data to be put into the buffer, whereas reading extracts it from the buffer. Unlike a file which has (almost) unlimited output capacity, the buffer used for a pipe has a modest size – only 4096 bytes. If a process writes a lot of data and fills the buffer, the process will be suspended until the reading process has caught up a little and removed some data from the buffer. Similarly, if the reading process reads fast enough to empty the buffer, it will be suspended when it attempts to read some more.

The only problem with *pipe* is that we usually want the standard output of one program to write into the buffer and the standard input of some other process to read from the buffer. And that is why we first went through all the details of how to rearrange file descriptors. Figure 12.1 gives a simple example of a program creating two child processes connected by a pipe. One process executes the *cb* program and the other executes the *lpr* program. All the calls to *dup2* and *close* will, no doubt, make this example seem rather confusing.[1] On the other hand, if you can follow the logic of this program, you will have an excellent understanding of file descriptors. Now for a quick tour through the program logic. First, if the executable form of the program has the name *cprint*, the program can be invoked with a command similar to

cprint prog1.c prog2.c

This command will send a beautified version of "prog1.c" to the printer, and then it will send a beautified version of "prog2.c" to the printer. One minor difficulty is that *cb* does not take a filename argument. Therefore, inside the main processing loop, our program replaces the standard input with input from the next argument file. It does this using *dup2* and then closes the superfluous

---

[1] Author's note: there was some trouble getting it to work too!

FIGURE 12.1. The cprint Program

```
#include <stdio.h>
#include <sys/file.h>

int cb_pid, lpr_pid, pid, status, i, fd[2], filefd;

void main( argc, argv )
int argc;  char *argv[];
{
    for( i=1; i<argc; i++ ) {
        filefd = open( argv[i], O_RDONLY, 0 );
        if (filefd < 0) {
            perror( argv[i] );  continue;
        }
        dup2( filefd, 0 );
        close( filefd );
        pipe( fd );
        if ((cb_pid = fork()) == 0) {  /* 'cb' */
            dup2( fd[1], 1 );
            close( fd[0] );  close( fd[1] );
            execl( "/usr/bin/cb", "cb", 0 );
            _exit( -1 );
        }
        if ((lpr_pid = fork()) == 0) {  /* 'lpr' */
            dup2( fd[0], 0 );
            close( fd[0] );  close( fd[1] );
            execl( "/usr/ucb/lpr", "lpr", 0 );
            _exit( -1 );
        }
        close( fd[0] );  close( fd[1] );
        do {
            pid = wait( &status );
            if (pid == cb_pid)  cb_pid = 0;
            if (pid == lpr_pid) lpr_pid = 0;
        } while( cb_pid != lpr_pid && pid != -1 );
    }
}
```

file descriptor. Next, we create the pipe. The *pipe* function stores two file descriptors in the array *fd*. The first entry is for reading and the second for writing.

A child process to run *cb* is now forked off. This process will be reading from the standard input and we have already taken care of that. (Recall that a child process inherits standard input and output from its parent.) We have to redirect standard output, however, to go into the pipe. Therefore, we use *dup2* to perform the substitution and then we close the duplicate file descriptor and the (superfluous) file descriptor for the read side of the pipe. Then the child can transfer control to an invocation of *cb* via the *execl* call.

Next, a child process to run *lpr* is forked off. Its standard input has to be replaced with input read from the pipe. The code used to achieve this is similar to that found in the first child. Then control is transferred to the *lpr* program.

The main program closes its file descriptors for the pipe, since it will not be using the pipe itself, and then waits for both child processes to complete. Subsequently, the main processing loop can be repeated for the next file provided as an argument in the command line. Note that it is quite important for superfluous file descriptors to be closed in all processes. If, for example, we do not close all the extra descriptors for writing to the pipe, the process that is reading from the pipe will never be given an end-of-file indication. And that causes the *lpr* process in our example to hang, waiting for more input.

12.2. SOCKETS

12.2.1. What Are Sockets?

Two processes cannot communicate via a pipe unless they have inherited file descriptors for that pipe from a common ancestor. This means that the *talk* program, for example, cannot use pipes to communicate between two users. Communication between two unrelated processes could, conceivably, take place through files. Process A could append its message to a file, and process B could check that file at regular intervals and read from it whenever it contains anything new. This approach would be rather inefficient though. The Berkeley UNIX system provides a better solution to the problem in the form of *sockets*.

A socket is like the end point of a UNIX pipe. We can describe a pipe as being comprised of two sockets that are linked by some sort of communications software.[2] A single socket is used in exactly the same way as a file descriptor. When a socket is created, it is allocated a slot in the object descriptor table exactly as for an open file. After the socket has been linked to another socket, the slot number may be used as the file descriptor parameter in calls to the *read* and *write* functions.

---

[2] Indeed, Berkeley UNIX implements a pipe as a pair of sockets.

Two (or more) sockets must be connected before they can be used to transfer data. There are many kinds of connection to choose from. We can begin, though, by grouping connections into two categories. First, we can have a connection that is implemented just as a pipe is. That is, the system allocates a buffer; writes to a socket cause the data to be stored in the buffer; and reads from a socket at the other end cause that data to be removed from the buffer. Secondly, we can have a connection between processes on two different computers where writes to a socket cause the data to be sent out over a transmission line to the process on the other computer. It is becoming common for several computers running the UNIX system to be linked in a *local area network* (LAN) using coaxial cable for high-speed communication. Transmissions over communications lines are usually grouped into message packets constructed and transmitted according to special rules known as a *protocol*. Several different protocols are supported by the Berkeley UNIX system. Most system software which performs socket communication between computers uses either the *Internet Transmission Control Protocol* (TCP) or the *Internet User Datagram Protocol* (UDP).

To make matters more confusing, the different kinds of protocol are grouped into families. The TCP and UDP protocols both belong to the Internet family (INET). The INET family is known as a *communications domain*. Development of the INET communications domain was funded by the Defense Advanced Research Projects Agency (DARPA) of the United States government. There are several other domains which have protocols corresponding to standards set by private manufacturers or standards organizations. A list of domain names can be seen in the file "/usr/include/sys/socket.h". These names all begin with the prefix *AF_*, which is short for *address family*. Not all the communications domains listed in this file may actually be implemented on your system. And, within any domain, not all the protocols listed in documentation for that domain may be implemented. The reason is that intercomputer communications is a relatively recent UNIX facility and still subject to ongoing development.

It would be inappropriate to go into details about communications and protocols in this book. This chapter will continue with just a brief glimpse at the two most important domains on the Berkeley UNIX system and give only two small program examples.

12.2.2. Types of Socket

There are three kinds of socket which may be used in one or more of the communications domains. They are named SOCK_STREAM, SOCK_DGRAM and SOCK_RAW. The first kind provides byte-by-byte stream communication in a manner similar to pipes. Sockets of this kind may be used for transmission in either direction.

The second kind, SOCK_DGRAM, is used for datagram transmission, again, in either direction. A datagram is nothing more than a packet of data along with some control information, such as a packet sequence number. However, the normal user would probably not wish to use datagrams directly because the system does not guarantee delivery of datagrams in the order that they are transmitted or any delivery at all! To use datagrams, you would either have to limit communications to a single packet or else you would have to implement your own datagram-handling protocol to put packets into the correct order, to request retransmission of missing packets and to ignore duplicate packets.

The third kind, SOCK_RAW, is provided only for users who want a high degree of control over message transmission. For example, this raw interface might permit the user to specify the exact path to use when sending packets over a complicated network.

This chapter does not give any information about the usage of the SOCK_DGRAM nor SOCK_RAW form of sockets. For more information, you should consult the references given at the end of this chapter.

12.2.3. The UNIX Domain

When both ends of a socket connection are located in the same computer, we can use a simple communications domain called the UNIX domain. A simple example of the use of sockets in the UNIX domain appears in Figures 12.2 and 12.3. Our example is motivated by the following situation. We imagine that there is a user, user A, who wishes to receive files or data sent by other users on the system. Possibly, user A uses a hardcopy terminal and is providing a line printer service for other people; or, possibly, user A has connected a special hardware device such as a bit-mapped raster display and wishes to have other users send picture images to him. In order to receive the data, user A starts the *Receive* program shown in Figure 12.2, which sets up a socket ready to receive data. The received data is generated as the standard output of this program. User A might invoke the program as

```
Receive > data_in
```

Later, another user, user B say, would execute the *Send* program of Figure 12.3, which connects with A's socket. User B might execute the program as

```
Send A < some_data
```

where *A* represents the user id of A. Any data provided to the standard input of *Send* will be transmitted to A. Although the two programs start similarly, they soon diverge. Let us begin with the *Receive* program in Figure 12.2. This program acts as a server, passively waiting for client processes (invocations of the *Send* program) to connect with it. *Receive* creates the socket with a call to the *socket* function. The first parameter gives the communications domain (or address family) as UNIX. The second parameter specifies SOCK_STREAM

FIGURE 12.2. The Receive Program

```
#include <stdio.h>
#include <sys/types.h>
#include <sys/socket.h>

#define SOCK_PREF "/tmp/#"
#define oops(msg) {perror(msg);   exit(-1);}

struct sockaddr saddr;
int    slen, s, rfd, ch;
FILE   *rf;

void main( argc, argv )
int argc;  char *argv[];
{   /* construct the socket name & length */
    saddr.sa_family = AF_UNIX;
    strcpy( saddr.sa_data, SOCK_PREF );
    strcat( saddr.sa_data, getenv("USER") );
    slen = sizeof(saddr);
    unlink( saddr.sa_data );

    s = socket( AF_UNIX, SOCK_STREAM, 0 );
    if (s == -1) oops("socket");
    if (bind(s, &saddr, slen) != 0) oops("bind");
    if (listen(s,1) != 0) oops("listen");

    for( ; ; ) {  /* wait for a connection */
        rfd = accept( s, NULL, NULL );
        if (rfd == -1) oops( "accept" );
        rf = fdopen( rfd, "r" );
        if (rf == NULL) oops("fdopen");
        ch = '\f';  /* start with a form-feed */
        do {
            putchar( ch );  ch = getc(rf);
        } while( ch != EOF );
        fclose( rf );  fflush( stdout );
    }
}
```

FIGURE 12.3. The Send Program

```
#include <stdio.h>
#include <sys/types.h>
#include <sys/socket.h>

#define SOCK_PREF "/tmp/#"
#define oops(msg) {perror(msg);   exit(-1);}

struct sockaddr saddr;
int     slen = sizeof(saddr);
int     s, ch;
FILE    *sf;

void main( argc, argv )
int argc;  char *argv[];
{
    if (argc != 2) {
        fprintf(stderr,
            "Usage: %s  recipient\n", argv[0]);
        exit(-1);
    }
    saddr.sa_family = AF_UNIX;
    strcpy( saddr.sa_data, SOCK_PREF );
    strcat( saddr.sa_data, argv[1] );

    s = socket( AF_UNIX, SOCK_STREAM, 0 );
    if (s == -1) oops("socket");
    if (connect(s, &saddr, slen) != 0) oops("connect");
    sf = fdopen( s, "w" );
    if (sf == NULL) oops("fdopen");

    /* send data to socket */
    fprintf(sf,"Data from %s::\n", getenv("USER"));
    while( (ch = getchar()) != EOF )
        putc( ch, sf );
    fclose( sf );
    exit( 0 );
}
```

type sockets. The third parameter could be used in other domains for specifying a particular protocol, but it is inapplicable here.

After creating the socket, we must give it a name. If it did not have a name, there would be no way for the *Send* program to say what socket it wanted to connect to. Just as you can choose names for files, you can choose names for sockets in the UNIX domain. In fact, in the current Berkeley implementation of sockets, socket names and file path names share the same name space. That is, the program must choose a socket name that could also be a valid name for a new file. Our program chooses a path name that begins "/tmp/..." because files (and hence sockets) in the "/tmp" directory should be accessible to all users. The name is constructed and copied into a structure, whose name and size are passed to the *bind* function. Our call to this function will cause an entry in the "/tmp" directory to be created and associated with the socket. Next, *Receive* tells the UNIX system that it will be listening for connections on this socket. The second parameter in the call to *listen* tells the system how big a backlog of waiting connections it should be prepared to handle. Then, *Receive* calls *accept* to wait for a connection to be made. The process will be suspended until the connection occurs, or until some interrupting signal arrives.

If a connection is made, the *accept* function returns a file descriptor as its result. This file descriptor may be used for both input and output communication with the client process at the other end of the communications link. In our simple example, we will only use the file descriptor for reading. Our *Receive* program converts the file descriptor into an ordinary stream pointer, using *fdopen*, and reads from the stream. At the end of input from the stream, it closes the stream. Closing the stream causes the file descriptor to be closed and that breaks the socket connection. But breaking the connection does not delete the entry we created in the "/tmp" directory. This is why the program began by attempting to delete (unlink) this entry – in case there was a socket left from a previous invocation of *Receive*.[3] After closing the connection, the program goes back to wait for another connection.

The sending program, *Send*, in Figure 12.3 is a little less complicated. It creates a socket, just as *Receive* did. This socket, however, needs to be connected to the socket created by *Receive*. Therefore, *Send* constructs the same socket name as that used by *Receive* and passes this name to *connect*. If the connection can be made (i.e. the entry in the "/tmp" directory exists), the call will return a zero result. After a successful connection, the *Send* program can use the socket as though it were a file descriptor. (Both file descriptors and sockets are implemented as indexes into the same object descriptor table.) Our program converts the file descriptor to a stream for convenience, writes data to

---

[3] The documentation hints that the need to unlink sockets after use may disappear in some future release of the Berkeley UNIX system.

the socket and closes the stream when finished. Closing the stream causes *Receive* at the other end to receive an end-of-file indication.

12.3. THE INET DOMAIN

There are several networking programs provided with the Berkeley UNIX system. They include *rlogin, rwho* and *talk*. All the networking programs use the Internet communications domain. Within this domain, the commonly used protocols are TCP and UDP. TCP (Transmission Control Protocol) provides reliable byte-stream message transmission and is used to support the SOCK_STREAM form of socket. UDP (User Datagram Packet) is used to support the SOCK_DGRAM form of socket. UDP is more efficient, in that there is less software overhead associated with its use, but it is unreliable; the system does not guarantee that packets will arrive at the other end. Our example programs will use SOCK_STREAM sockets and therefore the TCP protocol.

A major difference between the UNIX and INET domains is the form of the socket names. In the UNIX domain, file pathnames are used to name sockets. In the INET domain, network addresses must be used. A network address consists of three numbers. The first number specifies the network or address family (INET in our case), the second number identifies the computer and the third identifies a port on that computer.

A program that communicates with a program on another computer needs to know the network address of that other program. But how does it find out what address to use? For the networking programs that form part of the UNIX system, there is a facility akin to the directory assistance service provided by a telephone company. Most networking software fits the client/server model. For example, on each UNIX machine in a network, there is a remote login server (the *rlogin* daemon) waiting for clients on other computers to make a connection. When a user on some machine executes the *rlogin* program, it determines the number for the machine specified as the *rlogin* argument by searching for the machine name in a small database that lists the machines on the network. This database is the file "/etc/hosts". The program then determines the port number for the *rlogin* service by searching another small database. This other database corresponds to the file "/etc/services". The file also says which protocol each service uses for communication. The numbers found in the two databases are combined to create an INET address. Then *rlogin* attempts to make the connection. (There is an assumption that the port numbers for *rlogin* service are the same on all machines.)

Our small programming example of the use of sockets in the INET domain takes the form of a computerized bulletin board. The idea is that a server program on our machine will send today's bulletin board announcements (copied from a file) to any client located on any machine in the network. Unless we have *super-user* privileges, we cannot add the port number for our bulletin board service to the "/etc/services" database. Therefore, we have just picked a port number and built it into the program. With luck, no-one else will have already taken this port number. (At the end of this section, we tell you what to do if you do not want to rely on luck.) Now let us begin with the client program. We call the program *b_board* and it appears in Figure 12.4. We have hard-coded into the program the assumption that the bulletin board server program is located on a machine named "mega-vax", and uses port number 2000. Probably, the program should be generalized so that the name of the computer is provided as a command-line argument. (It would not be inconceivable to have different bulletin boards on different computers.) The program begins by constructing the network address in the structure named *bba*. This structure has a different format to that used in the previous example for the UNIX domain. First, our program uses the *bzero* function to clear the structure to hold zeros. (This is actually unnecessary here because static storage is initialized with zeros anyway.) Second, the address format code (the network number) is set to indicate INET. Next, we need to know the number for the machine with name "mega-vax". We use a library routine, *gethostbyname*, to look up the number in the database and we put the number into the network address. A routine, *bcopy*, is used to copy the number because this makes our code independent of the number of bytes in the number. Finally, we put the port number into the address. The function *htons* (host-to-network, short) is used to convert the number into a standard form used in network communications. This function overcomes a potential problem caused by different computer manufacturers having chosen to order the bytes within an integer differently. The host-to-network conversion function puts the bytes in the order that all computers on the network are programmed to expect. (There was no need to convert the machine number because *gethostbyname* returns the number with the bytes in the proper network order.) If we had desired to connect to a standard service rather than our own unofficial one, we would have used a library function, *getservbyname*, to look up the proper port number to use.

Having constructed the network address, the *b_board* program creates a socket and attempts to connect it to the address. In the call to *socket*, there is again no need to specify a protocol in the third parameter because TCP will be used automatically for a SOCK_STREAM socket. If we had wanted, we could have used a function *getprotobyname* to look up a code number for the TCP protocol and passed that number as the third argument.

After establishing a connection, we can use the socket as though it were a file descriptor. Our program reads from the socket and copies the data to the standard output.

Now we can turn our attention to the server program which will be left running on the computer named "mega-vax". The source code for this program is given in Figure 12.5. We call the program *b_board_d* (the *d* suffix indicates that the program is a *daemon* – a permanently running process that watches

FIGURE 12.4. The b_board Client Program

```
#include <stdio.h>
#include <sys/types.h>
#include <sys/socket.h>
#include <netinet/in.h>
#include <netdb.h>

#define HOSTNAME "mega-vax"
#define PORTNUM   2000
#define oops(msg) { perror(msg);   exit(-1); }

struct sockaddr_in bba;
struct hostent *hp;
FILE *rf;   int  s, rfd, ch;

void main()
{
    /* build the network address */
    bzero( &bba, sizeof(saddr) );
    bba.sin_family = AF_INET;
    hp = gethostbyname( HOSTNAME );
    if (hp == NULL) oops( "no such computer" );
    bcopy( hp->h_addr, &bba.sin_addr, hp->h_length );
    bba.sin_port = htons(PORTNUM);

    /* make the connection */
    s = socket( AF_INET, SOCK_STREAM, 0 );
    if (s == -1) oops("socket");
    if (connect(s, &bba, sizeof(bba)) != 0)
        oops( "connect" );

    /* read and print data read from the socket */
    rf = fdopen( s, "r" );
    if (rf == NULL) oops("fdopen");
    while( (ch = getc(rf)) != EOF)
            putchar(ch);
    fclose( rf );
}
```

out for client connections). The *b_board_d* program begins in a similar way
to the client program. It builds a network address, its own address. Rather
than explicitly use the machine name, "mega-vax", in the program, we use a
function, *gethostname*, which returns the name of our own machine.

FIGURE 12.5. The b_board_d Server Program

```
#include <stdio.h>
#include <sys/types.h>
#include <sys/socket.h>
#include <netinet/in.h>
#include <netdb.h>

#define PORTNUM 2000
#define BBD_FILE  "/u0/jack/bulletin.brd"
#define oops(msg) { perror(msg);  exit(-1); }

struct sockaddr_in saddr;
struct hostent *hp;
char    hostname[256];
int     slen, s, sfd, ch;
FILE    *sf, *bbf;

void main( argc, argv )
int argc;  char **argv;
{   /* build our own network address */
    bzero( &saddr, sizeof(saddr) );
    saddr.sin_family = AF_INET;
    gethostname( hostname, sizeof(hostname) );
    hp = gethostbyname( hostname );
    bcopy( hp->h_addr, &saddr.sin_addr, hp->h_length );
    saddr.sin_port = htons(PORTNUM);

    /* create the socket and bind the address */
    s = socket( AF_INET, SOCK_STREAM, 0 );
    if (s == -1) oops("socket");
    if (bind(s, &saddr, sizeof(saddr)) != 0)
        oops( "bind" );

                        /* continued on next page ... */
```

```
/* ... continued from previous page */


    /* repeatedly wait for clients to connect */

    if (listen(s,1) != 0) oops("listen");
    for( ; ; ) {
        sfd = accept( s, NULL, NULL );
        if (sfd == -1) oops( "accept" );
        sf = fdopen( sfd, "w" );
        if (sf == NULL) oops( "fdopen" );
        bbf = fopen( BBD_FILE, "r" );
        if (bbf == NULL) {
            fputs("Empty bulletin board\n",sf);
        else {
            while( (ch = getc(bbf)) != EOF)
                putc(ch,sf);
            fclose(bbf);
        }
        fclose( sf );
    }
}
```

After building our network address, we create a socket and bind the address to it. Next, we tell the system that we are prepared to listen for connections and wait in the *accept* call for some client process to make a connection. When a connection is made, we copy the contents of the bulletin board file to the socket, close the connection, and return to the beginning of the loop to wait for a new connection.

You may have disliked the arbitrary assumption made in this example that we could use port number 2000 for the bulletin board service. If you want to eliminate the assumption that a particular port number is free for use, the B_BOARD_D program should be modified to use port number zero. When the program makes the *bind* call, the UNIX system will automatically substitute the number of an available port. After the *bind* call, the program can call the *getsockname* function to determine what port number was assigned. This number can be printed and made available to all potential users of the bulletin board service. That is, code like the following can be inserted in the program just before the call to *listen*:

```
slen = sizeof(saddr);
if ( getsockname(s, &saddr, &slen) != 0 )
        oops( "getsockname" );
printf( "Service available on port %d\n",
        ntohs( saddr.sin_port ) );
```

12.4. MULTIPLEXED INPUT-OUTPUT

It is not hard to conceive of programs that have two sources of input and must respond, without delay, to input that becomes available from either source. The *talk* program provides a good example. After *talk* has established a socket connection with another instance of *talk*, perhaps on another computer, the program has two sources of input and two destinations for output. The program must wait for input to come from either the socket or from the keyboard. Input received from the socket must be copied onto the lower half of the screen. Input received from the keyboard must be echoed to the upper half of the screen and also written to the socket. Clearly, the *talk* program must respond instantly, or nearly instantly, to a new character becoming available from either source.

But how do we write a program that accepts input from either source without knowing in advance which source will provide some input first? If the program calls *getc* (or some similar function) to read from one source, the program will be suspended until input from that source arrives, while ignoring the other source of input. A possible solution to the problem is to use a *non-blocking* read instead of *getc*. You could program your own version of *getc* which returns an input character if one is available or returns a special code, say '\0', if one is not available. (Such a function can be programmed because it is possible to test to see how many input characters could be read before the program would be suspended.)[4] By alternating non-blocking reads on both input sources, we could be sure of seeing an input character as soon as it arrives. But, this approach would be very wasteful of CPU time.

A better solution, and the normal solution used in non-Berkeley versions of the UNIX system, is for the program to fork into two processes. One process reads from one source and the second process reads from the other source. This way, a process would be unblocked and would read as soon as input became available. If we were trying to implement *talk*, we would still have a small problem trying to prevent the two processes from writing to the screen simultaneously. But with a little effort, the problem can be solved using signals to synchronize the actions of the two processes.

---

[4] Better still, the *fcntl* function or the *ioctl* function can be used to modify the behaviour of standard input to become non-blocking.

However, the Berkeley UNIX system provides a simpler solution to the problem of reading from two or more sources simultaneously. The system function, *select*, can be passed a mask which has one bits in positions corresponding to the file descriptors for these input sources. When control returns, there will be one bits set only for the input sources that you can read without having to wait. Actually, *select* takes three separate masks. One for reading, one for writing (remember that writes to pipes or slow output devices can cause the writing process to be suspended), and a third for watching for exceptional conditions associated with a file descriptor. There is also an optional time-out value that can be passed. This specifies a limit on how much time the process should be blocked waiting for possible input-output or exceptions on the selected file descriptors. A simple example of the use of *select* follows:

```
int  rmask, wmask, xmask, nf;
int  fd;   /* a socket or file descriptor */
...
rmask = (1 << fd) | (1 << 0);
wmask = xmask = 0;
nf = select(fd+1, &rmask, &wmask, &xmask, NULL);
if ( (rmask >> 0) & 1 ) {
    /* read from standard input */
    ...
}
if ( (rmask >> fd) & 1 ) {
    /* read from descriptor fd  */
    ...
}
```

In this example, we wait for input from either the standard input (descriptor 0) or from the source associated with descriptor *fd*. The first parameter to *select* is a limit on the range of descriptor values to check. In our call, we are saying that only descriptors with values in the range 0 to *fd* are relevant. (There are *fd+1* descriptors in the range to check.) The result stored in *nf* is the total number of bits that are set in the three masks on return from the function.

FURTHER INFORMATION ON SOCKETS

- Stuart Sechrest. "Tutorial Examples of Interprocess Communication in Berkeley UNIX 4.2bsd." Report UCB/CSD 84/191, Computer Science Division, University of California, Berkeley 94720.

- S.J. Leffler, R.S. Fabry and W.N. Joy. "A 4.2bsd Interprocess Communication Primer." Supplementary documentation supplied with Berkeley UNIX 4.2bsd system, July 1983.

- S.J. Leffler, W.N. Joy and R.S. Fabry. "4.2BSD Networking Implementation Notes." Supplementary documentation supplied with Berkeley UNIX 4.2bsd system, July 1983.

QUESTIONS

1. The *pipe* system function is actually implemented as a call to the *socketpair* function which returns a pair of connected sockets usable for stream communication. Sockets, however, support bi-directional communication. Does this mean that programs can write to the read side of a pipe and vice versa?

2. The server program, *Receive*, shown in Figure 12.2 is open to all users on the system. How could we restrict access to a particular group of users?

3. Some telephone companies provide a service that allows subscribers to dial a special number and join in a group conversation. How would you design a similar facility for the UNIX system where an INET address and a terminal take the place of the telephone number and telephone?

CHAPTER 13

TERMINAL HANDLING

13.1. THE TERMINAL DRIVER

The characters that you type on the keyboard of your terminal do not go directly to the program you are running. They are first processed by an interface program known as the terminal driver or the TTY driver.[1] Similarly, output characters to the terminal are also subject to some processing.

When operating in its normal mode, the terminal driver reads characters from the keyboard, echoes these characters to the screen and also saves them in a line buffer. When the line is completed with a linefeed or carriage return character, the line is made available to whatever program you are currently executing. Certain characters you type are treated specially by the terminal driver. One special character is the backspace character. If the terminal driver is operating in a mode suitable for CRT terminals, typing a backspace causes three characters to be echoed to the screen and a character to be deleted from the line buffer. When you type a backspace, the driver echoes a backspace, then a space to blank out the position on the screen that you are about to overwrite and then another backspace to put the cursor back on the space. Another special character is your *kill* character, usually '@' or *Control-U*, which causes the line buffer to be cleared. Other special characters, such as *Control-*, cause signals to be sent to whatever program is currently executing (and therefore has control of the terminal). The character sent by the *return* key of your

---

[1] TTY is an abbreviation for teletypewriter, once the only kind of terminal supported by the UNIX system. Even though teletypewriters are rarely seen now, the abbreviation occurs throughout the system documentation.

keyboard is also subject to processing: the terminal driver echoes both a carriage return and a linefeed to the screen and sends a linefeed character to the program. This is why programs that read several lines of data might check for the linefeed character, '\n', in the input but not for the carriage return character, '\r'.

Output processing by the terminal driver is not as sophisticated as the input processing. For the most part, characters are transmitted unchanged to the terminal screen. One action is that when a program outputs a linefeed character, the terminal driver will normally insert a carriage return character. The translation of tab characters into spaces is an optional service provided by the driver for terminals which do not understand the concept of tab stops. The driver will also optionally create time delays to slow the transmission rate to terminals that have trouble keeping up after certain screen actions. For example, some terminals can accept characters at a very rapid rate as long as the characters appear one after the other on the same line. But when a linefeed character is received by the terminal, it may be temporarily unable to receive new characters until it has finished scrolling the screen image up by one line.

There are actually two different terminal drivers available with the Berkeley UNIX system, the old driver and the new driver. The new driver must be used if you use the *csh* command shell, since only the new driver supports the *Control-Z* control character and understands job control. The old driver is perfectly usable, however, if you use the *sh* shell. We will assume that you use *csh* and therefore also need to use the new terminal driver. To force use of the new driver, you should include a line similar to

    stty new crt

in your ".login"file. The *stty* command is the normal method of changing modes or options for the terminal driver. The argument *crt* in our command, above, requests that all options suitable for a CRT terminal should be selected. The command can also be used to see what the current options are set to. If you execute

    stty everything

you will get a rather complete list.

The terminal driver operates in one of three main modes: *cooked, cbreak* or *raw*. The cooked mode (called so because it is the opposite of raw) is the normal mode. In raw mode, no processing is performed at all on input characters. Each character is passed immediately to the executing program without being echoed. The cbreak mode is intermediate between the other two. Characters are immediately passed to the executing program without being buffered, but they are echoed as normal and most special characters still have effect.

Most programs that you write will operate quite happily when they read from or write to a terminal in the normal cooked mode. The only feature of the cooked mode that might get in your way is the fact that the program cannot read any characters from a line until you type the carriage return at the end of the line. Some programs, such as the *vi* editor, use raw mode. The *vi* editor must read each character as you type it so that it can immediately update information on the screen. The cbreak mode is unsuitable for *vi* because many characters that have special meaning to *vi* are intercepted by the terminal driver and may cause unwanted effects.

If you write a program, such as a game or a full-screen editor, where you need to read and respond to characters immediately, you should avoid using raw mode. If your program puts the terminal into raw mode and then goes wrong, you will find out that there is no way to stop the program. All the usual methods of stopping a program, such as typing *Control-C*, *Control-* or hitting the break key, do not work. These characters are simply sent as input to your program. (Hitting the break key in raw mode generates a null byte.) If you do not believe this, just enter the two commands

```
stty raw
yes
```

and then try to stop the output! All you can do to stop the *yes* program is disconnect the terminal. (When the terminal driver detects the disconnection, it sends a SIGHUP signal to the program and that will finally stop it.)

If you are writing a program like a full-screen editor, you should set the terminal mode to cbreak and turn off the echoing of characters. If you want to perform actions such as moving the cursor up one line when a letter *k* is typed, you do not want to have the *k* echoed on the screen. It is possible to set the terminal driver to this mode with the *stty* command. You would just need to execute

```
stty cbreak -echo
```

However, if you do this, the next command that you type will not be echoed – and that can be a little disconcerting. Ideally, of course, you want your program to change the terminal driver modes at the start of its execution and to reset the modes at the end. Hence, you could include the function call

```
system( "stty cbreak -echo" );
```

in your program initialization and include the call

```
system( "stty -cbreak echo" );
```

at the end of the program.

A greater degree of control over the terminal driver modes can be obtained, and rather more efficiently too, with the *ioctl* function. The code to set the cbreak mode and disable echoing is

```
#include <sgtty.h>
struct sgttyb oldmode, newmode;
...
ioctl( 0, TIOCGETP, &oldmode );
newmode = oldmode;
newmode.sg_flags |= CBREAK;
newmode.sg_flags &= ~ECHO;
ioctl( 0, TIOCSETP, &newmode );
```

The first argument to *ioctl* is a file descriptor associated with the terminal. If the terminal is associated with the standard input of our program, as it normally would be, we can use zero. The second parameter is a service request code. The names for these codes are included by the "<sgtty.h>" header file. The TIOCGETP code requests that the current terminal modes be copied into the structure specified in the third argument. After this first call to *ioctl*, we create a modified copy of this structure where we have set a bit to turn on cbreak mode and unset a bit for echoing (to turn echoing off). Then, we call *ioctl* with the TIOCSETP request code to set the new modes from our modified structure. After our program has finished its work, it can reset the terminal driver back to its original state by executing

```
ioctl( 0, TIOCSETP, &oldmode );
```

For changing the current erase character (usually *backspace* or *delete* on a CRT terminal), the current line kill character (usually @ or *Control-U*), or a wide variety of processing flags, the *sgttyb* structure is used in the *ioctl* call. For changing other options, different request codes are passed as the second argument and different structures passed as the third argument. More complete details can be obtained by looking at the header files for use with *ioctl* and from the on-line manual entry under the heading *tty*. You must type

```
man 4 tty
```

to see this entry because there is a command named *tty* too.

When you are debugging a program that changes terminal driver modes, you are likely to find that it sometimes leaves your terminal in a strange state. If your program has terminated and you have received a prompt for a new command, but nothing you type appears on the screen, the terminal driver is either in no-echo mode or in raw mode. If your characters echo but backspacing over characters to correct them does not seem to work, the driver is in cbreak mode. The sure-fire method to get your terminal back into a usable state is to type the following sequence of 7 characters:

Control-J   r   e   s   e   t   *Control-J*

You must type these characters whether or not anything is echoed on the screen. If your keyboard has a key labelled *linefeed*, you may use that instead of *Control-J*. The *reset* command resets the terminal driver modes, as its name suggests. The linefeed (or *Control-J*) character should be used to terminate the command rather than a carriage return. The reason is that the terminal driver translates the carriage return character (which is the same as a *Control-M* character) into a linefeed in the cbreak and cooked modes, but not in raw mode. Thus only a linefeed is guaranteed to work.

13.2. THE TERMCAP DATABASE

Each manufacturer of terminals seems to have a different idea as to what capabilities a terminal should have. Some CRT terminals recognize special control character sequences that cause a line to be deleted in the middle of the screen (with the bottom half of the screen being scrolled up) and others do not. Some terminals support underlining of characters on the screen, others do not, and so on. Even if two terminals support the same capability, such as character underlining, they may use different control sequences to perform the underlining action. Although there is a standard for terminal control sequences, the ANSI X3.64 standard, only about 50% of terminals conform to the standard. Of those that conform, most do not implement all the control sequences defined in the standard and most have their own special extensions.

To enable programs to take advantage of special terminal capabilities, the Berkeley UNIX system provides a database that describes most terminals in common use. This database is the file "/etc/termcap". The format of a terminal description in this file is described in the on-line manual. You should execute

```
man 5 termcap
```

to see the manual entry. Each terminal description lists various kinds of terminal attributes or capabilities, organized as fields separated by colon characters. There are three kinds of attribute or capability. The simplest kind is a Boolean flag to indicate whether the terminal has the corresponding capability or not. For example, the presence of the `pt` capability indicates that the terminal understands tab characters. A second kind gives a numeric value for some attribute or capability. For example, the field `co#80` indicates that the terminal has 80 columns. (If a terminal can be switched from 80 columns to 132 columns, say, there would be two separate entries for this terminal in the database.) The third kind of entry gives control sequences for performing various actions. For example, a field such as `dl=\e[M` gives the three character control sequence for deleting a line in the middle of the screen. (The notation `\e` is a readable way of specifying the ASCII *escape* character.)

It is not a good idea for ordinary programs to make extensive direct use of the terminal capability database. If the program assumes the existence of certain capabilities, such as *dl*, on the terminal, the program will only be able to work on terminals that have that capability. If the program must work on a wide variety of terminal types, the program must provide alternate methods of performing actions on terminals that lack various capabilities. For example, if the program does need to delete a line in the middle of the screen when there is no *dl* capability, it could erase and rewrite the entire bottom half of the screen or it could take advantage of the scrolling region capability provided on VT100-compatible terminals. All these considerations are best left to sophisticated full-screen programs such as the *vi* editor.

Generally speaking, an ordinary program should use the terminal capability database only for simple operations. A program that wants to produce menu-like screen layouts needs only the capability to clear the screen and to move the cursor to arbitrary coordinate positions on the screen. These are capabilities that almost all CRT terminals have. If your program needs to perform more sophisticated screen updating operations, it should use the family of library functions known as *curses*. The curses library is described briefly in the next section of this chapter.

There are functions in a special program library for extracting terminal capabilities and working with them. When you compile a program that uses these functions, you should supply the −ltermcap flag on the *cc* command that performs the final linking operation. Figure 13.1 shows code needed to fetch the clear screen (*cl*) and cursor motion (*cm*) capabilities and determine the screen size for our terminal. The routine that performs the actual cursor motion requires that a few more capabilities are loaded too. The principle behind the various function calls is fairly simple. First, the *tgetent* function is called to read the terminal description into a local array. Like most terminal handling software, it is assumed that the environment variable *TERM* gives the name of the kind of terminal in use. If the entry cannot be found or the termcap file cannot be read, the function returns error codes 0 and -1 respectively. Success is indicated by a result of 1.

The other functions, *tgetstr*, *tgetnum* and the unused *tgetflag*, search the local array to find values of capabilities. The *tgetnum* function returns an integer value for a capability/attribute, or -1 if the capability is not present. The *tgetstr* function returns a pointer to a string containing a command sequence, or *NULL* if the capability is not present. This string is copied into a buffer supplied by the caller, which explains the second argument to the function. The *tgetflag* function (not used in our example) is used similarly to *tgetnum* to obtain a Boolean value for a capability. A result of 1 indicates that the capability is present; 0 indicates that it is absent.

Using these capabilities is not completely straightforward. The control sequences cannot (always) be sent directly to the terminal because some sequences are preceded by integers that indicate a time delay to allow the terminal to complete the screen update. A function named *tputs* is provided to output control sequences. Another problem is that the control sequence for cursor motion is parameterized. Somewhere in the sequence encoded values of the desired line number and column number must appear. Different manufacturers

FIGURE 13.1. Loading Terminal Capabilities

```c
#include <stdio.h>
char  PC;          /* padding character */
char *BC;          /* backspace character */
char *UP;          /* cursor up sequence */
char *CM;          /* cursor motion sequence */
char *CL;          /* clear screen sequence */
int   LI;          /* number of lines */
int   CO;          /* number of columns */

void read_termcap()
{
    char  tc_entry[1024];
    static char tcbuff[256], *tcbuffp = tcbuff;
    char *term, *temp;

    term = getenv( "TERM" );
    if (term == NULL) {
        fprintf(stderr, "No TERM env. variable\n");
        exit(-1);
    }
    if ( tgetent( tc_entry, term ) != 1 ) {
        fprintf(stderr, "Cannot get %s capabilities\n",
            term ); exit(-1); }
    temp = tgetstr( "pc", &tcbuffp );
    PC = (temp != NULL)? *temp : ' ';
    UP = tgetstr( "up", &tcbuffp );
    CL = tgetstr( "cl", &tcbuffp );
    CM = tgetstr( "cm", &tcbuffp );
    LI = tgetnum( "li" );
    CO = tgetnum( "co" );
    if (LI < 0) LI = 24;  /* Some reasonable defaults */
    if (CO < 0) CO = 80;  /* for missing values       */
    if (CM == NULL || CL == NULL) {
        fprintf(stderr,"cm & cl capabilities needed\n");
        exit(-1);
    }
}
```

have chosen to encode the information in different ways. Therefore the *tgoto* function is provided to insert the line number and column number into the control sequence. The result is a string which can be passed to *tputs* to actually move the cursor. Note that the line and column numbers that you pass to *tgoto* are assumed to have a zero origin. For example, if there are 24 lines on the screen, you should specify line numbers in the range 0 to 23.

Figure 13.2 shows a function that could be used to output a menu onto a screen, using the capabilities extracted with the function of Figure 13.1. The *tputs* function requires three arguments. The first is the string to be output; the second specifies the number of lines on the screen that will be affected by the output (this information is needed to create appropriate time delays when dealing with certain kinds of terminals); and the third argument names a function that will output one character to the terminal. Our use of *tputs* to clear the screen affects all lines on the screen so we pass the value of *LI*, the number of lines on the screen.

13.3. THE CURSES SCREEN-HANDLING PACKAGE

As explained above, you would have to put a lot of effort into your program if you wanted it to perform full-screen output for a wide variety of terminals. Rather than expend this effort, you should acquaint yourself with a package of library functions called *curses*.

The curses package supports an interface to an idealized terminal that has most of the features that you would find on a sophisticated CRT terminal. It also supports multiple windows, although, in practice, most programs treat the terminal screen as being a single window. There are functions in the package for moving the cursor and writing characters at different positions on the screen, for inserting or deleting lines, for scrolling the screen, and so on. These functions will work regardless of whether the actual terminal in use has corresponding capabilities. The *curses* functions will translate your screen update requests into whatever control sequences are needed to produce the desired effect on the real terminal. In fact, *curses* makes some attempt to produce the shortest possible control sequences that accomplish the screen update.

Curses also provides functions to help with input from the terminal. It will, on request, disable echoing and enable cbreak mode in the terminal driver. For full details about the use of the *curses* package, you should refer to the document named below.

FIGURE 13.2. Use of Terminal Capabilities

```
typedef struct menu_item {
        int y, x;   /* coordinates for the item */
        char *item;
    } MENU_ITEM;

/*  Table entry == ( Line #, Col #, Text )  */
MENU_ITEM menu1[] = {
    {  0, 25, "MAIN MENU" },
    {  5, 10, "1.  Quit" },
    {  7, 10, "2.  Edit" },
    {  9, 10, "3.  Compile" },
    { 11, 10, "4.  Link" },
    { 13, 10, "5.  Run" },
    { 0, 0, NULL } /* terminator */ };

void out1(ch) int ch; {
    putchar( ch ); }

void output_menu( menu )
MENU_ITEM menu[];
{
    MENU_ITEM *mp;  char *cstr;
    /* clear the screen */
    tputs( CL, LI, out1 );

    /* loop through the menu items */
    for( mp = menup; mp->item != NULL; mp++ ) {
        cstr = tgoto( CM, mp->x, mp->y );
        tputs( cstr, 1, out1 );
        fputs( mp->item, stdout );
    }
}
    ...
    /* display the menu */
    output_menu( menu1 );
    ...
```

FURTHER INFORMATION ABOUT curses

- Ken Arnold. "Screen Updating and Cursor Movement Optimization: A Library Package." Supplementary documentation supplied with Berkeley UNIX 4.2bsd system, July 1983.

QUESTIONS

1.   In the example program of Figure 13.2, why did we not pass the *putchar* function as the third argument to *tputs* (instead of using the intermediary function *out1*) ?

2.   Why is the **static** attribute needed in the declaration of *tcbuff* in Figure 13.1?

APPENDIX A

THE vi EDITOR

A.1. OVERVIEW

The *vi* editor is the standard full-screen editor provided with the Berkeley UNIX system. It has a rather large repertoire of commands, which makes it forbidding to a first-time user. In this appendix, only a selection of the *vi* commands will be covered. This selection includes all the facilities that one should need when editing C source code files or English text. For a full list of commands, you should obtain a copy of the document "An Introduction to Display Editing with Vi" by William Joy. It is included in the documentation supplied with the Berkeley UNIX system. Your system administrator should be able to help you locate the documentation.

Vi (often pronounced like the English word *vie*) may be used to edit files containing ASCII characters. It cannot handle files containing non-ASCII characters or the ASCII NUL character (the character '\0' in C). Apart from this, the only restriction on an ASCII file is that a single line cannot contain more than 1023 characters.

The *vi* program may be invoked under three different names: as *vi*, as *ex* or as *view*. Using the name *vi* (short for *visual*) gives you access to a very powerful screen-oriented editor. The name *ex* is used when you wish to use a line-editor similar to *ed* but which is a little more powerful and more user-friendly. However, *ex* has a subcommand (*vi* - what else?) which changes its mode of operation to be the same as *vi*. The name *view* is used if you wish to obtain read-only access to a file. The facilities of *vi* are very convenient for browsing, but when you invoke *vi* as *view*, you are not allowed to store the file back (unless you explicitly override). This restriction is useful protection against accidentally destroying your file.

The concept of a full-screen editor is reasonably simple. The screen always shows a range of consecutive lines in the file. With standard terminals that have a display area of 24 lines, *vi* usually shows 23 lines of the file.[1] One line on the screen, at the bottom, is used for displaying information messages and for entering some types of command. *Vi* has simple, one-letter commands which move the cursor around on the screen. If your terminal keyboard has arrow keys, these keys should be usable as cursor movement commands too. Other commands may be used to change the information displayed on the screen at the current cursor position. These changes will be reflected in the edited file only when the file is subsequently saved. In addition to commands in the cursor movement and text replacement categories, there are many more commands for controlling *vi*.

A.2. GETTING STARTED WITH vi

Before you try to use *vi* for the first time, you should make sure that *vi* will know what kind of terminal you are using and whether this terminal is suitable. CRT terminals have command sequences that perform actions such as clearing the screen, moving the cursor and for changing information displayed on the screen. Unfortunately, different kinds of terminals may use completely different control sequences. If *vi* assumes the wrong terminal type, you are likely to see some bizarre results when *vi* is in operation.

The *vi* program will normally try to determine your terminal type from the environment variable named *TERM*. You can see the current value of this environment variable by executing the command

```
printenv
```

The value of *TERM* should be a short string that looks like an abbreviation for the name of your terminal. A typical setting might be "vt100" (for the DEC VT100 terminal) or "h1500" (for the Hazeltine 1500 terminal) and so on.

If the value looks like an abbreviation for some terminal type but does not match the kind of terminal you are using, it is not necessarily an error. Some terminals emulate other kinds of terminal and if your terminal is emulating the one listed for *TERM*, *vi* should work. If *TERM* is shown with a value like "dumb" or "su", you will definitely have to change its setting.

Before you attempt to set the value of *TERM*, you can read through the standard list of terminal types by executing

---

[1] This number can be reduced in some circumstances. For example, fewer lines may be displayed if you are using the terminal at a low baud rate.

```
setenv TERM dumb
more /etc/termcap
```

Note that *TERM* needs to be set to some safe value for *more* to operate properly! In the "/etc/termcap" file (the terminal capability database), lines beginning with a hash mark, #, are comments. Some of these comments make amusing reading. The file is very long, containing descriptions of scores of different kinds of terminal. These descriptions contain the command sequences needed to control the terminals. It is easy to recognize the beginning of a new terminal description in the file because a line that has a printing character in the first column is either a comment line or is the first line of a terminal description. Continuation lines for a terminal description are all indented by one tab character.

The first line of a description contains various names for the terminal, separated by vertical bars. The last name listed is intended to be the full name, readily recognizable by humans. You may set *TERM* to be the same as any of these names except for the last name. They are treated as synonyms by *vi* and other UNIX system software. However, it is not a good idea to use the first name, which is always a two-character abbreviation.

If you scan through "/etc/termcap" you should be able to find a suitable abbreviation for your terminal. If you cannot, it might be a good idea to ask for assistance. You can set the *TERM* environment variable to some string value, say *vt100*, by executing one of the *csh* commands:

```
setenv TERM vt100
```

or

```
set term = vt100
```

The latter command is somewhat preferable for reasons that will be explained in Appendix B.

The easy way to test whether your setting of *TERM* is suitable is to invoke *vi*. Just type the command

```
vi
```

At this point, there are four different outcomes. If your screen is cleared, tilde (˜) characters are written down the left column and the cursor is moved to the left of a line at the top of the screen, *vi* is working quite normally. However, you should insert a few lines and edit them a little to make sure. Sometimes a wrong terminal description is sufficiently similar to the correct one that *vi* will go wrong only in certain situations. If *vi* updates the screen incorrectly for some editing operations, then the terminal type is unsuitable. If starting up *vi* gives you the message "Visual needs addressible cursor or upline capability," your terminal must be an obsolete model that is too primitive to be used by full-screen programs. If you see the message "Using open mode" (accompanied by some other message) there is something wrong with the entry for your terminal in the terminal capability database and you should ask for assistance. Finally, if your terminal seems to go wild, scribbling strange characters over the screen in random positions, you must have an unsuitable terminal type.

Whatever the outcome of your test, you can exit from *vi* by typing the following four characters:

> *Escape* : q !

The character *Escape* denotes the ASCII escape character. You should be able to find a key on your keyboard labelled *Esc* or *Escape* which transmits this character. If you cannot find such a key, you can transmit the escape character by pressing the *Control* key (perhaps labelled *Ctrl*) and the left square bracket key ([ ) together. However, if your terminal keyboard really does not have an Escape key, it would be a good idea to find another terminal to use. The ASCII escape character is used in *vi* to terminate all text input or text replacement commands.

A.3. INVOKING vi

If you have an existing file, say "prog.c", you can edit it with the command

```
vi prog.c
```

This command causes *vi* to make a temporary copy of the file, to display the first screenful of the file, to place information about the size of the file on the bottom line of the screen and finally to place the cursor at the beginning of the first line of the file.

If you wish to use *vi* to create a new file, say "newprog.c", the same form of command is used, namely

```
vi newprog.c
```

This command causes *vi* to clear the screen, place tilde characters down the left side of the screen, put an information line at the bottom of the screen that tells you that you are creating a new file, and to move the cursor to a blank line at the top of the screen. Each tilde character represents a non-existent line in the file. As you add lines to the file, the tildes will gradually be displaced from the screen. *Vi* does not leave completely blank lines on the screen, because you may be fooled into thinking that the file contains blank lines. In some circumstances, *vi* may also use the 'at' symbol (@) to represent a non-existent line in the file. It will usually be displayed after you have deleted lines from the file.

A.4. CURSOR MOVEMENT COMMANDS

The simplest cursor movement commands are those that move the cursor one position vertically or horizontally. If there are keys labelled with arrows on your keyboard, these *ought* to work as cursor movement commands. However, nothing is guaranteed. Depending on the terminal type, *vi* may not be able to use any or all of the arrow keys. Not all keyboards have arrow keys in any

case. Consequently, there are other ways to move the cursor. First, the space
and backspace characters will move the cursor horizontally in the way one
would expect. The space character does not overwrite any characters displayed
on the screen; only the cursor moves. If the keyboard has a linefeed key, it may
be used to move the cursor down. In addition, the four lower-case letters, h,
j, k and l, can be used as cursor movement commands. For example, when
you type h, the cursor immediately moves left by one column. You do not
have to hit the carriage-return key after the command. The h command does
not have any effect if the cursor is at the first character on a line. Instead, you
will probably hear your terminal beep.[2] The beep is simply a warning from *vi* –
perhaps in case you are not looking at the screen.

Many useful cursor movement commands are listed in Table A.2. This
table and two others have, for convenience, been collected together in a "Vi
Reference Guide" section at the end of this appendix. To gain experience with
vi, it is probably a good idea to experiment with these commands on a sample
file. Some of the cursor movement commands are relatively sophisticated. A
simple step up in sophistication is the w command (short for *word*). This command advances the cursor to the beginning of the next word in the file. Two
related commands are b (*back one word*) and e (*end of word*).

A command which is extremely useful to C programmers is %. If the cursor is currently located on a bracket character (one of { , } , (or)), the
cursor is moved onto the matching bracket in the program. This command
makes it relatively easy to check whether your brackets are properly matched.
If *vi* cannot find a matching bracket, it will not move the cursor and it should
beep. Be aware, however, that *vi* can become confused if your C program has
macros that generate unbalanced brackets or has comments or string constants
that contain unbalanced brackets.

An important command is / which is used for searching. When you type
/, the cursor jumps to the bottom line on the screen. Next you must type a
pattern, terminated either by a carriage return or the *escape* character. This
pattern has the same style as that used in the *ed* editor. If all you want to do is
locate the next occurrence of some identifier, say *foo*, you would type

        /foo

and this will cause *vi* to advance the cursor to the beginning of the next
occurrence of *foo* in the file. If you then want to repeat the same search, you do
not have to repeat the full command. The single letter command n (*next*)
repeats the last search. The single letter command N is similar, except that it
repeats the last search backwards through the file. If you want to search backwards initially, you should use ? instead of /. After performing a backwards

---

[2] For some terminal types, a *visible bell* may be used instead of a beeping sound. A visible bell shows
up as a momentary flashing of the screen.

search, n will repeat the search scanning backwards through the file. If you use N after a search begun with ? , the search will be repeated forward through the file.

The string following the / or ? command is a *pattern*, using the same conventions as patterns in the *ed* and *sed* editors. It is important that you know which characters have special meanings in a pattern. If you do not want to have to learn the details of pattern construction, you can simply avoid using the special characters, or you can remember to precede these characters with the escape symbol (\) or you can set the *nomagic* option (see below). The special pattern characters are

    ^ $.   *   [\

If, for example, you want to search for the character sequence $bill$, you have to type the *vi* command as

    /\$bill\$

We will not discuss patterns here. A full description is provided in the system documentation for *ed*.

A.5. TEXT REPLACEMENT COMMANDS

In a moment, we will look at some commands for inserting, deleting and replacing text in the file. These commands are summarized in Table A.3, which appears at the end of the appendix. But before running through these commands, we should point out that the commands fall into two main categories. Commands from the first category operate on characters within a line and commands from the other category operate on entire lines. For example, the command i may be used to insert characters into the middle of a line, whereas the o command is used to insert entire lines into the file.

A.5.1. Insertion

If you wish to insert characters into the current line, you would normally use either the i (*insert*) command or the a (*append*) command. The former, i, inserts characters at the current cursor position. The a command is similar except that it adds characters at the position immediately after the cursor position. Any number of characters may be inserted. Text insertion ceases only when the escape character is typed. You may even insert the carriage-return character, which causes the current line to be split into two lines. Variations on the character insertion commands are A, used to append characters to the end of the current line, and I, used to insert characters at the beginning of the current line.

To insert one or more lines into the file, either the o or the O command is used. These are known as the *open* commands because they cause the text on the screen to be opened up. When you type o, a blank line is created below the current line and the cursor is positioned at the beginning of this new line. Any text you type is now entered on the new line. Whenever you hit the carriage-return key, another blank line is inserted. Text insertion is halted only when you type the escape character. The O command is similar, the difference being that the new line is inserted immediately above the current line in the file.

A.5.2. Deletion

The normal command used for deleting a character from the middle of a line is x. Presumably the command name is chosen because its effect is analogous to deleting words on an ordinary typewriter by typing letter x's over the text. When x is typed, the character underneath the cursor is simply deleted.[3] The character defined as your terminal delete character, often the key labelled *Del* on your keyboard, may also be used to delete a character. If you wish to delete several characters, you may precede the delete command with the character counts, as in 5x.

If you wish to delete an entire word from the line, you should position the cursor to the start of the word and then type dw (the *delete word* command). Finally, the D command will delete all characters from the current cursor position to the end of the line. Deleting an entire line is accomplished with the dd command. This deletes the current line. Several lines can be deleted by preceding this command with a number. For example, 13dd will delete thirteen lines.

A.5.3. Replacement

With the exception of the r and R commands, replacement is equivalent to a deletion followed by an insertion. Therefore, we will look at these two commands first. The r command is used to replace a single character. The character underneath the cursor is replaced with whatever single character you type after the r. For example, if you type rq, the character at the current cursor position is changed to a letter q. There is no need to type an escape character after using r. If you press the *return* key after typing r, you will replace the current character with a linefeed. This has the effect of splitting the current line into two lines, causing a re-arrangement of the displayed lines on your screen.

The R command is used to effect a one-for-one replacement of several characters. After you type R, the next character you type overwrites the character that is currently underneath the cursor. After this, the cursor is advanced by one column and you can replace a second character, and so on. Replacement stops only when an escape character is typed. Note that you can replace text only on the same line. You cannot, for example, jump down to the line below

---

[3] Note that, unlike editors on some other operating systems, you cannot directly delete a linefeed character (\n) from the file. Deleting this character is equivalent to joining two lines together and there is a special command, J, to perform this action.

by typing a *return* or a *linefeed* character and carry on replacing text there. The effect of typing a *return* is actually to split the current line.

If you wish to replace one character with several characters, you would use the s (*substitute*) command. After typing s, all characters, up to an escape character, replace the one character that was underneath the cursor. If you wish to replace, say, three adjacent characters with several characters, you could use the command 3s. When you type the substitute command, the last character to be replaced is changed to a dollar character. This indicates the extent of the change that you are about to perform. The dollar symbol will disappear if you enter replacement text over the top of it, or when you terminate the replacement text.

If you wish to replace an entire word on the line, you would position the cursor at that word and type the command cw (*change word*). As before, the last character of the text to be replaced is temporarily changed to a dollar symbol and, as before, your replacement text continues until an escape character is typed. A group of consecutive words may be replaced if the command is preceded by a count, as in 3cw.

Replacing an entire line is performed with either the S or the cc command. After typing either command, you may enter any number of replacement lines, stopping when an escape character is typed. Several lines may be replaced by preceding the command with a count. For example, 5cc is used to replace five consecutive lines.

A.5.4. Other Editing Actions

We will now look at some actions which change the file but which cannot be properly classified under the previous headings. The most important command of all, especially to a novice user, is the u (undo) command. If you have just executed a command that changed the file and you can see that your change is incorrect, you simply have to type u to undo the effect of the change. The file is instantaneously changed back to its state before your previous command. Unfortunately, you cannot repeat u to undo earlier changes, a second u simply undoes the previous *undo*.

A frequently required action is that of moving or copying a block of lines to another place in the file. These two actions are performed similarly in *vi*. The instructions for moving a block of lines are as follows. First position the cursor onto either the top line or the bottom line of the block to be moved (it does not matter which). Then type the command

        mz

which *marks* the current line and gives the name z to this line. Second, move the cursor to the line at the other end of the block. Now type the command

        d'z

which deletes all the lines from the current line to the line marked with the name *z*, inclusive. These lines are not irretrievably lost because *vi* retains a copy of them in a special buffer. Finally, position the cursor to a line immediately before the desired destination for the block of lines and type

       p

which puts all the lines contained in the buffer back into the file. If you wanted to move the lines to the top of the file, you would have to move the cursor to the topmost line and use the command

       P

This command puts back lines immediately before the current line. As a final note, any letter may be used instead of *z* to mark a line.

    Copying a block of lines is almost exactly the same as moving them. The difference is that the **y** (*yank*) command should be used instead of the **d** (*delete*) command. That is, the second command should be

      y'z

The *yank* command causes lines to be copied into the same buffer that deleted lines are moved to.

    If you only want to move or copy a few lines, the preceding instructions can be simplified a little. If, say, you wish to move three lines, you could move the cursor to the first of the three lines and type

      3dd

to delete the lines. Then you can move the cursor to the desired insertion point and type **p** as before. To copy three lines, you would use the command

      3yy

to copy the lines into the buffer, rather than deleting them.

A.5.5. Command Structure

It should be obvious from the examples already given that commands can usually be preceded by a count. You can type a number before your command whenever it makes sense: **8k** moves the cursor up eight lines; **8dw** deletes eight consecutive words; **5rx** replaces five consecutive characters with the letter *x*, and so on.

    What may have not been so obvious is the general structure of the *change*, *delete* and *yank* commands. When you type **dw** to delete a word, you are not using a *delete word* command as such. You are using a *delete* command, **d**, with an operand, **w**, that specifies how much is to be deleted. This operand may be recognized as the command to move the cursor to the next word. The general structure of the delete command is

    d *<motion command>*

In other words, any command that causes cursor motion may be placed immediately after the *d*. For example, you may type `d51` to delete five consecutive characters, `dj` to delete the current line and the following line, and `dG` to delete all lines up to the end of file. You may experiment for yourself to discover useful combinations.

The yank command has a structure exactly like the delete command, and the change command is very similar. Its general structure is

c <*motion command*> <*replacement text*>

A.6. MISCELLANEOUS COMMANDS

When you type a colon character, the cursor jumps to the command line at the bottom of the screen. Then you may type a command, which will be displayed on that line. There is a large repertoire of commands, of which only a few are listed in Table A.1 at the end of the appendix. The most important commands are those used to save the file and to terminate the edit session. Usually, you would use the command `wq` at the end of the session. If, however, you have changed your mind about editing the file and wish to abandon your changes, you will have to use the command `q!`.

If you wish to merge another file into the file being edited, you would first move the cursor onto the line that precedes the desired insertion point, and then use the `:r` command.

If you wish to exit temporarily from the *vi* editor to execute some shell commands, you have a choice of methods to use. Perhaps the easiest method is hitting the *Control-Z* key combination, an action that suspends the edit session and returns you to your command shell. You can later resume the edit session with the `fg` command of the *csh* command shell. Another method uses the shell escape mechanism of *vi*. All you have to do is type the command

:shell

which creates a subshell for you to use. If you wish to execute only one shell command (say the *ls* command), you may execute it with

:!ls

Vi has a large number of options that control its operation. These options may be displayed or changed with the `:set` command. To see all the option settings that are in effect, type the command

:set all

To set an option on, you give the name of that option after the `set` command. For example, to have line numbers displayed on the screen, you would type

:set number

And to disable an option, you should precede the name of the option with the word *no*. Thus, to turn off the display of line numbers, you can type

```
:set nonumber
```

A.7. USING ex COMMANDS

As mentioned earlier, *vi* and *ex* are two names for the same program. If you use the shell command

> **ex** *filename*

to begin the edit session, you will invoke an editor that is much like the *ed* editor. All the *ed* commands are supported by *ex*.

When you invoke the editor with the name *vi*, you can still use all the *ex* commands. Some of these commands are easier to use than the equivalent full-screen commands. For example, if you wish to change all occurrences of the identifier *jack* to *jackie*, you can use the single command

```
:1,$s/jack/jackie/g
```

As before, the colon character causes the cursor to jump down to the command line at the bottom of the screen. The remainder of the command line is a use of the *substitute* command of the *ed* editor (and hence also of *ex*).

You can obtain more details about this command and other *ex* commands from the documentation for *ed* or *ex*.

A.8. RECOVERING FROM PROBLEMS

Soon after you first began to use a computer, you probably discovered that even the simplest program was likely to lead to unexpected problems. If you encounter some difficulty with *vi*, there is usually a way to recover from it. In this section, we will run through the recovery techniques – starting with the easy problems first.

First, what do you do if your screen becomes garbled? One common cause is a communications failure. If you are using a terminal connected to a computer via a modem and a telephone line, you will find that noise on the telephone line can cause many strange characters to be displayed. There is a simple command to redraw the screen correctly, but first you must make sure that any text you are about to type will not be inserted into the file. Therefore, you should type the *escape* character. (If you were not inserting text, *vi* will merely make the terminal beep.) Then typing *Control-L* will clear the screen and cause it to be completely redrawn. If *Control-L* does nothing, try *Control-R* instead. If your screen is consistently garbled in the same way, the reason is probably that the entry for your terminal in the terminal capability database, "/etc/termcap", is incorrect or that you have selected the wrong terminal type. It would be wise to ask for some assistance if this is the case.

Second, what do you do if you accidentally delete a large chunk of your file? If you realize what you have done immediately after executing the offending command, you can undo its effect with the u command. However, if you are a fast typist or do not look at the screen, you may already have typed commands after the one that deleted half your file. In this case, the undo command will not help you. But do not worry, *vi* keeps the last nine blocks of deleted text in named buffers. To re-insert the block of lines that were most recently deleted, type the command

> `"1p`

To re-insert the last-but-one block of deleted text, use the command

> `"2p`

and so on. You can even step through the buffers, inserting them into the file and deleting them again, until you hit the buffer that contains the text you want. You just have to continue the sequence

> `"1pu.u.u.u.`

until you are successful. The u command undoes the insertion and the dot repeats the last command,p, but applies it to the next buffer.

Third, what do you do if you lose your place in the file? This can happen if you are editing a very large file and you accidentally hit a key that sends you to a completely different region of the file (as happens with the G command). It may take some time to find your way back to the previous position in the file with scrolling commands. Fortunately, there is a command that allows you to return directly to the previous position in the file. This command is

> `''`

(two single quote characters).

Fourth, what do you do if you lose your connection to the computer or if the system crashes? Fortunately, *vi* always makes a temporary copy of your file to work with. Even if the system crashes or if you accidentally hang up your connection to the computer, this temporary file is preserved. Next time you log into the system, you can resume editing your file by initiating *vi* with the command

> `vi -r` *filename*

where *filename* is the name of the file that you were previously editing. (*Vi* will inform you of this possibility by sending UNIX mail to you.) When you restart the edit, you will probably find that the last couple of input lines or the last couple of minor changes in the file have been lost. It should only be a minor inconvenience to re-enter these last few changes.

A.9. vi REFERENCE GUIDE

Although we have not stated it explicitly, *vi* is in one of three states at any moment. The normal state is called *Command* state. In this state, you can enter cursor movement commands, text deletion commands, etc. When you type a command like o (open) or i (insert), *vi* switches to *insert* state. In this state, all text that you type is inserted into the file. Only the *Escape* character or an interrupt (hitting the *Break* key for example) takes *vi* out of this state and back to command state. When you type one of the characters: :, /, ?, or !, the cursor jumps to the bottom line on the screen and all further text is echoed on that line. When the cursor is on the bottom line, *vi* is in the *last-line* state. Hitting the *Return* key or the *Escape* key at the end of the line causes the command to be executed and then *vi* returns to the normal command state. A partially typed command on the last line can be cancelled by backspacing back past the beginning of the line or by an interrupt (hitting the *Break* key).

All the *vi* commands described in this Appendix are collected together here in three separate tables on the following pages. Remember that only about half of all the *vi* commands are listed. It is suggested that you become familiar with these commands before advancing to the full *vi* command language.

TABLE A.1. vi Control Commands

Command	Description
:w	write the file back
:w *name*	write to the named file
:q	quit the editor
:wq	write the file and then quit
:q!	quit, discarding unsaved changes
ZZ	quit, saving the file only if any changes were made
:r *name*	read in the named file
:shell	temporarily escape to a subshell
:!*cmd*	execute the shell command *cmd*
:set *number*	display line numbers
:set *nomagic*	disable special characters in patterns

TABLE A.2. vi Cursor Movement Commands

Command		Description
h	*backspace*	move cursor left
j	*linefeed*	move cursor down
k		move cursor up
l	*space*	move cursor right
+	*return*	move cursor to first non-white character on next line
–		move cursor to first non-white character on previous line
^		move cursor to first non-white character on current line
$		move cursor to end of line
w		move cursor to next word
e		move cursor to end of word
b		move cursor to previous word
%		move cursor to matching bracket (in C code)
59|		move cursor to column 59
G		move cursor to last line in file
99G		move cursor to line number 99
Ctrl-B		scroll up one screenful
Ctrl-D		scroll down several lines
Ctrl-F		scroll down one screenful
Ctrl-U		scroll up several lines
/*pattern*		move to next occurrence of *pattern*
?*pattern*		move to previous occurrence of *pattern*
n		repeat previous / or ? search
N		repeat previous search in opposite direction

TABLE A.3. vi Text Editing Commands

Command	Description
x	delete one character
D	delete characters up to end of line
dw	delete one word
dd	delete one line
i *text*	insert text at cursor position
a *text*	insert text after cursor position
I *text*	insert text at start of line
A *text*	append text at end of line
o *text*	insert lines after current line
O *text*	insert lines before current line
r *c*	replace current character with *c*
R *text*	replace several characters
s *text*	substitute text for current character
S *text*	substitute text for current line
cc *text*	substitute text for current line
cw *text*	change one word
J	join current line to next line
u	undo last change made
.	repeat the last edit command
yy	yank a copy of the current line into a buffer
m *c*	mark the current line with the name *c*
d '*c*	delete lines from here to line marked with *c*
y '*c*	yank lines from here to line marked with *c*
p	put contents of buffer at cursor position
P	put contents of buffer before cursor position

APPENDIX B

THE csh COMMAND SHELL

B.1. INTRODUCTION

B.1.1. What is the Shell?

Commands typed on the keyboard of your terminal are read by a command interpreter program. This program analyzes each command, determines what actions are to be performed and then performs the actions. For example, if you type the command

```
wc -l file1 > file2
```

the command interpreter performs all the actions in the following list, though not necessarily in the same order. First, it parses the command line and determines that the command to be executed is named *wc*, that it has two arguments (`-l` and `file1`), and that its output is to be directed to a file named "file2". It searches one or more directories determining that the *wc* program is located in the program library named "/bin". The command interpreter next makes a request to the operating system that a new *process* be created. This involves duplicating the current program (the command interpreter) and scheduling the copy (called a *child process*) for execution. The original copy of the program now waits for its child to finish. (If we had followed the command with an ampersand, it would not wait.) The child process opens *file2* for output (creating the file if necessary) and requests that the operating system re-direct its standard output to the open file. Then it asks the operating system to replace the currently executing code with the executable code found in "/bin/wc" and to pass it two strings (the command line arguments) as parameters. The *wc*

227

program is now loaded into memory and scheduled for execution. When the operating system finishes executing *wc*, it sends a signal to the parent process (the original copy of the command interpreter). Sending the signal involves little more than restarting the program and providing a status value to indicate whether the child successfully completed execution. The re-awakened program now outputs a command prompt to the terminal and waits for a new command to be typed.

What you should observe from all of the above is that the command interpreter is, by no means, a magic program. You can write a C program that does everything the command interpreter can do. From within a C program, you can, for example, make requests to create child processes (look up the *fork* and *vfork* system calls). You can request that another program be loaded into memory and control be passed to it (look up *execl* and related system calls). The command interpreter has no special privileges in the UNIX system; it is just another a C program. In fact, if you do not like the command interpreter, you are quite free to program your own. The purpose of the command interpreter is not to provide the user with special facilities – all its facilities are already available in the UNIX system as system calls. Its purpose is to make these facilities accessible. In other words, the command interpreter program is like an outer layer of software, or a *shell*, surrounding the system that provides a interactive interface for you to use. In standard parlance, a *shell* is a command interpreter.

Now that the command shell concept has been demystified to some extent, let us look at what is available. In the Berkeley UNIX system, you get a choice of at least two different shells. First, there is the standard shell available on all UNIX systems. It is sometimes called the *Bourne shell* (after its author, Steven Bourne) and its program name is "/bin/sh". The other shell was written at Berkeley and is called the C shell. Its program name is "/bin/csh". The two shells support command languages that, for simple command execution, are very similar. Our sample command with the *wc* program is the same for either shell. The two shells differ in what extra facilities they offer. The Bourne shell has better facilities for redirecting input-output and for intercepting interrupts. The C shell has, amongst other things, better job control facilities. It, for example, lets you switch jobs between foreground execution and background execution.

In this appendix, we describe the C shell command language. The Bourne shell language has been covered in many books, whereas the C shell has received relatively little coverage. If you are currently using the C shell, you can try out the Bourne shell by invoking it as a program. You just have to type the command

      sh

And when you have tired of using this shell, you just have to type the end-of-file character, *Control-D*, instead of a command to terminate *sh* and return to your previous shell. Conversely, if you are currently using the Bourne shell, you can invoke the C shell by typing

```
csh
```

To exit from *csh*, you can use the *Control-D* character instead of a command unless you have set the shell variable *ignoreeof* (see below). In this case, you must use the *exit* command.

When you log into the UNIX system, a shell program is automatically started for you. If you care to inspect your entry in the "/etc/passwd" file, you will see your default shell specified at the end of the line that represents your entry. If your login name is *joanie*, say, you can see your entry in the password file with the command

```
grep joanie /etc/passwd
```

And if you should wish to change your choice of default shell from *sh* to *csh*, you should use the command

```
chsh joanie csh
```

The next time you logged in, you would be given *csh* as the start-up shell.

B.1.2. Overview of Shell Facilities

As we explained above, the purpose of the shell is to provide a convenient interface to the UNIX operating system. The commands that you type at your terminal form a language with its own syntactic and semantic rules. This language is, in some respects, similar to a programming language. The main difference between the shell language and an ordinary programming language is that you are dealing with different kinds of objects. You are mostly concerned with requesting that programs be executed, with providing arguments to the programs, and with manipulating files. Thus, the facilities of the shell language are oriented towards providing easy access to programs and providing convenient notations for accessing files.

The *csh* shell includes the following facilities:

- Automatic command searching
  When you type the name of a program to be executed, *csh* will search several directories to find an executable file with the given name. A hash table implementation is used to make these searches very fast.

- Input-output redirections
  The standard input of a program may be redirected so that the program reads from a file. Similarly, the standard output may be redirected into a file.

- Pipelining commands
  The standard output from one program may be directly fed into the

standard input of another program.

- Command aliasing
  This feature allows you to provide aliases for commands (possibly including arguments).

- Job control
  When you enter a command, you may indicate whether the command is to be run as a foreground or a background job. *Csh* permits you to suspend an executing job, to restart it, and to convert a job from foreground execution to background or vice versa.

- Command history
  If you request it, *csh* keeps a list of the most recent commands you have executed. *Csh* provides convenient notations for repeating one of these commands (possibly with minor changes made to the command).

- Shell Control Flow
  When *csh* commands are read from a file, it is desirable to be able to specify the conditions that must be satisfied before a program is to be executed. This is analogous to an *if* statement in an ordinary programming language. The *csh* shell language provides an *if* statement as well as other control flow constructs similar to those found in the C language (namely, the *while* loop, *switch* statement, and the *goto* statement).

- Shell Script Files
  Any collection of *csh* commands may be stored in a file and *csh* invoked to execute the commands in that file. Such a file is known as a *shell script*. Either a new instance of the shell can be created to execute the shell script or the commands in the file can be executed by the current invocation of the shell.

B.2. INPUT-OUTPUT REDIRECTIONS AND PIPELINES

It is fairly standard practice for UNIX programs to read from their standard input (the file named *stdin* or the file that has descriptor number 0) and to write results to their standard output (*stdout* or descriptor number 1). When such a program is invoked by *csh*, the default is for the standard input of the program to be connected to the same source as the standard input of the shell (usually the terminal keyboard). Similarly, the standard output of the program is, by default, connected to the same destination as the shell's standard output (usually the screen of your terminal). However, the *csh* language provides simple notations for redirecting input or output.

As a sample program, let us use *fmt*. What *fmt* does is largely irrelevant, except inasmuch as it reads the standard input and writes to the standard output. In fact, *fmt* is a simple-minded text formatter which moves words from one line to another to try to make lines as long as possible without exceeding 72 columns. If you type the command

```
fmt
```

the program is invoked and, by default, it reads standard input (your keyboard) and writes to standard output (the screen). To see any results, you must type some input to the program, terminated by *Control-D*. Unless you type a lot of input, the output will not appear on the screen until you hit *Control-D* because the program buffers its output.

Re-directing input to come from a file requires the use of the < operator. For example, to format text taken from a file, say the file "personal_letter", you would enter the command as

```
fmt < personal_letter
```

This causes a reformatted version of your file to be displayed on the screen.

Re-directing the standard output requires the use of the > operator. If you typed the command

```
fmt > new_file
```

a reformatted version of the input you type at the keyboard will be stored into the file called "new_file". If this file did not already exist, *csh* will attempt to create it for you. If it did already exist, *csh* will attempt to let you overwrite the file.[1]

Of course, you can redirect both the input and the output in the same command. For example,

```
fmt < personal_letter > new_file
```

will reformat your file, storing the result in a new file. But be careful. You might think that a command like

```
###  DO NOT EXECUTE THE FOLLOWING!
fmt < personal_letter > personal_letter
```

could be used to reformat the file in place. This does not work! *Csh* opens the file for output before *fmt* is ever invoked. Opening a file for output has the side effect of emptying the file. The *fmt* program will therefore read an empty file and produce no output. In other words, the command will destroy the file without producing any error messages.[2]

A variation on output redirection is the appending of output to the end of a file. The appropriate *csh* operator is >> . For example, the command

```
fmt >> personal_letter
```

---

[1] The word *attempt* has been used because it is possible that access permissions on the current directory or on an existing file with the name "new_file" prohibit you from creating or overwriting the file.

[2] If this should worry you, there is a way to prevent files from being accidentally destroyed. See the *noclobber* variable under the *SHELL VARIABLES* heading, below.

will reformat any input you type at the terminal and append it to the file, "personal_letter". If the file did not previously exist, *csh* will attempt to create it before invoking *fmt*.

You may recall that typical UNIX programs use two output files. As well as the standard output, used for results, there is a standard error output file (corresponding to file descriptor number 2 or the name *stderr*). By default, the error output from any program you run is directed to the same destination as error output for your shell, which is usually the terminal screen. When you redirect the standard output, the error output file remains unaffected. Thus, if *fmt* should create any error message when it is invoked with

```
fmt < personal_letter > new_file
```

the message will still come to your terminal instead of being buried in the middle of your output file. This is probably the behaviour you want for commands typed at the terminal. However, if the command is being run when you are not sitting at the terminal[3], there is a danger that the message will be lost. Therefore, it is desirable to be able to redirect error messages into a file. This redirection is accomplished with the `>&` operator in the *csh* language. If you type the command

```
fmt < personal_letter >& new_file
```

then both the standard output and the error output are directed into the same file. No error messages generated by *fmt* are sent to the terminal. The operator `>>&` has a similar effect to `>&` except that both kinds of output are appended to the specified file.

The practice of chaining programs together so that the output of one program is passed to the input of the next is encouraged in the UNIX system. Let us take text formatting with *troff*, for example. If you have a *troff* input file that contains both tables and mathematical equations, it needs to be processed by three successive programs: *tbl*, then *eqn* and finally *troff* itself. A sequence of commands to run the programs, using temporary files for communication[4], would look like

```
tbl < text_input > #tmp1
eqn < #tmp1 > #tmp2
troff -me < #tmp2
```

But there is a tidier way to achieve the same effect, using *pipelines*. A pipeline can be thought of as a conduit through which data flows. The *csh* symbol that represents a pipeline is `|`. Using this operator, we can rewrite the earlier command sequence as

---

[3] Look up the *at* command to see how to run a command after you have logged out.

[4] It is recommended practice to give temporary files names that begin with a hash symbol. If you forget to delete these files, the system is supposed to remove them for you after a day or two.

```
tbl < text_input | eqn | troff -me
```

As it happens, all of the programs *tbl, eqn* and *troff* have been programmed to take their inputs either from their standard input or from any files that are provided as arguments. The rule is that if a file argument is provided, the program reads that. If no file is provided, the program reads its standard input. Thus, our last command is normally typed as

```
tbl text_input | eqn | troff -me
```

Finally, we note that the operator |**&** has the expected effect. It causes both the standard output and the error output of the program on its left to be piped into the standard input of the program on its right. However its use is inappropriate in a normal pipeline. If we use

```
tbl text_input |& eqn ...
```

and the *tbl* program generates an error message, the error message will be read by *eqn*. This situation is obviously undesirable. Yet there is a way to extract error messages from a command pipeline and redirect them elsewhere. Here is how it would be done for our text formatting example:

```
(tbl text_input | eqn | troff -me) >& msgs
```

Error messages generated by any of the three programs in this pipeline will be written to the file "msgs". This is our first use of parentheses in a command line. They cause the shell to fork and create a subshell which executes whatever commands are enclosed by the parentheses. The >**&** redirection after the parenthesized command redirects any output generated by the subshell. This output should consist only of error messages generated in the subshell.

A table of the file redirection and piping operators appears at the end of this appendix.

B.3. FILENAME EXPANSIONS

Shell commands usually perform operations on disk files. Therefore it is reasonable to expect that *csh* should provide some convenient notations for referring to files. Suppose, for example, you wish to compile all the C source files in your current directory and retain the object files for each of them. You could certainly list all the source files in the command, as in

```
cc -c file1.c file2.c file3.c
```

and so on. But you will not be glad of all the typing if you have twenty source files to list. The normal way to enter the command in the *csh* language is as

```
cc -c *.c
```

The asterisk character **∗** is often called a *wild card* character because the shell will take the asterisk as representing any sequence of characters at all.[5] *Csh* takes the string *.c as a pattern and attempts to match it against the names of all the files in your directory. If your directory contains the six files

file1.c	file2.c	file4.o
file3.c	abc.xyz.c	rubbish

then the pattern matches against "abc.xyz.c", "file1.c", "file2.c", and "file3.c". Therefore *csh* substitutes this list of file names, in alphabetic order, for the pattern before executing the *cc* command.

You can use more than one wild card character in a pattern. For example, the command

        cc *.*

will include the file "file4.o" as well as the four listed previously. (One command to watch out for is

        rm *

which deletes *all* the files in your current directory.)

Other pattern features of file names are as follows. First, ? is a wild card which matches any single character. Therefore,

        cc file?.c

will compile three files in the example directory, and

        rm file?.?

will delete four files. Second, if you want to match one character but you want to accept only certain characters (rather than any character as implied by "?"), you can enclose these characters in square brackets. Thus,

        rm file[134].?

will remove "file1.c", "file3.c" and "file4.o" from the example directory and leave "file2.c" intact. You can also use a hyphen to denote a range of characters, as in

        rm file[1-3].?

Another special character for file name expansions is the tilde (~). In a command such as

        cd ~/bin

the tilde represents the full path name for your home directory. Therefore, the command will change the current directory to the subdirectory "bin" in your home directory. Similarly,

---

[5] There is an exception: *csh* will not expand either * or ? to match a period at the beginning of a filename.

```
echo ~
```

will print the full path name of your home directory. The tilde character can be used as a prefix for the user id of another user on the system, in which case, *csh* will expand the combination to the full path name of that user's home directory. If there is a user named *cathy* on your system, you can execute a command like

```
ls ~cathy
```

to see what files this user has in her home directory. (The command will work only if you have read permission on this user's home directory.)

A table of *magic* characters, including filename matching characters, appears at the end of this appendix.

B.4. COMMAND ALIASES

The *csh* alias command provides a simple means for you to give alternate names, or aliases, to commands. If, for example, you have trouble remembering that the command to delete a file is *rm*, you can provide an alias as in

```
alias delete rm
```

After the shell has executed this command, you can freely use the name *delete* as a synonym for *rm*.

A slightly more advanced use of aliasing is to force certain options to be provided on commands. For example,

```
alias ls ls -F
```

causes *csh* to expand all subsequent uses of the *ls* command to include the −F option. That is, if you subsequently typed the command

```
ls /bin
```

the shell expands the command to

```
ls -F /bin
```

before proceeding to interpret the command further. The −F option is a useful one that causes the types of files to be indicated in any directory listing. This feature lets you see at a glance which members of a directory are executable programs and which are subdirectories.

Another alias which many people find useful is

```
alias rm rm -i
```

It causes the *rm* program to double check with you before deleting any files. This provides useful protection against the accidental deletion of files.

Of course, you should not have to retype all the aliases you use every time you log into the UNIX system. If you place your collection of alias commands in a special file named ".login" or ".cshrc" (see section B.11 below), the commands will be executed as soon as your shell is started up.

If you have created an alias for the *rm* command like that above, how can you ever execute *rm* without the −1 flag? One way is to remove the alias with the command

        `unalias rm`

The only other simple answer is to access the *rm* program under a name that *csh* will not recognize as aliased. For example, you can type the command as

        `/bin/rm *`

to remove all your files non-interactively.

We will now look at a couple of trickier aspects of aliasing. First, aliases can expand to be several commands. For example,

        `alias status 'uptime; stty all'`

causes *status* to expand to two commands which are executed one after the other. (The semicolon character is an alternative to the newline character as a command delimiter.) Second, there may be situations where you want to insert arguments into the middle of an alias expansion. For example, suppose that you frequently execute command pipelines like

        `tbl document | eqn | troff -me`

It would be nice to provide an alias to reduce the amount of typing and to avoid having to remember whether *tbl* precedes *eqn* in the pipeline or vice versa. We cannot set up an alias like

        `alias format 'tbl | eqn | troff -me'`

because when we use the command with arguments, as in

        `format doc1`

the shell will expand the command to

        `tbl | eqn | troff -me doc1`

To circumvent this problem, *csh* provides a notation for referring to command arguments. The correct way to create the alias is

        `alias format 'tbl \!* | eqn | troff -me'`

Now our use of the *format* alias will expand with the argument in the correct place.

In fact, the notation `!*` represents *all* arguments. We can use a command like

        `format doc1 doc2 doc3`

and this will be equivalent to executing

        `tbl doc1 doc2 doc3 | eqn | troff -me`

Alternatively, you can use `!:1` to refer to just the first argument, `!:2` to refer to the second, and so on. Thus, you can create a command to exchange the names of two files as follows:

```
alias exch 'mv \!:1 #t; mv \!:2 \!:1; mv #t \!:2
```

A backslash (\ ) is required in front of the exclamation mark character to prevent *csh* from recognizing the exclamation mark as a special operator when the alias is defined. As in the C language, the backslash is used as an escape character. You might have noted that we enclosed some of our alias definitions within single quotation marks. Doing so was no accident. If the text is not enclosed within single quotation marks, *csh* attempts to perform filename expansion on the text. For example, if you try making the alias

```
alias print pr \!* | lpr
```

you will probably get the nasty message "No match." from *csh*. This means that *csh* tried to match `\!*` against the names of files in your directory but did not succeed. Thus, we have been using single quotation marks to prevent the asterisk character from being expanded and the backslash to delay interpretation of the exclamation mark.

Finally, it is useful to know that typing

```
alias
```

all by itself causes *csh* to print a complete list of current alias definitions. Typing

```
alias jack
```

will print out just the definition for *jack*, if there is one.

B.5. JOB CONTROL

Berkeley UNIX and *csh* provide convenient mechanisms for controlling several simultaneously executing jobs. A job is just a program whose execution has been initiated by you. At any moment, the job can be either

1) *Running* – which means that the program is active and being executed at regular intervals (i.e. receiving time slices of the CPU), or

2) *Stopped* – execution of the program has been suspended, perhaps because it is blocked waiting for an I/O device, but it can be restarted later.

In addition, a program may be running in the foreground or running in the background. A foreground job is a program which has control of your terminal. Anything you type at the keyboard is available for input by the program (although the program may not necessarily read it). While a foreground job is running, your keyboard input is not seen by the command shell. The command shell is simply in a wait state, waiting for the foreground job to terminate. Obviously there can be only one foreground job at any moment. On the other hand, there can be any number of background jobs or stopped jobs.

Csh gives you the ability to start and stop jobs and to switch them between foreground execution and background execution. A background job can be initiated by appending an ampersand (**&**) to the end of a command, as in

```
cc bigprog.c &
```

The shell will output a single information line about this job (specifying the UNIX process number or numbers for this job), and then it will give you a prompt for another command. Eventually the background job will complete and *csh* will output a one-line message to inform you of the job completion. This message will normally come to you at a convenient moment, just before the prompt for a new command.[6]

If we have started a background job, we can convert it into a foreground job with the **fg** command. For example, a session at the terminal which starts up two background jobs might look like

```
% cc bigprog.c &
[1] 2974
% troff -me big_doc.roff &
[2] 2993
% jobs
[1] - Running              cc bigprog.c
[2] + Running              troff -me big_doc.roff
% fg %1
cc bigprog.c
```

The notation [1] printed by *csh* shows that the C compilation is job number 1. Similarly, the *troff* job is assigned number 2. We can ask *csh* for the status of all current jobs with the *jobs* command, as above. If we had used *fg* without an argument, we would have brought the most recently activated job (the *troff* job) into the foreground. (The most recently activated job is distinguished in the output of the *jobs* command by the plus symbol.) If we want to be explicit or to bring some other job into the foreground, we can supply an argument to *fg*. The argument can be written as **%1** for job number 1, or it can be written as **%cc** to denote the most recent *cc* command.

To convert a job from foreground execution to background execution, we must first suspend execution. Suspending execution is normally accomplished with the *Control-Z* key combination which, by default, sends a *stop* signal to the program. Unless the program is deliberately intercepting and ignoring stop signals, the program is suspended and the shell will give you a prompt for a new command. A continuation of our previous terminal dialogue might look like

---

[6] If you set the shell variable, *notify*, *csh* will tell you as soon as a background job terminates.

```
^Z
Stopped
% jobs
[1] + Stopped              cc bigprog.c
[2] - Running              troff -me big_doc.roff
% bg %cc
[1]     cc bigprog.c &
% jobs
[1] + Running              cc bigprog.c
[2] - Running              troff -me big_doc.roff
```

The shell has echoed the *Control-Z* character and output the message "Stopped". If we ask for a job status, we see that the C compile is shown as *stopped*. A stopped job can only be restarted or be killed. It can be restarted as a foreground job by using the *fg* command or as a background job with the *bg* command, as in the sample session at the terminal. When we restart a program, *csh* outputs a line to remind us what it is we are restarting. The use of the *jobs* command once more would verify that the program is indeed running again.

A stopped job or a background job can be terminated with the *kill* command. If we should change our minds about running the *troff* job, for example, we can kill the job with the command

```
kill -9 %2
```

or with a command similar to

```
kill -9 %tr
```

The notation **%tr** refers to the most recently created active job whose command name begins with the letters 'tr'. (The argument **-9** should be included if you want to guarantee that the program is actually killed.)

Finally, we should note that the shell automatically stops a running background job that attempts to read from the terminal. Here is a sample session where this happens:

```
% mail fred &
[1] 34211
% Subject:
[1] + Stopped (tty input)  mail fred
```

You can leave the program halted at the point where it is trying to read the subject of the mail message for as long as you like. Eventually, you will either have to kill the job or restart it by bringing it into the foreground. Once the program is brought into the foreground, you can enter the input that it was expecting and it will resume execution.

B.6. THE HISTORY MECHANISM

When you use the computer, you probably find yourself repeating commands. For example, when you are developing a new program, the sequence of commands you enter is likely to be something like edit a file, attempt to compile the file (but the compiler reports some errors), re-edit the file, attempt re-compilation, and so on. When you wish to repeat commands in this manner, you may avoid retyping each command in its entirety. *Csh* maintains a *history list*, a list of the most recent commands executed by you, which provides a notation for re-executing any command in this list. The number of commands in the list is controlled by a shell variable called *history*. By default, only the last command is remembered. To make use of the history mechanism, you must make sure that the variable is set to a suitably large number. (See the section on shell variables for more details.)

A reference to a command in the history list is introduced by the exclamation mark character. The exclamation mark may be followed by another exclamation mark to refer to the most recent command, by a number to refer to a specific command or by a few letters which identify the command. An example of a session at the terminal that uses the history mechanism is shown in Figure B.1. In this sample command sequence, we simply had to type `!!` to repeat the *vi* edit command. *Csh* echoes the full version of this command before executing it. Later on, we used the notation `!vi` to repeat the most recently executed *vi* command and `!c` to repeat the C compile.

An alternative, but less usable, notation is to follow the exclamation mark with a command number. For example,

`!23`

will re-execute the 23rd command that you gave to the shell, provided that this command is still in the history list. Also, you can use the command form

`!-2`

to re-execute the last-but-one command, and so on. But for commands used much further back, you need to know the command numbers. One way to see what they are is to type the command

`history`

which gives a list of commands in the history list along with command numbers. Another means of knowing command numbers is to change the shell command prompt to always include the number of the next command. See below for the command which will change the prompt string to do this.

Finally, it is useful to know that there are ways to modify a command line before it is re-executed. If all you want to do is append some extra arguments, I/O redirections and the like to a command, you may do so easily. For example, if you have recently executed the command

FIGURE B.1. Example of the History Mechanism

```
% vi bigprog.c
        .
        .    { perform some edits on the file }
        .
:wq       { save the file back }
% !!
vi bigprog.c
        .    { re-edit the file, we forgot }
        .    { to change something! }
        .
:wq       { save the file back }
% cc -c bigprog.c
bigprog.c: line 29: variable i not declared
% !vi
vi bigprog.c
        .
        .    { edit the file again !! }
        .
:wq
% !c
cc -c bigprog.c
%
```

```
cat somefile
```

you can repeat that command but with redirection and in the background as follows:

```
!ca > newfile &
```

If you have made a mistake in a command, there is a notation for changing the command before re-executing it. A short session might proceed as follows:

```
% cc -c -DDEBUG bigproh.c
0: No source file bigproh.c
% !!:s/oh/og/
cc -c -DDEBUG bigprog.c
%
```

The suffix :s/oh/og/ indicates to *csh* that you wish to substitute the two characters "og" for "oh" in the command that you referenced. Actually, it is such a common occurrence to modify and re-execute the previous command that *csh* provides a shorter notation for it. The example command

`!!s/oh/og/` could have been typed as

      `^oh^og`

B.7. SHELL VARIABLES AND SHELL EXPRESSIONS

Just as a programming language like C has variables, the *csh* language also has variables. Some variables are used to control the operation of the shell. For example, a variable named *prompt* contains the string that is printed as your command prompt. Other variables can be created and used to control the operation of a shell script file (see below) or they can simply be used as a method of abbreviating commands.

B.7.1. Setting Values

Shell variables have values which are lists containing zero or more elements. Elements of the lists are called *words* in the *csh* documentation, but words are really just character strings. Words may be used to represent either decimal or octal integer values. If the word consists of decimal digits, without a leading zero, it may be used as an operand for arithmetic operations listed below. If the word contains only octal digits and begins with a zero, it is treated as an octal integer (just as in C).

      Shell variables are often used in a manner akin to Boolean variables. If the variable has a value, no matter what it is, the variable is used to represent *true* and if the variable is unset, with no value, then it implicitly represents *false*. The value that is commonly used to set such a variable is the empty list. A special test must be used to determine whether the variable has a value or not because it is an error to attempt to access the value of an unset variable.

      The *set* command is used to change the value of a shell variable. The command has several forms, as illustrated in the following examples. The command

      `set V`

will set variable *V* to have an empty list as its value. The command

      `set V = abc`

will set *V* to have the string `"abc"` as its value. To be more precise, the value would be a list with one element and the value of this element is `"abc"`. The command

      `set V = (123 def ghi)`

sets the value of *V* as a list with three elements, these elements being the strings `"123"`, `"def"` and `"ghi"`. If *V* has been set to a list of words, as in the previous assignment, we can change one of the elements as follows:

      `set V[2] = xxxx`

This command changes the second word in the list. Finally, if you type the command

```
set
```

csh will give you a listing of the values of all variables which are currently set.

B.7.2. Referencing and Testing Shell Variables

The value of a shell variable is accessed by placing a dollar character before the name of the variable. Thus,

```
echo $term
```

will output the value of the variable *term*. This particular shell command should usually yield the same result as the command

```
printenv TERM
```

because *csh* maintains a one-way correspondence between the shell variables *term*, *path*, *user* and the environment variables *TERM*, *PATH* and *USER*. That is, if you change the shell variable *term*, you will find that the environment variable *TERM* has been changed to match. However, if you change *TERM* (with the *setenv* command), the *term* shell variable is unaffected. *Csh* does not maintain an equivalence for any shell or environment variables other than those listed above.

An alternative notation for accessing a shell variable is to enclose the variable name in curly brace characters and then to prefix the dollar symbol. Our previous example of the *echo* command could be typed as

```
echo ${term}
```

It has exactly the same effect. The need to use curly braces arises only when a string of alphabetic characters is to be catenated to the contents of the variable (see the section on expressions).

If a variable holds a list of words, a subscripting notation may be used to access one word or a range of consecutive words in the list. For example, if variable *V* holds a list of words, we may write shell commands like

```
echo $V[1]
```

to print the first word in the list, and commands like

```
echo $V[2-3]
```

to print the words in positions 2 through 3 inclusive. The command

```
echo $V[2-]
```

prints all words from the second position on. All these subscripting notations can be enclosed in curly braces, when necessary, as in the command

```
set W = ${V[3]}
```

Shell variables may be tested in a number of ways. The notations $#*name* or ${#*name*} may be used to find out how many words are in the list. For example, after executing the two commands

```
set V = (abc def ghi 123)
set N = $#V
```

the variable *N* will have the value 4.

The notations $?*name* or ${?*name*} can be used to test whether a variable has been set or not. The result of the test is 0 for *not set* and 1 for *set*.

B.7.3. Shell Variables that Control the Shell

Some shell variables affect the way that the shell executes your commands. Some of the more useful control variables are briefly listed below.

- *prompt*

    contains the string which prints as your command prompt. The default value for this string (**%**) is rather uninteresting and many UNIX users change it. In environments where there are several computers, users frequently redefine *prompt* to remind them which computer they are using. For instance, if your computer is known to you as *Sun B*, say, you might set *prompt* with

    ```
    set prompt = 'B>> '
    ```

    If you want the prompt to show command numbers, you should use an assignment like

    ```
    set prompt = '\!> '
    ```

    The backslash is needed to protect the exclamation mark from being expanded at the time the *set* command is executed. And if you truly want your prompt to contain an exclamation mark, you will have to set the prompt in a manner similar to

    ```
    set prompt = 'HI THERE\\! '
    ```

- *ignoreeof*

    disables *Control-D* as a command input for terminating the shell. When the variable is set, the only commands to terminate the shell are *logout* (if this is the invocation of the shell that was initiated when you logged in) and *exit* (if this is not a login shell).

- *history*

    controls the number of previous commands retained in the history list. A reasonable number of commands is fifty and such a list can be set with

    ```
    set history = 50
    ```

- *mail*

    controls how often *csh* checks for new mail messages that have arrived for you and controls where it looks for the mail. If your login name is *joanie*, you would normally set *mail* with a command like

```
set mail = (60 /usr/spool/mail/joanie)
```

which specifies that *csh* should check the named file for new mail every sixty seconds. The directory containing incoming mail normally has the pathname shown in the example, but it would be wise to check whether a different path is needed for your particular UNIX system.

- *path*

  is a list of directories where *csh* will look for programs named in your commands. A fairly typical setting for *path* is

  ```
  set path=(/bin /usr/bin /usr/ucb .)
  ```

The first three elements of the list are system directories where the standard commands are kept. The fourth element, a period, represents your current directory. If you are at all concerned about security, you should always put the period at the end of the path list.[7] If you have your own directory containing executable programs, say a subdirectory of your home directory called "bin", you would include it in the path list[8] as follows:

```
set path=(~/bin /bin /usr/bin /usr/ucb .)
```

A position at the front of the list is preferable because it gives you the freedom to create and use your own versions of system commands.

- *noclobber*

  is a flag which protects you from accidentally overwriting a file in a file redirection. If this flag is set and if the file "junk" already exists when you type a command like

  ```
  cat garbage > junk
  ```

then *csh* will refuse to execute the command. If you really wish to perform this file redirection, you have to use a special override form of redirection:

```
cat garbage >! junk
```

(There is a similar override form for appending, namely >>! .) To set the flag, you need only execute

```
set noclobber
```

---

[7] This helps guard against the *Trojan Horse* subterfuge, in which some nasty person creates a program named *ls* and leaves it lying around in a directory that you might visit. This fake *ls* program could perform very malicious actions such as deleting all your files or it could be more subtle and create, unknown to you, a permanent loophole in the security of your files.

[8] If you do include one of your own directories in the path list, make sure that you know about the *rehash* command, which is described later.

- *noglob*

    turns off the filename expansion process of *csh*. This operation is useful if
    you are about to enter commands whose arguments contain wild card
    characters and you do not want to be bothered with enclosing the argu-
    ments in quotation marks or using backslash escape characters.

B.7.4. Expressions

Shell variables have values which are lists of words. To the shell, a word is
nothing more than a string of ASCII characters. These lists can be combined to
create longer lists as in the following short extract from a session at the terminal:

```
% set single = xxx
% set List1 = (abc def)
% set List2 = (ghi jkl mn)
% set M   = ($single $List1 $List2)
% echo 'value of M = ' $M
value of M = xxx abc def ghi jkl mn
%
```

The use of the *echo* command in this example illustrates that strings can be
combined (or catenated) by juxtaposing them. More usually, strings are
catenated to create file names. Given the assignment to *single*, above, the command

```
set PROG = /tmp/${single}zz.c
```

would cause *PROG* to be assigned the filename "/tmp/xxxzz.c". This example
also illustrates the need for the alternate (curly brace) notation for accessing a
shell variable. Without the braces, the shell would look for a variable with the
name *singlezz*.

Csh expressions use a syntax that is similar to that of the C language.
Expressions may only be used in commands that begin with the keywords *if*,
while, *exit* or the symbol @ . All the *if* and *while* commands are explained in
the following section of this appendix. The @ command form will be discussed
presently.

The most important expressions for controlling conditional execution of
commands are those that yield results representing true or false. As in C, false
is represented by the integer 0 and true by any non-zero integer. Comparison
operations yield either 0 or 1 as their results. The operators == and != may
be used to compare either string values or number values. The other comparison operators that occur in C, namely <, <=, > and >=, may only be used
to compare numeric values. There are two more comparison operators: =~ and
!~. The former operator, =~, is used to compare strings and is similar to ==.
It is a more powerful comparison operation, though, because the right-hand
operand can include wild card characters such as * and ?. For example, the

expression

        abcdefgh =~ a*d*

will evaluate to 1 (true). The other operator, !~, just yields the opposite result to =~.

    Boolean values may be combined with the && and || operators, which operate in exactly the same way as they do in C. And a Boolean value may be inverted with the ! operator. Note that it is necessary to have a space following the exclamation mark to avoid confusion with the history mechanism notation.

    Integer forms of all the arithmetic operators of C, including assignment, are available too. Although arithmetic expressions can be used as operands for the *if* and *while* commands, they are most often used in a special kind of shell command that is marked by having an "at" symbol (@) in the first column. The symbol indicates an arithmetic assignment statement. Here are some examples:

        @ i = 10
        @ j = $i * 2 + 5
        @ i++
        @ j *= ($i - 5) / 2

The first of these assignments is equivalent to

        set i = 10

None of the other assignment statements, however, can be reexpressed as a *set* command.

B.7.5. Testing File Characteristics

Another form of shell expression is a test on a file. For example, the following expression

        -w ~joanie/junk

is a test to see if the file "junk" in the home directory of *joanie* is writable. If the file can be written to, the result is 1, otherwise it is 0. The complete list of tests is given at the end of the appendix.

B.8. csh CONTROL STRUCTURES

The *csh* command language includes facilities for conditionally executing a command and for repeatedly executing a group of commands. These facilities are most useful if you, yourself, are not sitting at the terminal to type these commands yourself or if you have to type the same group of commands repeatedly. That is, these shell facilities are needed for when the commands have been collected into a shell script file.

The *csh* control structures are modelled after those found in the C programming language. (Presumably this is how the *C shell* obtained its name.) The command language has two forms of the **if** statement, the **while** loop, a variation on the **for** loop, the **switch** statement, and the **goto** statement.

B.8.1. The Shell if Command

There is a one-line form of the *if* command, which has the structure

    if (expression) simple-command

The expression is evaluated and if it is a non-zero integer, the following command is executed. If the expression is zero, no command is executed. If the expression does not evaluate to an integer, the shell reports an error. An example of the command is

    if (-w $file2) mv $file1 $file2

The one-line form of *if* command is not general because the following command must be simple and must not use pipes or I/O redirection. Furthermore, this form of *if* command is occasionally inappropriate because the shell expands uses of the history mechanism and of shell variables in the entire command line before determining whether the command after the test should be executed. Sometimes the occurrence of such an expansion in a command that will not be executed is unwanted and may result in an error message from *csh*. For example,

    if ($?FILE) rm $FILE

will yield an error message if the variable *FILE* is not set.

To avoid problems, the multi-line form of *if* is recommended. The general structure for an *if* command without an *else* clause is

    if (expression) then
            zero or more lines
            containing shell commands
    endif

The first line in this layout must be typed as a single line. The line cannot be split into multiple lines (unless the end-of-line is escaped with a backslash) and no commands should appear after the keyword *then* on the same line. Similarly, the *endif* keyword must appear on a line by itself.

Just as in most programming languages, an *else* clause may be provided. The structure is then

```
if ( expression ) then
        zero or more lines of shell commands
else
        zero or more lines of shell commands
endif
```

Again, the *else* keyword must appear on a line by itself.

If statements may be nested. But if the *else* clause contains just a single *if* statement, there is a shorthand form. The lines beginning with the keywords *else* and *if* that appear consecutively may be joined and one of the *endif* lines eliminated. This leads to a structure like

```
if ( expression ) then
        shell commands
else if ( expression ) then
        shell commands
else
        shell commands
endif
```

B.8.2. The Shell while Command

The *while* command may be used to repeat a group of commands. The general structure is

```
while ( expression )
        shell commands
end
```

The first line and last line must be typed as single lines, as shown. Within the loop body, the shell command *break* may be used to exit the loop (just as in C) and the command *continue* may be used to cause a transfer to the test at the top of the loop (again, just as in C).

B.8.3. The Shell foreach Command

The shell provides a second form of looping construct. This loop has an index variable which takes on successive values from a list of words. The general structure is

```
foreach variable ( list of words )
        shell commands
end
```

Just as with the *while* loop, the commands within the loop body may include *break* and *continue*.

A simple example of the *foreach* command appears in Figure B.2. This loops runs through all the C source code files in the current directory and prints

FIGURE B.2 An Example Use of foreach

```
foreach F (*.c)
        set SIZE = `wc -l $F`
        if ($SIZE > 10000) then
                echo "$F too big to print"
                continue
        endif
        echo "Printing $F ..."
        pr $F | lpr
end
```

only those that are not excessively large. The first command uses a *csh* feature that has not yet been mentioned. It is possible to access the output of a program in a shell command. If the command to invoke the program is written within a pair of backquote characters (`), the program will be executed and its output treated as a list of words. The command invokes the *wc* program to count the number of lines in a file. The result is a single number which we assign to a shell variable.

B.8.4. The Shell switch Command

The *switch* command selects from among several possible groups of commands according to a selecting expression. The general structure is

```
switch ( string )
case string:
        shell commands
        breaksw
case string:
        shell commands
        breaksw
            .
            .

default:
        shell commands
endsw
```

The *default* clause is optional. If it is provided, it should appear after all other case labels. The *breaksw* causes an exit to the bottom of the *switch* construct, just like the *break* statement in C. If a *breaksw* command is omitted, execution will drop through to the next clause of the *switch* construct.

Although this structure is obviously modelled after C, the *csh* version of the *switch* statement is more powerful in two important ways. The first reason is that the values appearing as *case* labels need not be constants. Since lines read by the shell are subject to expansion (of shell variables, of references to history events, etc.), the labels can be formed by catenating various substrings together. The shell interprets the *switch* command by first expanding the selector string in the first line. Then the shell scans forward finding lines beginning with the keyword *case*, expanding these lines and comparing the selector string against the string appearing after the keyword. If the strings match, the following command lines are executed. Since the search proceeds sequentially, it is not an error for two *case* strings to be the same, the shell simply stops at the first one that matches. The second reason this *switch* statement is more powerful than the one in C is that strict equality matching between the selecting expression and case labels is not performed. Instead, pattern matching between the selecting expression and the case label expression is performed (exactly as with the ˜= operator). In other words, case label expressions may contain wild card characters.

B.8.5. The Shell goto Command

A label may be placed anywhere within a file containing shell commands. It is typed as an identifier followed by a colon and placed on a line by itself. A *goto* command may occur anywhere else in the file, either before or after the line where the label is defined. The general format is

>   *label* :

>   .
>   .
>   .

>   goto *label*

B.9. THE INTERPRETATION PROCESS

When *csh* reads a command line, it performs various manipulations on the text of this line before any commands get executed. It is necessary to know something about how this processing of the text proceeds if you want to become an adept shell programmer.

There are several stages to the processing of a command line. In the first stage, the command line is read and split into words.[9] Words are normally separated by one or more white space characters (blanks and tabs). However, some shell operator symbols will be recognized as separate words regardless of whether they are surrounded by white space. These symbols are

---

[9] The command line may consist of several input lines if all but the last of these lines end with the backslash character.

      &   **&&**   **|**   **||**   **;**   **<**   **<<**   **>**   **>>**   **(**   **)**

In addition, text enclosed within pairs of single quote characters, pairs of double quote characters or pairs of backquote characters is not split into words.

The second stage is for *csh* to deduce the basic command syntax. That is, the line is decomposed into commands separated by semicolons. Components of pipelines are recognized, I/O redirections are recognized, and so on.

The third stage is for *csh* to perform alias substitution. The first word in a command line is checked to see if it has an alias definition. If it has, the substitution is performed.

The fourth stage is for *csh* to perform history substitutions. The words in the line that have not been recognized as shell operators are scanned to search for exclamation mark characters. Any exclamation mark followed by another exclamation mark, by an integer or by alphanumeric text causes a search of the history list for the matching command. If the reference to a history event is followed by a colon (as in `"!!:s/fred/jack/"`), editing on the matching command is performed. The possibly edited command is then substituted into the command line.

The fifth stage is for *csh* to search words for references to shell variables. This search is keyed by the dollar character. The values of variables or the results of tests on variables are substituted as appropriate.

The sixth stage is for commands supplied as strings between pairs of backquote characters to be executed. The standard output of a command given between backquotes is substituted for the entire string (including the quotes). Unless the backquoted command itself appears inside a pair of double quotes, the command output is split into words at white space or at newline characters. If the command appears inside double quotes, only newline characters cause a split into separate words.

The seventh stage is filename expansion. The words in the command are scanned for the magic characters

       *   **?**   **{**   **[**

and appropriate expansions are performed. In addition, if the word begins with the tilde character (˜), the the name of the specified home directory is substituted.

Finally, the command is executed. *Csh* checks the first word on the line to see which command has been given. Many commands, such as *echo* and all the control flow commands, are handled directly by the shell. Three of these commands, namely the *if, while* and **@** commands, require *csh* to perform expression evaluation before execution of the command is completed. A command that is not built into the shell causes *csh* to search the directories in the $*path* list for a program with that name. If the program is found, the shell forks and the child process executes the program.

It is frequently necessary to prevent the shell from performing some or all of the expansions listed above. How, for example, could we use the *echo* command to print a line containing an asterisk? The command

```
echo ***    WAKEUP!!    ***
```

is quite incorrect because *csh* will perform both history and filename substitution. One mechanism to prevent a character from being treated as magic or special in some way is to precede it with a backslash character. Our example *echo* command could be written as

```
echo \*\*\*    WAKEUP\!\!    \*\*\*
```

and it will work. It, perhaps, does not work perfectly because *csh* does not preserve the original spacing of our message. Remember that the line is split into words at white space. If we use three spaces to separate two words, that fact is forgotten. The proper way to write the command is as

```
echo '***    WAKEUP\!\!    ***'
```

The single quote characters protect the enclosed text from being split into words and from all forms of expansion except history expansion. (Hence the need to retain backslash characters before the exclamation marks.)

If double quote characters are used, they protect the enclosed string only from being split into words at blanks and tabs. The string is still subject to all forms of expansion. Thus, we could personalize our sample *echo* command to include the name of the person at the terminal with

```
echo "\*\*\* WAKEUP $user\!\!    \*\*\*"
```

Finally, we should mention that the order in which the parsing and various expansions are performed may not suit our needs. If this is the case, it may be necessary to force *csh* to reprocess the line. Reprocessing is requested with the *eval* command. An example of its use appears in the next section.

B.10. SHELL SCRIPT FILES

Although all the commands described above can be entered at the terminal, many of them are sensibly used only within shell command files. A file that contains shell commands is called a *shell script* file. If you have such a file named "SCRIPT", say, you can execute the script with the command

```
csh SCRIPT
```

If you are developing a new script and you have trouble getting it to work properly, you can enable trace output. Using either command form

```
csh -x SCRIPT
```

or

```
csh -v SCRIPT
```

will cause each command line in the script to be printed after some expansions have been performed and before the shell actually tries to execute the command. The −x flag causes the line to be printed at the latest possible moment, whereas −v causes the line to be printed immediately after history substitution.

We will now introduce shell script programming with the help of a couple of examples.

B.10.1. Example of a Parameterless Script

A shell script for a program named ZAP is listed in Figure B.3. If this script is held in a file named "ZAP", then as mentioned earlier, we can execute the commands in the file by typing

csh ZAP

But if you prefer (and most people do), you can make the file executable by first executing the command

FIGURE B.3. Csh Script for ZAP

```
 1.    # csh shell script for zapping processes
 2.
 3.    set ps_out = "'ps g'"
 4.    @ i = 1
 5.
 6.    while ( $i < $#ps_out )
 7.    @   i ++
 8.        set line = ($ps_out[$i])
 9.        set proc_no = $line[1]
10.        if ($proc_no == $$) continue
11.
12.    RETRY:
13.        echo -n "Kill this process?  $line    "
14.        set ans = $<
15.        if ($ans =~ n* || $ans =~ N*) continue
16.        if ($ans =~ q* || $ans =~ Q*) break
17.        if ($ans =~ y* || $ans =~ Y*) then
18.            kill -9 $proc_no
19.        else
20.            echo 'Respond with y (yes), n (no) or q (quit)'
21.            goto RETRY
22.        endif
23.    end
```

```
chmod +x ZAP
```

and then you should be able to execute the commands in the file with the simpler command

```
ZAP
```

When the UNIX system tries to execute this file, it will discover that the file does not contain executable binary and report this back to your current shell. (UNIX checks for a *magic number* in the first two bytes.) The *csh* shell then looks to see what the first line of the file contains. If a *csh* comment is recognized, a new instance of *csh* is created and given the file to read.[10]

What does the ZAP shell script do? It finds out what active processes you have and then runs through these processes and asks you if you want to kill each one in turn. (You may occasionally find that you have a need for a script like this one.) We will now run through this shell script and explain all the mysteries in it.

For reasons just explained, the first line is a *csh* comment. The first executable command occurs in line 3 and invokes the *ps* program to obtain a list of all your processes. The output of *ps* when invoked from inside our shell script might look something like

```
PID TT STAT   TIME COMMAND
8609 h9 S     0:23 -csh (csh)
11258 h9 R    4:11 wild_program
11341 h9 I    0:00 csh ZAP
13342 h9 R    0:00 ps g
```

where the first process listed is your login shell, the second process is the one that you want to kill, the third process is a second instance of the shell that was created to run our script and the fourth process is the *ps* program itself. All this output replaces the string written with the backquote characters in the command line. Now this string is itself contained within double quote characters. The use of the double quotes is important to the shell script. If we had used the line

```
set ps_out = `ps g`
```

the output of *ps* would be broken up into words wherever there was white space (blanks, tabs or newline characters). With our sample output from *ps*, there would be twenty-eight words. However, when text is enclosed within double quotes, the shell splits the text into words only at newline characters. Thus, the command in the shell script will actually assign a list of five words to *ps_out* for our sample *ps* output. Of course, each of these words contains blanks and tabs.

---

[10] If you forget to begin your script with a *csh* comment, the shell will pass your file to an instance of the *sh* shell instead. This is likely to produce many strange error messages.

The remainder of the shell script is a loop to run through the second and subsequent words in the list held in *ps_out*. We use an index variable *i*, initialized in line 4, and a *while* loop, occupying lines 6 to 23, to sequence through these words. Instead of this particular method of controlling the loop, we might equally well have used the *foreach* construct. Lines 4 through 7 could be replaced with the one line

```
foreach i ( $ps_out[2-] )
```

We will now trace through the first iteration of the loop, assuming that *ps_out* was assigned the five words above.

Line 6:   This line is expanded by *csh* (as a result of variable substitution) to become

```
while ( 1 < 5 )
```

and, because the test evaluates to 1 (true), the loop body is executed.

Line 7:   This one simply increments *i*, to give it the value 2.

Line 8:   On the first loop iteration, this line expands to the command

```
set line = ( 8609 h9 S 0:23 -csh (csh) )
```

and so becomes a command which assigns a list of six words to *line*.

Line 9:   The first of the six words in *line* is picked out and assigned to *proc_no*. Thus, *proc_no* is given the value 8609, which is the process number of the login shell.

Line 10:   Here, we have a one-line *if* command which is expanded to

```
if ( 8609 == 11341 ) continue
```

($$ expands to the process number of the shell executing this script.) This test is provided so that our ZAP script does not permit the user to kill the instance of the shell that is executing ZAP. The test fails, so control continues past a *goto* label to the echo command.

Line 13:   The echo command outputs the line

```
Kill this process?   8609 h9 S 0:23 -csh (csh)
```

and leaves the cursor at the end of this line on the screen. (The -n flag suppresses the newline character that is normally output at the end of the echoed line.)

Line 14:   This line contains a construct, $< , which is a request for *csh* to read a line from its standard input. The user must type a line which *csh* will substitute for $< . This response is assigned to *ans*.

Lines 15
-22:
There are three lines of tests on the current value of *ans*. Pattern matching forms of comparisons are used so that our ZAP script will recognize *n*, *no* and even *no thankyou* as being equivalent ways of saying "no". A *no* response causes the *continue* command to be executed and this would cause *csh* to return to the top of the *while* construct. A *quit* response would cause the *while* loop to be immediately exited. A *yes* response would cause the *kill* program to be invoked. Any other response causes a line listing the valid responses to be printed and then control goes back to the *RETRY* label to prompt for a new response.

B.10.2. Example of a Script with Parameters

There are many applications for which we can use a shell script file instead of writing a special program in C. We could, for example, write a C program that is equivalent to the ZAP script. The only discernible difference to the user would be that a C code version of ZAP would execute much faster. But for applications that are infrequently used or for applications that are subject to change, a shell script may be the sensible way to attack the problem.

To make shell scripts as usable as C programs, there needs to be a facility for accessing command line arguments. This facility is provided by the shell variable *argv*, which is a list containing the arguments. The first argument can be accessed by writing `$argv[1]` or `${argv[1]}` and similarly for the other arguments. Alternatively, there is a shorter notation. `$1` is equivalent to `$argv[1]`, and so on. The notation `$*` is equivalent to `$argv[*]`, a list containing all the arguments. An example shell script with arguments is reproduced in Figure B.4. Our FORMAT script is designed for people who can never remember the correct order to run the various text preprocessors used on *troff* input. If your computer installation has *pic* (a preprocessor that lets you create pictures in your documents), you have a choice of at least three preprocessors to use. Of course, you could set up an alias that always runs all three preprocessors

```
alias FORMAT 'pic \!* | tbl | eqn | troff'
```

but this alias will not let you pass any options to *troff*. They would be given to *pic* instead. And there is a certain amount of inefficiency in invoking a preprocessor unnecessarily.

If the FORMAT script has been made executable with the command

```
chmod +x FORMAT
```

it can be invoked with commands like the following one:

```
FORMAT -T -o5- doc1 doc2
```

On this example, our shell script would set up and execute the following pipeline:

FIGURE B.4. The FORMAT Shell Script

```
# csh script to control 'troff'

set tropts = ()         # options for ntroff
set files = ()          # list of troff source files

foreach arg ($*)
    switch ($arg)

    case -P:            # run PIC processor
        set pic;  continue
    case -T:            # run TBL processor
        set tbl;  continue
    case -E:            # run EQN processor
        set eqn;  continue
    case -?*:           # troff options
        set tropts = ($tropts $arg)
        continue
    default:
        set files = ($files $arg)
        continue
    endsw
end

set cmd = ()
if ($?pic) then
    set cmd = (pic $files |); set files = ()
endif
if ($?tbl) then
    set cmd = ($cmd tbl $files |); set files = ()
endif
if ($?eqn) then
    set cmd = ($cmd eqn $files |); set files = ()
endif

eval "$cmd troff $tropts $files"
```

```
tbl doc1 doc2 | troff -o5-
```

We have used the flags, $-P$, $-T$ and $-E$, to indicate that *pic*, *tbl* and *eqn*, respectively, are to be applied to all source files provided as arguments. Any other flags are assumed to be meant for *troff*.

How does it work? We begin with a *foreach* loop which looks at every command line argument in turn. A *switch* statement tests for our preprocessor flags and remembers if any of them are seen. Any other flags are appended to a list built up in the *tropts* variable. Any arguments which do not look like flags are assumed to be file names and appended to a list built up in the *files* variables. After the loop, we run through each preprocessor in the order in which they should be applied and build up a command pipeline to process the file arguments. The pipeline is built as a list in the *cmd* variable. Finally, we append *troff* and any flags for *troff* to the end of *cmd* and execute the command that is now contained in the variable. The shell command *eval* is needed to make *csh* look at the line twice. Unless the shell is forced to process the line twice, it will not recognize the vertical bars as representing pipelines. It would, instead, pass the vertical bars as command line arguments to the first program listed in our pipeline. (This program would look for a file whose name consists of just the vertical bar character and report an error.)

B.11. THE .login AND .cshrc FILES

After you have become familiar with *csh*, you will undoubtedly find that there are several variables that you would like to set and several aliases that you would like to use. It would, of course, be inconvenient to have to type all the *set* and *alias* commands every time you log in. The obvious solution is to keep these commands in a file. So, if you have such a file named "my_aliases", say, how should you execute the commands in this file? If your answer to this question is to type the command

```
csh my_aliases
```

you are wrong. This command creates a new instance of *csh* to read and execute the commands. After *csh* has read the last line in the file, this instance of *csh* terminates and all the useful aliases are forgotten. Executing a new instance of *csh* simply has no effect on your login shell. And it does not help to make "my_aliases" executable because a new instance of *csh* will still be created to execute the commands.

The correct answer is to use the *source* command. If you enter the command

```
source my_aliases
```

the current shell will read the lines in the file as though you had typed them at the terminal.

But it is still a little inconvenient to have to type a command like

    `source my_aliases`

every time you log in or create another instance of the *csh* program. Therefore, there is another mechanism. If you have a file named ".cshrc" in your home directory then every time *csh* is invoked, it will begin by reading and executing the contents of this file. In addition, if this invocation of *csh* is your login shell, it will look for and read a file named ".login" in your home directory immediately after reading the ".cshrc" file (if there was one). A fairly typical pair of ".cshrc" and ".login" files are reproduced in Figures B.5 and B.6. It is a good idea to keep the ".cshrc" file as short as possible. New shell instances are created fairly often, and a long ".cshrc" file can slow down your work at the terminal quite noticeably. All work that need be done once only should be performed in the ".login" file. It should be noted that those shell variables which have corresponding environment variables (*term*, *path* and *user*) are automatically inherited by subshells. Therefore they do not have to be reset in ".cshrc". Similarly, environment variables are inherited too. They do not need to be reset either.

Our ".login" file may need a little explanation. The first part of the file is concerned with initializing tty modes and setting the *term* shell variable (and therefore setting the *TERM* environment variable too). The most important part of this process is invoking the *tset* program in order to make a guess at the kind of terminal in use. In our example, the arguments of *tset* have been set up so that if you log in at a baud rate greater than 1200, it will guess the terminal type to be a DEC VT100. Otherwise, it will guess a NEC spinwriter. (The question mark symbols cause *tset* to output its guess and wait for you to confirm the guess by hitting the return key or to override it by typing a different terminal type.) The result of the *tset* command is a terminal name which is used to set the shell variable *term* (and thus the environment variable *TERM*). Note that the shell variable *noglob* is set before invoking the *tset* program. When this variable is set, *csh* does not expand any wild card characters

FIGURE B.5. A Typical .cshrc File

```
# set up our favourite aliases
  alias ls      ls -F
  alias rm      rm -i

# initialize various shell variables
  set history=50 time=5
  set ignoreeof notify
```

FIGURE B.6. A Typical .login File

```
# initialize for our terminal type
  set noglob
  set term = 'tset - -e -m '>1200:?vt100' '?nec''
  unset noglob
  if ($term != nec) stty new crt
# initialize various shell variables
  set path=(~/bin /usr/ucb /bin /usr/bin .)
  set savehist=50
  set prompt='> '
  set mail=(60 /usr/spool/mail/$user)
# set environment variables used by misc. programs
  setenv EDITOR /usr/ucb/vi
  setenv MORE -c
# define an alias needed in the login shell
  alias off      logout
# check for system messages
  msgs -fp
# show current system load
  uptime
```

in command lines. Although it actually does not need to be set in our particular example, it is a wise precaution because arguments to *tset* frequently contain characters that are special to the shell. Our terminal initialization is completed by testing the terminal type, and if the terminal is not a spinwriter, we invoke the *stty* program to initialize the tty modes so that they will be suitable for a CRT terminal.

B.12. csh REFERENCE GUIDE

The remainder of this appendix contains several lists of commands, operators and variables that briefly summarize the *csh* command language. Some entries in these tables are not discussed elsewhere in this appendix. Further information can be obtained from the on-line manual entry for *csh*.

B.12.1. Special Characters in csh

Listed below are all the special characters that you should use with care in *csh* commands. The special meaning of most of these characters can be removed by using a backslash before the character. Note that characters that only have meanings within expressions (such as + and -) are not included.

\#   Start of a comment which continues up to the end of the line. A comment cannot be continued onto a second line. The first line of a *csh* script file should be a comment with the \# character in the first column.

@   Perform expression evaluation. The @ character must appear in the first character position of the command line.

\$ Access to the value of a shell variable or a test on a shell variable.

!   Access to an event in the history list or to an argument of an aliased command.

*   Wild card character in pattern matching or a range of list indexes.

?   Wild card character in pattern matching.

[Introduces a list of characters to match. A matching right square bracket character must be provided.

~   When used at the beginning of a word, a tilde causes expansion to the pathname of a home directory.

{   There are two uses. It may be used with a matching right brace to form a *string product* when generating a list of file names. For example, `abc{x,y,z}def` is expanded to the list of three words,
         `abcxdef abcydef abczdef`
Its other use, again with a matching right brace, is to test the termination status of an enclosed command. For example,
         `{cmp -s file1 file2}`
may be used within expressions as a subexpression with value 0, 1 or 2.

\\   The escape symbol to disable the meaning of a special character. It may also be used as the last character on a line to permit an overly long command to continue onto the next line.

&   Background command execution.

| Pipeline symbol.

<   I/O redirection symbol.

>   I/O redirection symbol.

;   Command terminator symbol. It terminates any command line except a comment.

(The left parenthesis must be matched with a right parenthesis. There are two uses. The parentheses are used to enclose commands that must be run in a subshell and they are also used for grouping operations within expressions.

'   A pair of single quote characters protects enclosed text from variable substitution and being split into words.

" A pair of double quote characters protects enclosed text from being split into words (except at embedded newline characters).

' A pair of backquote characters is used to enclose a command. When command substitution occurs, the output of the command replaces the quoted string.

B.12.2. I/O Redirection and Pipeline Operators

< *file*	Take standard input from *file*.
> *file*	Send standard output to *file*.
>> *file*	Append standard input to *file*.
>& *file*	Send both standard output and error output to the named *file*.
>>& *file*	Like >&, but append to *file*.
>! *file*	Like >, but report an error if *file* exists and *noclobber* is set.
>&! *file*	Like >!, but redirect both standard output and error output.
>>! *file*	Like >>, but report an error if *file* does *not* exist and *noclobber* is set.
>>&! *file*	Like >>!, but redirect both standard output and error output.
<< *word*	Redirect standard input of the program on the left to come from the command input of the shell, up to an input line which is identical to *word*. It is normal to have quotes around *word*, which stops *csh* from expanding the input lines.
|	Pipe standard output from program on left to standard input of program on right.
|&	Pipe both standard output and error output from program on left to program on right.

B.12.3. Shell Expressions

Shell expressions may appear in the *if, while* and @ commands. Expressions may contain the following string comparison operators

$$== \quad != \quad =\tilde{} \quad !\tilde{}$$

the following Boolean operators

$$! \quad \&\& \quad ||$$

the following integer operators

$$+ \quad - \quad * \quad / \quad \%$$

and the following bitwise integer operators

$$\tilde{} \quad \& \quad | \quad \hat{}$$

Parentheses may be used for grouping operations within an expression.

Expressions may include the following tests on files. To avoid confusion with the subtraction operator, it may be necessary to parenthesize these tests. The result of a test is 1 to indicate success or 0 to indicate failure.

−r *file*   Test if *file* can be read.

−w *file*   Test if *file* can be written to.

−x *file*   Test if *file* can be executed.

−d *file*   Test if *file* is a directory.

−e *file*   Test if *file* exists.

−o *file*   Test if you are the owner of *file*.

−z *file*   Test if *file* is empty.

−f *file*   Test if *file* is an ordinary file, that is, not a directory, not a character special and not a block special file.

Finally, it is possible to execute a command and use the status code set by that command within an expression. An example of a command which sets the status code in a useful way is *cmp*. You can use the construction

```
{ cmp −s file1 file2 }
```

as a component of an expression. The value of this subexpression will be 0 if the two files are identical and 1 otherwise. However, it is probably a better idea to run a program in a separate command line and to test the status code set by this program by using the *status* shell variable.

B.12.4. Special Shell Variables

$$ Contains the process number of the shell.

$<   An input line read from the standard input of the shell and supplied as the value of this variable.

$argv   A list of command line arguments to the shell.

$cdpath   A list of directories to search for subdirectories if the *cd* command cannot find the subdirectory in the current working directory.

$cwd   The pathname of the current working directory.

$echo   Causes command lines to be echoed after all expansions have occurred but before execution.

$history   The number of commands remembered by the history mechanism.

$home   The pathname of the home directory.

`$ignoreeof`	Disables end-of-file (^D) from terminals as a means of terminating the shell.
`$mail`	Controls the frequency of checks for new mail and gives the names of files to check for mail.
`$noclobber`	Prevents > redirections from destroying existing files and >> from using non-existent files.
`$noglob`	Disables filename expansions.
`$nonomatch`	Disables error reporting when filename expansion fails to match any file.
`$notify`	Causes *csh* to report completion of a background job as soon as the event occurs.
`$path`	Provides a list of directories that *csh* searches for executable programs.
`$prompt`	Contains the command prompt string.
`$savehist`	Specifies the number of commands to be remembered as history from one login session to the next.
`$shell`	The file containing the shell program.
`$status`	The completion status of the last command. Normally, zero means that the last command was successful and non-zero implies that it was unsuccessful.
`$time`	Causes a summary of resource utilization to be printed for any job that uses more than $*time* CPU seconds.
`$verbose`	Causes command lines to be echoed after history substitution has occurred.

B.12.5. Control Flow Commands

`if (`*expr* `) command`	Conditional execution of *command*, which must be a simple command.

`if (`*expr* `) then`
    commands
`else if (`*expr* `) then`
    commands
`else`
    commands
`endif`
	Conditional execution of groups of commands.

```
while (expr )
     commands                    Conditional repetition of commands.
end
```

```
foreach vrbl (list )            Definite repetition of commands with an index
     commands                   variable, vrbl, that takes on successive values
end                             from list.
```

```
break                          Exit from an enclosing while or foreach loop.
```

```
continue                       Return to the top of an enclosing while or
                               foreach loop.
```

```
switch(string )
case pattern:
     commands
     breaksw
case pattern:                  Selection among groups of commands accord-
                               ing to the results of successively matching
         .                     string against case label patterns.
         .
default:
     commands
endsw
```

```
repeat count command           Repeatedly execute command count times.
                               The command must be simple.
```

```
goto label                     Unconditional transfer to label.
```

```
onintr label
```
Transfer to label if an interrupt occurs. If *label* is omitted from this command, all interrupts will be ignored. If a minus sign character is used instead of *label*, default handling of interrupts is restored.

label:

Define a *label* used as a target of *goto* and *onintr* commands. The label definition must appear on a line by itself.

B.12.6. Shell Commands for Directory Management

The current working directory provides the starting point for relative path-names used in references to files. *Csh* keeps track of your working directory in the variable $*cwd* and provides commands (*cd* or *chdir*) to change the working directory. *Csh* actually maintains a stack of working directories. The top element of this stack (with position number 0) is the current working directory. Two commands to manipulate this directory stack are provided.

In addition, *csh* maintains two lists of directories. One list, $*path*, contains the names of all the directories that should be searched to find an executable program. Because searches for programs are very frequent, *csh* compiles a hash table which lists all the programs in the search path. This hash table is compiled when the shell is started. For the most part, you need not be aware that command searches are being implemented as hash table look-ups. The exception arises if new programs are added to any directories in your search path. If this happens, *csh* will be unaware of the existence of these programs and will fail to find them. Therefore, the *rehash* command is provided to force *csh* to recompile its hash table. A second list of directories can be held in the variable $*cdpath*. If the *cd* (or *chdir*) command cannot find the specified subdirectory in the current directory, it will search all the directories named in $*cdpath* for it.

A list of all the commands associated with the management of directories is as follows:

cd
: Change working directory to $*home*. (*chdir* is an alternate command name for *cd*.)

cd *name*
: Change working directory to *name*. (*chdir* is an alternate command name for *cd*.)

dirs
: Print the directory stack.

popd
: Pop the directory stack.

popd +*n*
: Delete the *n*-th entry in the directory stack.

pushd
: Exchange the top 2 elements in the directory stack.

pushd *name*
: Push *name* onto the directory stack.

pushd +*n*
: Exchange the *n*-th entry with the top entry of the directory stack.

rehash
: Recompile the hash table of programs in the $*path* list of directories. This command is required after you have added new programs to any of the directories in $*path*. (Otherwise the shell will say that these programs cannot be found when you try to use them.)

hashstat
: Print hash table statistics.

unhash   Stop using hash table searching for commands. This means
                that *csh* takes longer to invoke a command, but you no longer
                need to execute *rehash* every time you add a new program to
                a library on your search path.

B.12.7. Commands for Job Control

bg   Put current job into background.

bg %*job*   Resume the specified job in the background. The same effect
                can be achieved by just typing %*job* &

fg   Bring current job into foreground.

fg %*job*   Bring specified job into foreground. The same effect can be
                achieved by just typing %*job*

history   Print the history list.

jobs   List all active jobs.

kill %*job*   Send the TERM (terminate) signal to the specified job.

kill -9 %*job*   Definitely kill the specified job.

notify   Report when the current job terminates.

notify %*job*   Report when the specified job terminates.

stop   Stop the current job.

stop %*job*   Stop the specified job.

wait   Wait for all background jobs to complete before reading and
                executing another command.

B.12.8. Other Shell Commands

alias   List all aliases in effect.

alias *name*   List any alias for *name*.

alias *name wordlist* Set an alias for *name*.

unalias *pattern*   Remove all aliases with names matching *pattern*.

echo *wordlist*   Print the arguments on the standard output.

echo -n *wordlist*   Print the arguments without a terminating newline.

eval *wordlist*   Reparse and execute *wordlist* as a command.

exit   Exit from the shell with termination status 0.

exit(*expr*)   Exit from the shell with status *expr*.

login   Terminate the current (login) shell and login again.

logout   Terminate a login shell.

`set`	Print the values of all shell variables. Just typing the at symbol (`@`) as a command by itself has the same effect.
`set` *name*	Set the value of *name* to be an empty list.
`set` *name=word*	Set the value of *name* to be *word*. The same effect is achieved with the command form

$$@name{=}expr$$

set *name=(wordlist)*	Set the value of *name* to be a list.
`set` *name*[*index*]*=word*	
	Change the value of one list element. (*name* must have a list value and *index* must be a valid index.) The same effect is achieved with the command form

$$@\ name[index]{=}expr$$

`unset` *pattern*	Unset all variables whose names match *pattern*.
`setenv` *name value*	Set the specified environment variable.
`unsetenv` *pattern*	Unset all environment variables whose names match *pattern*.
`shift`	Delete the first element of the *argv* list (in effect, shifting the list left).
`shift` *variable*	Delete the first element of the *variable* list.
`source` *file*	Read and execute shell commands contained in *file*.
`suspend`	Suspend the current shell (which cannot be a login shell).
`time`	Summarize CPU time usage of this shell and all its child processes.
`time` *command*	Report CPU time usage of *command*.
`umask`	Print the value of the current file creation mask.
`umask` *value*	Set the file creation mask to *value*. When *csh* creates a file as a result of an I/O redirection, it uses the *umask* value to set the access permissions on the new file.

FURTHER READING

- William Joy, "An Introduction to the C Shell." Supplementary documentation supplied with Berkeley UNIX 4.2bsd system, July 1983.

- "*Csh* On-Line Manual Entry." Berkeley UNIX 4.2bsd system, July 1983. This must be the longest and most detailed manual entry in the system. You should be able to print your own copy with the command

```
nroff -man -Tlpr /usr/man/man1/csh.1 | lpr
```

APPENDIX C

AN EXTENDED BNF
DEFINITION FOR C

C.1. WHAT IS BEING DEFINED

When the *cc* command is invoked to compile a C source file, the file is first processed by the C preprocessor. It is the result of the preprocessing that is actually compiled to produce binary object code. The syntactic definition of C given in this appendix describes the structure of the C program *after* it has been processed by the preprocessor. Consequently, you will not see symbols like #define appearing anywhere in our definition.

C.2. INTRODUCTION TO BNF NOTATION

Our syntactic notation is an extended version of BNF. In case you have not encountered BNF (Backus-Naur Form) notation before, we begin with a short introduction. You should not find BNF notation to be difficult to read, but a reasonable amount of familiarity is necessary before you will properly appreciate the full implications of all the grammatical rules.

A BNF description for a language is comprised of a number of grammatical rules or *production rules*. For an example, let us consider how we might define the structure of an **if** statement in C. In BNF notation, we would write down one or more lines that look somewhat like equations. We might write the following:

$$<\text{if statement}> \quad ::= \quad \textbf{if} \ `(' \ <\text{expression}> \ `)'$$
$$<\text{statement}> \ <\text{else part}>$$
$$<\text{else part}> \quad ::= \quad <\text{empty}>$$
$$| \ \texttt{else} \ <\text{statement}>$$

The concept or language construct that we wish to describe is the **if** statement. In our example, this construct is named by the symbol *<if statement>*. The symbol is technically known as a *non-terminal* symbol. In BNF notation, non-terminal symbols are always written as one or more English words enclosed by angle brackets. Our first line, above, defines an instance of *<if statement>* to consist of six items. It consists of the keyword **if** followed by a left parenthesis followed by an instance of an *<expression>* followed by an instance of a *<statement>* followed by an instance of an *<else part>*. The keyword **if** and the parentheses are symbols that actually appear in a C program; they are known as *terminal symbols*. In contrast, *<expression>*, *<statement>* and *<else part>* are non-terminal symbols which themselves require BNF definitions. To keep the example reasonably short, we have given a definition only for *<else part>*. A complete C grammar would contain definitions for all the non-terminal symbols that are ever used in the grammar.

Our example of a definition for *<else part>* illustrates another aspect of the BNF notation. As you may know, the else-part of an **if** statement is optional in C. Thus, there are two choices for what an *<else part>* might be. It might be absent, in which case, the right-hand side of the definition is empty. Rather than leave a blank line, we explicitly show the emptiness with the special symbol *<empty>*. The other possibility for an *<else part>* is that it might consist of the keyword **else** followed by an instance of a *<statement>*. The two alternatives for *<else part>* are separated by a vertical bar, "|". When you read grammar rules to yourself or out loud, you might like to read the BNF symbol "::=" as the English word "is" and read the symbol "|" as the English word "or".

We have adopted some typographical conventions that are intended to make the production rules easier to read. A character or character pair used as an operator or punctuation symbol of the C language (such as an addition symbol or a semicolon) is enclosed in quotation marks. A keyword of the C language, which is another kind of terminal symbol, is not enclosed in quotes. It is, however, printed in a distinctive type face (that used for all program examples throughout the book). Non-terminal symbols are easily recognizable because their names are always enclosed in angle brackets. The terminal symbols for an identifier and for the various constants of C (such as integer constants and so on) are exceptional because we also write them as names enclosed by angle brackets. If, for example, we were to use the printed form

```
identifier
```

one might object that it would imply the existence of a C keyword named

identifier. Therefore it is written as

$$<\text{identifier}>$$

Similarly, the various kinds of constants in the C language are written as

$<\text{int const}>$ $<\text{float const}>$

$<\text{character const}>$ $<\text{string const}>$

The BNF notation has been extended in two ways. We use square brackets to enclose an optional symbol or group of symbols, and we use curly braces to enclose a symbol or group of symbols that may be repeated zero or more times. As an example of the use of square brackets, we can simplify our definition of the **if** statement to just one grammar rule:

$$<\text{if statement}> \quad ::= \quad \texttt{if} \;\; \text{'('} <\text{expression}> \text{')'} <\text{statement}>$$
$$[\;\; \texttt{else} <\text{statement}> \;\;]$$

As an example of the use of curly braces, we can define a list of statements in C as follows:

$$<\text{stmt list}> \quad ::= \quad \{ \; <\text{statement}> \; \}$$

This single rule says that a statement list (represented by the non-terminal symbol *$<$stmt list$>$*), is comprised of zero or more instances of the *$<$statement$>$* construct.

C.3. THE OVERALL STRUCTURE

The input to the C compiler (after preprocessing) must consist of a sequence of zero or more global definitions. These are definitions of names that will be visible throughout the source file and can only be hidden if there happen to be declarations for objects with the same name inside some function.

C.3.1. Global Definitions

There are three main possibilities for a global definition (*$<$global def$>$*). The first possibility is to introduce a new type without declaring any variables with that type (as when a structure is being defined); a second possibility is to define variables and their types or to declare the result types of functions; and the third possibility is to define a function in full, giving both the result type and the function body.

$$<\text{goal}> \quad ::= \quad \{ \; <\text{global def}> \; \}$$
$$<\text{global def}> \quad ::= \quad [\; <\text{attributes}> \;] \; \text{';'}$$
$$| \; [\; <\text{attributes}> \;] \; <\text{init dcl list}> \; \text{';'}$$
$$| \; [\; <\text{attributes}> \;] \; <\text{function def}>$$

C.3.2. Function Definitions

A function definition, *<function def>*, consists of a heading (*<fn declarator>*) that gives the function type and names the formal parameters, followed by the function body. The function body (*function_body*) consists of zero or more declarations for the formal parameters, followed by a compound statement (*<compound stmt>*). A compound statement is formed from a sequence of local declarations and a list of executable statements, all enclosed within curly braces.

<function def>   ::=   <fn declarator> <function body>

<function body>   ::=   <formal decls> <compound stmt>

<compound stmt>   ::=   '{' <local decls> <stmt list> '}'

<local decls>   ::=   { <attributes> [<init dcl list>] ';' }

<formal decls>   ::=   { <attributes>
                        [<declarator list>] ';' }

C.3.3. Basic Declaration Attributes

A declaration normally begins with a basic data type (like **int**) and may be modified by a storage class adjective (such as **register**). The type information and storage class information can be combined in various ways to form attribute combinations that are legal in declarations.

Up to three basic type attributes may be combined, as in the data type **unsigned short int**. A storage class may intermingled, as in the data type **unsigned register int**. Note that **typedef** does not really denote a storage class in the same way that **register** does, but this is the most convenient place in the grammar to introduce the construct. The **fortran** class appears to have no use and is completely undocumented.[1]

<attributes>   ::=   [<type>] <class> [<type>]
                    | <type>

<class>   ::=   register
                    | static
                    | extern
                    | fortran
                    | auto
                    | typedef

---

[1] It does have an effect in that if it is supplied as an attribute on a function it can cause different parameter setup code to be emitted (but code that is unsuitable for linking to FORTRAN77 subroutines.)

```
<type>          ::=     <attribute> [ <attribute> ]
                        [ <attribute> ]
                    |   <struct dcl>
                    |   <enum dcl>

<attribute>     ::=     unsigned
                    |   short
                    |   long
                    |   int
                    |   float
                    |   double
                    |   char
                    |   void
```

C.3.4. Data Declarations with Storage Initialization

The non-terminal *<init dcl list>* represents a sequence of declarations for variables or declarations of result types of functions. Each declaration in the sequence is represented by the non-terminal *<declarator>* in the grammar, below. This non-terminal is shown as having two possible expansions. It can be a declaration of a function result type (*<fn declarator>*) or it can be a declaration of a variable (*<var declarator>*) with optional initialization.

The storage initialization part of a declaration consists of a list of values enclosed within braces. To permit initialization of arrays of structures, etc., these lists of values may be nested.

```
<init dcl list>     ::=     <init declarator>
                            { ',' <init declarator> }
<init declarator>   ::=     <fn declarator>
                        |   <var declarator> [ '=' <initializer> ]
<init list>         ::=     <initializer> { ',' <initializer> }
<initializer>       ::=     <const expr>
                        |   '{' <init list> [ ',' ] '}'
```

C.3.5. Function Types

A declaration for the result type of a function, represented by the non-terminal *<fn declarator>*, begins with a type specification for the result of the function. This type specification may begin with some basic attributes, such as **int**, and may then continue with a further definition for the function type. For example, here is the beginning of a function definition:

```
struct list_tag *next_element( list )
```

The basic type **struct list_tag** corresponds to the non-terminal *<attributes>* in the grammar. The remainder of the function heading provides the rest of the information. Its structure is defined by the non-terminal *<fn declarator>*.

The same non-terminal is also used in declarations of a function type, as in these declarations:

```
extern char *malloc(), *strcat();
```

The first three possibilities for *<fn declarator>* apparently permit functions to return pointers, functions, or arrays. However, this is not strictly correct. It is illegal for a C function to return a function or an array result directly. There are restrictions, not incorporated into the syntax rules, that only permit functions or arrays to be returned indirectly. For example, a result type of *pointer to array* is legal.

The fourth possibility for *<fn declarator>* provides parenthesization within function type definitions, as in the declaration

```
extern void (*doodah)();
```

which declares *doodah* to be a pointer to a function that returns no result.

> \<fn declarator\>   ::=   '*' \<fn declarator\>
> | \<fn declarator\> '(' ')'
> | \<fn declarator\>
>   '[' [\<const expr\>] ']'
> | '(' \<fn declarator\> ')'
> | \<identifier\> '(' [\<identifier\>
>   { ',' \<identifier\> }] ')'

C.3.6. Type Declarations

A type declaration normally declares the types for one or more program identifiers. The non-terminal *<declarator list>* represents a list of the identifiers that are being declared. This list is shown as being optional as in

```
enum colours { red, green blue };
```

where we are introducing a new **enum** tag identifier. Similarly, we may wish to introduce a **struct** or **union** tag identifier without declaring any objects with the **struct** or **union** type.

> \<type declaration\>   ::=   \<type\> [\<declarator list\>]
>
> \<declarator list\>   ::=   \<declarator\> { ',' \<declarator\> }

Each identifier that is being declared is included in the *<declarator>* construct. There are three possibilities shown below. The first alternative provides for the declaration of the return type of a function, as in this declaration for *sprintf*:

```
char *sprintf(), nextch;
```

The second possibility provides for declarations of variables, as with the declaration of *nextch* in the example, above. The non-terminal $<var\ declarator>$ (for non-function declarator), represents the declaration of a single variable. The third possibility is legal only for declarations of fields inside a **struct** or **union** type. It represents a *bit field*.

> $<$declarator$>$ ::= $<$fn declarator$>$
> | $<$var declarator$>$
> | [$<$var declarator$>$] ':' $<$const expr$>$

The syntax of $<var\ declarator>$ mirrors the syntax for $<fn\ declarator>$, seen earlier. The first three alternatives cover pointers, pointers to functions and arrays. The fourth alternative introduces parenthesization in the declaration. Finally, the name of the variable is given in the last alternative.

> $<$var declarator$>$ ::=   '*' $<$var declarator$>$
> | $<$var declarator$>$ '(' ')'
> | $<$var declarator$>$
> '[' [$<$const expr$>$] ']'
> | '(' $<$var declarator$>$ ')'
> | $<$identifier$>$

C.3.7. Enumeration Types

The first alternative for an enumeration declaration, given below, references an enumeration type that has been defined earlier in the program. The other form introduces a new enumeration type. The enumeration tag identifier ($<enum\ tag>$) is needed only if this enumeration type will be referenced again later in the program. The definition consists of a list of identifiers, representing the constants of this enumeration type. Optionally, the internal integer representation for any enumeration constant may be specified. It is specified by following the identifier by the assignment operator and an integer constant (or an expression which can evaluate to an integer). Note that the actual PCC syntax permits a redundant extra comma at the end of the list of enumeration constants. This possibility is not shown in our syntax rules.

> $<$enum dcl$>$ ::=   **enum** $<$enum tag$>$
> | **enum** [$<$enum tag$>$]
> '{' $<$enum const list$>$ '}'
>
> $<$enum tag$>$ ::= $<$identifier$>$

$$<\text{enum const list}> \quad ::= \quad <\text{enum const}>$$
$$\{ \text{ ',' } <\text{enum const}> \}$$
$$<\text{enum const}> \quad ::= \quad <\text{identifier}> \ [\text{ '=' } <\text{const expr}> \ ]$$

C.3.8. Structure and Union Declarations

Declarations for structures and unions are identical, except for the introductory keyword. The first form of declaration for a structure type and the first form for a union type reference a structure or union type that has been previously defined. The other forms of declaration serve to introduce a new structure or union type. The tag identifier is needed only if this structure type or union type will be referenced again later in the program. The fields of the structure or union are defined by a list of declarations enclosed within curly braces. The production rules, below, imply that each such declaration must be terminated by a semicolon. In fact, the C compiler permits the last semicolon before the right brace to be omitted (perhaps as a concession to PASCAL programmers).

$$<\text{struct dcl}> \quad ::= \quad \textbf{struct} \ <\text{structure tag}>$$
$$| \ \textbf{union} \ <\text{union tag}>$$
$$| \ \textbf{struct} \ [\ <\text{structure tag}> \ ]$$
$$\text{'\{'} \ <\text{type dcl list}> \ \text{'\}'}$$
$$| \ \textbf{union} \ [\ <\text{union tag}> \ ]$$
$$\text{'\{'} \ <\text{type dcl list}> \ \text{'\}'}$$
$$<\text{structure tag}> \quad ::= \quad <\text{identifier}>$$
$$<\text{union tag}> \quad ::= \quad <\text{identifier}>$$
$$<\text{type dcl list}> \quad ::= \quad <\text{type declaration}> \ \text{';'}$$
$$\{ \ <\text{type declaration}> \ \text{';'} \}$$

C.4. EXECUTABLE STATEMENTS

A statement list ($<stmt\ list>$) consists of zero or more statements. Any statement may be prefixed with labels. Such a label may be a label referenced in some **goto** statement or, within a **switch** statement, it may be a **case** label or the special label **default**.

The various possibilities for an unlabelled statement are listed below. To start with, any expression followed by a semicolon forms a statement. In this way, an assignment may be written as a statement. Secondly, a compound statement (a group of local declarations and executable statements enclosed in curly braces) is a legal statement. All the other types of statement follow the compound statement alternative in the rules listed below.

```
<stmt list>    ::=   { <statement> }
<statement>    ::=   { <label> }  <unlab stmt>
<unlab stmt>   ::=   <expr> ';'
                   | <compound stmt>
                   | if '(' <expr> ')'
                     <statement> [ else <statement> ]
                   | while '(' <expr> ')' <statement>
                   | do <statement>
                     while '(' <expr> ')' ';'
                   | for '(' [ <expr> ] ';' [ <expr> ] ';'
                     [ <expr> ] ')' <statement>
                   | switch '(' <expr> ')' <statement>
                   | break ';'
                   | continue ';'
                   | return [ <expr> ] ';'
                   | goto <identifier> ';'
                   | ';'
<label>        ::=   <identifier> ':'
                   | case <const expr> ':'
                   | default ':'
<const expr>   ::=   <expr>
```

C.5. EXPRESSIONS

There are many operators in the C language and these operators are subdivided into many levels of precedence. It would be possible to provide grammar rules for expressions that incorporate precedence levels and associativity rules for the operators. But rather than do this, our grammar rules treat all binary operators and all unary operators uniformly. To decompose an expression that contains more than one operator properly, it is necessary to refer to the table of operators given at the end of Chapter 2.

C.5.1. Binary Operators

There are thirty binary operators and one ternary operator listed in the syntax rules below. The ternary operator, corresponding to a conditional expression (using the ? and : symbol combination), is included among the binary operators, below. Note that variations on the assignment operator, such as +=, are actually defined in the grammar as two separate terminal symbols. Thus it is legal to write += with an intervening space as + = or even as + /*comment*/ =.

```
<expr>        ::=   <expr>  <binary op>  <expr>
                |  <term>
<binary op>   ::=  '<'  |  '<='  |  '>'  |  '>='
                |  ','  |  '/'  |  '%'  |  '+'
                |  '−'  |  '<<'  |  '>>'  |  '*'
                |  '=='  |  '!='  |  '&'  |  '|'
                |  '^'  |  '&&'  |  '||'
                |  '='  |  '+' '='  |  '−' '='
                |  '*' '='  |  '/' '='  |  '%' '='
                |  '<<' '='  |  '>>' '='  |  '&' '='
                |  '|' '='  |  '^' '='
                |  '?'  <expr>  ':'
```

C.5.2. Unary Operators

There are two kinds of unary operator provided in the C language, prefix operators and postfix operators. Some constructs, such as array indexing and function invocation, are also included among our syntax rules. This situation is not unreasonable because the operation of indexing an array is a kind of postfix operation.

```
<term>        ::=   <term>  <unary postfix op>
                |  <unary prefix op>  <term>
                |  '('  <cast type>  ')'  <term>
                |  <term>  '['  <expr>  ']'
                |  <term>  '('
                   [ <expr>  { ','  <expr> } ]  ')'
                |  <term>  '.'  <identifier>
                |  <term>  '->'  <identifier>
                |  <factor>
<unary postfix op>  ::=  '++'  |  '−−'
<unary prefix op>   ::=  '*'  |  '&'  |  '−'
                |  '!'  |  '~'  |  '++'
                |  '−−'  |  sizeof
```

C.5.3. Variables and Constants

The basic constituents of expressions are either identifiers (usually representing variables) or constants. These possibilities are listed below for the non-terminal *<factor>*. In addition, a *<factor>* may be a parenthesized expression.

```
<factor>      ::=    <identifier>
              |    <int const>
              |    <float const>
              |    <character const>
              |    <string const>
              |    sizeof '(' <cast type> ')'
              |    '(' <expr> ')'
```

C.5.4. Type Specifications used in Casts

The syntax for a type specification has been defined earlier, as part of a variable or function declaration. However, a separate syntactic definition is needed for the form of a type specification used by the *cast* operator. The syntax is different because no variable name or function name appears in the specification. This special form of type specification corresponds to the non-terminal *<cast type>* in our grammar.

```
<cast type>    ::=    <type>  <null decl>
<null decl>    ::=    <empty>
               |    '(' ')'
               |    '(' <null decl> ')' '(' ')'
               |    '*' <null decl>
               |    <null decl> '[' [ <const expr> ] ']'
               |    '(' <null decl> ')'
```

FURTHER READING

- S.P. Harbison and G.L. Steele Jr. *C: A Reference Manual.* Englewood Cliffs, N.J.: Prentice-Hall, 1984. This book contains a grammar for C in a form more suitable for compiler implementers. It is in LALR(1) form to be precise. The book also explains many details of the C language that have not been fully covered here (on the grounds that these details are too technical).

APPENDIX D

LIBRARY FUNCTIONS

D.1. INPUT-OUTPUT

D.1.1. Stream Input-Output

The directive

        #include <stdio.h>

should appear in your program if you wish to use any of the functions listed below.

clearerr(fp)	reset error indication for stream fp.
fclose(fp)	close stream fp.
fdopen(fd, m)	open a stream in mode m corresponding to file descriptor fd.
feof(fp)	test for end-of-file on stream fp.
ferror(fp)	test for error indication on stream fp.
fflush(fp)	flush buffered output for stream fp.
fgetc(fp)	read one character from stream fp.
fgets(s, n, fp)	read one line, up to n-1 bytes, into array s from stream fp.
fileno(fp)	return file descriptor for stream fp.
fopen(s, m)	open file s with I/O mode m.
fprintf($fp, s, a, \ldots$)	
	output a ..., according to format s on stream fp.

fputc(*fp*, *c*)   output character *c* on stream *fp*.

fputs(*s*, *fp*)   output string *s* on stream *fp*.

fread(*a*, *m*, *n*, *fp*)
     read *n* items with size *m* bytes from stream *fp* into array *a*.

freopen(*s*, *m*, *fp*)
     close stream *fp* and then reopen for file *s* in I/O mode *m*.

fscanf(*fp*, *s*, &*a*, ...)
     input values from stream *fp* into variables *a* ... according to format *s*.

fseek(*fp*, *n*, *m*)   reposition stream *fp* to an offset of *n* bytes relative to position defined by *m*.

ftell(*fp*)   return current offset within file *fp*.

fwrite(*a*, *m*, *n*, *fp*)
     output *n* items of size *m* bytes from array *a* to stream *fp*.

getc(*fp*)   read one character from stream *fp*.

getchar()   read one character from *stdin*.

gets(*s*)   read one line from *stdin* into character array *s*.

getw(*fp*)   read one word (4 bytes) from stream *fp*.

printf(*s*, *a*, ...)
     formatted output on *stdout*.

putc(*fp*, *c*)   output character *c* on stream *fp*.

putchar(*c*)   output character *c* on *stdout*.

puts(*s*)   output string *s* on *stdout*.

putw(*i*, *fp*)   output one word (4 bytes), *i*, on stream *fp*.

rewind(*fp*)   reposition to beginning of file *fp*.

scanf(*s*, &*a*, ...)
     formatted input from *stdin* into variables *a*, ...

setbuf(*fp*, *a*)   force use of array *a* as a buffer for stream *fp*.

setbuffer(*fp*, *a*, *n*)
     force use of array *a* with size *n* bytes as a buffer for stream *fp*.

setlinebuf(*fp*)
     force line buffering for stream *fp*.

sprintf(*b*, *s*, *a*, ...)
     format arguments *a* ... according to format *s* and copy the string into character array *b*.

`sscanf`($b, s, \&a, \ldots$)

> read values from the character array b according to format s and assign to arguments a ...

`ungetc`(c, fp)   unread character c on stream fp.

D.1.2. General Input-Output

`access`(p, m)   test accessability of the file with pathname p in mode m.

`chdir`(p)   change working directory to the directory with pathname p.

`chmod`(p, m)   change access modes of the file with pathname p to m.

`link`($p1, p2$)   create a hard link, with pathname $p2$, to the file which has pathname $p1$.

`mkdir`(p, m)   make a new directory with pathname p and mode m.

`rename`($p1, p2$)   rename the file with pathname $p1$ to have pathname $p2$.

`rmdir`(p)   remove the directory with pathname p.

`truncate`(p, n)   truncates the file with pathname p to n bytes maximum size.

`unlink`(p)   delete the file with pathname p.

D.1.3. Low-level Input-Output

The directive

        `#include <sys/files.h>`

is needed for flag values to some of the functions listed below to be defined as preprocessor constants.

`close`(fd)   close the file with descriptor fd.

`dup`(fd)   duplicate file descriptor fd in lowest numbered empty slot.

`dup2`(nfd, fd)   duplicate file descriptor fd in the slot with index nfd.

`fcntl`(fd, r, a)   obtain information about or alter the state of file descriptor fd. The include file "fcntl.h" contains suitable definitions for use as the request code r. The meaning of the integer argument a depends on r.

`fsync`(fd)   force pending output on the file with descriptor fd to be sent to disk.

`ftruncate`(fd, n)

> truncates the file with descriptor fd to n bytes maximum size.

`getdtablesize`()

> return the size of the object descriptor table.

`ioctl`(fd, r, a)   test or change I/O processing characteristics of the file that has descriptor fd. The include file "sys/ioctl.h" defines the request codes usable for argument r. The third argument is the address of a buffer used for parameters.

`lseek`(fd, n, k)   reposition the file referenced by descriptor fd to offset n. The kind of offset is determined by k.

`open`(p, f, m)   open a file with pathname p according to flags f. If a new file is created, its mode is m.

`read`(fd, b, n)   read n bytes into buffer b from the file with descriptor fd.

`umask`(m)   set file creation mask to m.

`write`(fd, b, n)   write n bytes from buffer b to the file with descriptor fd.

D.2. MEMORY MANAGEMENT

`brk`(a)   resets the end of the data area to have address a (rounded up to a page boundary).

`calloc`(n, m)   returns the address of a block of storage, cleared to zeros, suitable for holding n objects of size m bytes each.

`free`(p)   releases storage, with address p, that was previously obtained via *malloc* or *calloc*.

`malloc`(n)   returns the address of a new block of memory with size n bytes beginning on a word boundary.

`sbrk`(n)   increases the size of the data area by n bytes and returns the address of the new storage.

D.3. STRING HANDLING

If the directive

        `#include <strings.h>`

appears in your program, suitable definitions for the following functions will be included.

`strcat`(ts, ss)   catenate string ss onto target string ts.

`strncat`(ts, ss, n)

        catenate at most n bytes of ss onto ts.

`strcmp`($s1, s2$)   compare strings $s1$ and $s2$.

`strncmp`($s1, s2, n$)

        compare at most n bytes of $s1$ and $s2$.

`strcpy`(ts, ss)   copy string ss into target string ts.

`strncpy`(ts, ss, n)

        copy at most n bytes of ss to ts.

`strlen(s)`   return length of string *s*.

`index(s, c)`   return pointer to first occurrence of character *c* in string *s*.

`rindex(s, c)`   return pointer to last occurrence of character *c* in string *s*.

`atof(s)`   convert string *s* to a floating-point (**double**) value.

`atoi(s)`   convert string *s* to an **int** value.

`atol(s)`   convert string *s* to an **long int** value.

D.4. CHARACTER TESTING AND CONVERSION

To use these functions, the directive

```
#include <ctype.h>
```

must appear in the program. This is because all the functions are actually defined as macros.

`isalpha(c)`   tests if *c* is alphabetic.

`isalnum(c)`   tests if *c* is alphanumeric.

`isupper(c)`   tests if *c* is an upper-case letter.

`islower(c)`   tests if *c* is a lower-case letter.

`isdigit(c)`   tests if *c* is a decimal digit.

`isxdigit(c)`   tests if *c* is a hexadecimal digit.

`isspace(c)`   tests if *c* is blank, tab or newline.

`ispunct(c)`   tests if *c* is a punctuation symbol.

`isprint(c)`   tests if *c* is a printable character.

`isascii(c)`   tests if *c* is an ASCII character.

`iscntrl(c)`   tests if *c* is a control character.

`toupper(c)`   translates the lower-case letter *c* to upper-case.

`tolower(c)`   translates the upper-case letter *c* to lower-case.

`toascii(c)`   forces *c* into the ASCII character set (by clearing its leftmost bit to zero).

D.5. PROCESS HANDLING

D.5.1. Process Management

`alarm(s)`   causes a SIGALRM signal to be generated after *s* seconds. The previous interval to an alarm signal is returned.

`execl(n, a0, a1..., 0)`
  replaces current process with a new process executing file *n* with arguments *a0*, *a1* ...

execle(*n*, *a0*, *a1* . . . , 0, *ep*)
> is like *execl* but provides environment *ep* as well.

execlp(*n*, *a0*, *a1* . . . , 0)
> is like *execl* except that the directories named in the *PATH* environment variable are searched to find program *n*.

execv(*n*, *ap*)   replaces current process with a new process executing file *n* with argument list *ap*.

execve(*n*, *ap*, *ep*)
> replaces current process with a new process executing file *n* with argument list *ap* and environment *ep*.

execvp(*n*, *ap*)   is like *execv* except that the directories named in the *PATH* environment variable are searched to find program *n*.

exit(*s*)   flush and close all open files and terminate the process with status code *s*.

_exit(*s*)   is similar to *exit* except the I/O buffers are not flushed.

fork()   create a new process, a duplicate of the current process.

getgid()   returns the real group id of the current process.

getegid()   returns the effective group is of the current process.

getitimer(*t*, *v*)
> returns the value of timer *t* in *v*. The include file "sys/time.h" gives definitions for *t* and *v*.

getpgrp(*pid*)   returns the number of the process group owning process *pid*.

getpid()   returns the number of the calling process.

getppid()   returns the number of the caller's parent process.

kill(*p*, *s*)   sends signal *s* to process *p*, or to all processes in the group if *p* is 0.

killpg(*g*, *s*)   sends signal *s* to all processes in group *g*.

setitimer(*t*, *v*, *ov*)
> sets timer *t* to hold value *v*. The old timer value is returned in *ov*. A SIGALRM, SIGVTALRM or SIGPROF signal is generated when a real timer, virtual timer or user/system timer hits zero. The include file "sys/time.h" gives definitions for *t*, *v* and *ov*.

setpgrp(*p*, *g*)   sets the group of process *p* to be *g*.

sigblock(*m*)   blocks receipt of signals according to bits set in mask *m* in addition to signals already being blocked.

sigpause(*m*)   wait until one of the signals permitted by mask *m* arrives.

`sigsetmask(m)`
> blocks those signals corresponding to bits set in mask m.

`signal(s,h)`   installs signal handler h for signal s, returning the old signal handler. The include file "signal.h" defines names for all the signals.

`sigvec(s,nh,oh)`
> is a more general version of *signal*. It installs the signal handler defined by nh for signal s, returning the previous handler oh. The include file "signal.h" provides a structure definition for nh and oh.

`vfork()`   is a more efficient version of *fork* to be used when the child process will immediately execute one of *execl, execve,* etc.

`wait(sp)`   waits until a signal is received or any child process terminates. The function result is the number of the child process (or -1 if there is no child). A status word referenced by sp gives the exit status of the child process.

`wait3(sp,op,ru)`
> is used to obtain the statuses of child processes. Option flags in op can inhibit waiting for child process terminations. Resource usage by a child can be obtained through ru.

D.5.2. Pipes and Sockets

The include files "<sys/types.h>" and "<sys/socket.h>" are required with most of the socket handling functions.

`accept(s,ap,alp)`
> indicates that the caller wishes to accept an incoming connection to socket s. The two other parameters point to a socket address and a name length which may be filled in with the name of the socket at the other end (depending on which communications domain is used).

`bind(s,n,nl)`   binds the name (socket address) n with length nl to socket s.

`connect(s,n,nl)`
> for SOCK_STREAM communication type, this call establishes a connection between the socket s and another socket with name n and name length nl.

`getpeername(s,n,nl)`
> returns the name of the party (peer) at the other end of the connected socket s. The name is returned in n and the length of the name returned via nl. This function does not work for UNIX domain sockets.

getsockname(s, n, nl)

>returns the current name for the socket s. The name is returned in n and the length of the name returned via nl. This function is useful if the system has been allowed to pick a port number for an INET address. It does not work for UNIX domain sockets.

listen(s, b)   informs the system that the socket s will be used to accept incoming connections and that a backlog of b such connections should be handled.

pipe(svp)   creates a communications path. The parameter svp refers to an array which is filled in with two file descriptors, one for the read side and the other for the write side of the pipe.

pclose(s)   closes a pipe, with stream pointer s, created by the *popen* function.

popen(cmd, m)   creates a pipe to read from or write to a shell command cmd. The direction of the I/O is indicated by m.

recv(s, b, bl, fl)

>reads a message from a previously connected socket s into buffer b which has size bl. A flags argument fl permits non-standard message access.

recvfrom(s, b, bl, fl, fr, flp)

>is like *recv* except that the socket need not have been connected. The buffer fr with length indirectly indicated by flp will be filled in with the address of the source of the message.

recvmsg(s, msg, fl)

>is a more general version of *recvfrom* where msg refers to a structure providing information controlling the message connection.

socket(af, t, p)

>creates a socket in communications domain af with communications type t and protocol p.

socketpair(d, t, p, sv)

>creates a pair of already connected sockets in communications domain d with type t and protocol p. The file descriptors are returned in the array sv.

APPENDIX E

ANSWERS TO QUESTIONS

Chapter 1

1. No, no token can contain white space.

2. 64, -63, 2748 and -240.

3. Four bytes (three linefeed characters plus the null terminator byte).

4. One byte (there is just a null terminator byte).

5. The constant .15e4 represents the value 1500, whereas the others represent the value 150.

6. Eight bytes. Recall that all floating point constants are stored in double-precision format.

Chapter 2

1. Two.

2. The possibilities include 3, 6 and 11. (No doubt there are more, depending on the compiler.)

3. If the less-than operator, < , were combined, it would yield <= which is another operator in the language. Although the unambiguous combinations could be supported, language consistency is important and it seems preferable to exclude all combinations with comparison operators.

4. x |= ((*(y++)) >= ((a-b)&1)

5. It behaves like the second possibility. The left-hand side is evaluated only once. (This question checks whether you read footnotes.)

Chapter 3

1. Zero. The **else** associates with the second **if**.

2. Ten lines.

3. Yes, it is legal and does absolutely nothing.

4. The loop is easier to set up if an additional variable is introduced, as in

```
for ( i=k=1;  k<=8;  k++, i = k*k ) {
```

6. For n in the range 0 to 7, the result is the factorial of n. Otherwise, the result is one.

Chapter 4

1. ```
char *(*papc)[];
```

2. ```
typedef char *pc;
typedef pc apc[];
typedef apc *papc;
```

3. b is a pointer to a ten-element array, where each element is a pointer to an integer.

4. Four bytes (all fields in the union have this same size).

Chapter 5

1. The caller would pass the address of the argument. At the beginning of the function, the parameter is dereferenced to obtain the value of the original argument. This value is saved in a local variable, and only this local variable is accessed or modified in the body of the function. At the end of the function, just before control is about to return to the caller, the local variable's value is copied back to the storage whose address was passed originally.

2. Not really, all calculations are performed in double-precision.

3. The function keeps calling itself and the stack from which local variables are allocated storage grows until there is no memory left. At this point, you should get the error message "Segmentation fault (core dumped)".

4. The array elements would need to be accessed via pointers which are declared with the type (char *) . These pointers have to be incremented or decremented in multiples of the array element size. Element values have to be copied by a function that copies the correct number of bytes (*bcopy* is suitable) and compared by the function that is passed in as an argument.

5. Recall that function invocation has higher precedence than the dereferencing operator. Thus, f will first be called as a function and it is the function result that can be dereferenced to yield an integer. That is, f is a function returning a pointer to an integer. In contrast, g must first be

dereferenced and it is the result of the dereferencing that can be invoked as a function (which then returns an integer). Therefore, g is a pointer to a function that returns an integer.

6. The obvious error is that the types of the arguments supplied in the call of *foo* do not match the types declared for the corresponding formal parameters. The C compiler does not notice these mismatches, the *printf* call will simply produce some strange output. A suitable correction would be to interchange the arguments in the call to *foo* (or interchange the formal parameters in the declaration of *foo*).

Chapter 6

1. For example, `increment( *cp )` would increment the pointer *cp* and not the location to which *cp* points.

2. The preprocessor goes into a loop repeatedly expanding the macro name. (The preprocessor eventually detects this as an error when an internal buffer overflows.)

3. The formal parameter x appears twice in the macro expansion. This means that the side effect of incrementing s (because of the ++ operator) may occur twice.

4. The preprocessor eliminates all the characters from /* up to */ as being a comment. Thus the second definition is never seen and the first definition defines *comment* as being an empty string.

5. This definition does not work too well for `swap(*cp1++,*cp2++)` because each parameter is evaluated twice in the macro body (see question 3, above). It does not do what one would expect for `swap(i,a[i])` either.

Chapter 7

1. For integer output, *printf* exepects to receive the *value* of that integer. For integer input, *scanf* needs the *address* of an integer variable. Strings are different because they are passed via a pointer to the first character in the string. This pointer suffices for *printf* to extract the string value and for *scanf* to know where to copy an input string to.

2. If some C source code contains a string like

   ```
   stringptr = "/* this is a bug\n";
   ```

   the program will incorrectly delete text starting at the /* character combination continuing until the end of the next comment in the code.

3. Yes, the file exists as long as any hard links to it remain.

4. The symbolic link remains but becomes unusable. If it is used, the system reports that the file is inaccessible.

5.   The function can fail if you do not possess read permission for one of the directories between the current directory and the root directory.

6.   The *du* command and the *rm -r* command may fail.

Chapter 8

1.   Any argument that *cc* does not understand (an unknown flag or a file without a suffix) is passed to the system *ld* program. This program expects *prog* to be a previously loaded program (i.e. like an *a.out* file). But such a file has a special code (a magic number) in the first two bytes. Since our file does not have this code, the message is produced.

2.   *Lint* works from a file that contains dummy definitions for all the standard library functions. The dummy definition for *malloc* declares the argument as being **unsigned**, whereas most users of *malloc* would pass an ordinary (signed) integer. This explains the complaint about argument 1. The dummy definition also declares the function result as `(char *)` and this is rarely the same type as that needed by the caller, hence the complaint about the function value.

Chapter 9

1.   The C compiler prefixes every C program with a small section of code that sets up the environment and then passes control to a label named _*main*. The *main* function must have the **extern** attribute or else the label _*main* will not be visible from any other program modules (including the code at the beginning of the program).

2.   No storage should actually be allocated for a variable by a declaration in a *.h* file because the same *.h* file may be included several times in the same program. The **extern** attribute implies that storage for a variable is allocated by some other declaration. (The C compiler on the Berkeley UNIX system is rather forgiving in this regard; it is not an error to omit the **extern** attribute.)

3.   *Mkmf* deduces the dependency rules be reading all the files in the directory to see which file includes which.

4.   The first declaration specifies that *table* is a label on a block of storage organized as an array. The second declaration specifies that it is a label on a single word of storage that holds a pointer. When the compiler sees a use of *table* as in

```
table[3] = 3;
```

it generates different machine code for the two cases.

Chapter 10

1. The simple answer is to pass the array name to the index check function. This implies that a macro to access an array element might be defined in a similar manner to

   ```
   #define ARR(x) arr[ XCHK(x,80,"ARR") ]
   ```

2. By using *malloc* to obtain sufficient storage for many words and many *listitem* nodes at once. If we obtain a large chunk of memory and subdivide it ourselves, we would eliminate much of the overhead in using *malloc*.

3. One method would be to check whether the first character is the same in each string before proceeding to call *strcmp*. Since this check would be very fast, it would usually save time overall. A second (and better) method would be to keep the hash code of the word in the *listitem* structure. Only if the new word has the same hash code as a word in the linked list would it be worthwhile to call *strcmp*.

4. Because the inclusion of profiling code considerably slows down the speed of the program (particularly function calls).

Chapter 11

1. Each user has a limit on the number of processes that may be simultaneously active. (This limit is around twenty-five.) After the loop has created this many processes, further calls to *fork* will fail.

2. The process would not receive the SIGTSTP signal that it sends itself, so control would continue past the call to *kill* on to the call of *signal* and continue to the end of the signal handler. When control exits the signal handler, SIGTSTP signals are unblocked and the signal that the process sent itself is now delivered. Control re-enters the signal handler and ... we have an infinite loop.

3. The easy method is to call the *abort* system function, which generates an illegal instruction interrupt. Another method, more in accordance with the contents of the chapter, is to restore default signal handling for SIGQUIT and then use the *signal* function to send this signal to ourselves.

4. Not really (but you could come close if you really tried). The problem is that there is only one system stack from which storage for functions is obtained. The *longjmp* function only works reliably if this stack is popped (corresponding to simultaneous exits from several active functions occurring.) Thus, the local storage of a *coroutine* executing *longjmp* is lost. To implement coroutines, one stack per coroutine is required.

5. One of the actions performed by the *exit* function is to close any open files. If a child process created by a *fork* call terminates by calling *exit*, all of its files are closed while the files belonging to the parent process remain open. But when a child process is created by *vfork*, the data area is not

duplicated. Therefore, if the child process calls *exit*, the action of closing the files owned by the child process also closes the files owned by the parent process.

Chapter 12

1. Yes. The Berkeley UNIX system does permit writes to the read side of a pipe, and vice versa.

2. The easiest method would be by means of file permissions attached to the socket or to the directory containing the socket. (Recall that sockets in the UNIX domain are implemented via file path names.)

3. We could create a server demon, much like the *B_BOARD_D* program, that accepts connections from users. However, the program would not complete a service for one user before calling *accept* to accept the next connection. It would use the *select* function to read input from any user *or* to accept a new connection. (This is one of the possible uses of *select*.) If a new connection is accepted, that simply provides one new file descriptor from which input is possible.

Chapter 13

1. Because *putchar* is not a true function, it is defined as a macro in the "stdio.h" include file.

2. Because the strings to which the global variables *BC*, etc., refer are allocated storage by *tgetstr* inside the *tcbuff* array. It would be unfortunate if the storage for this array were to disappear when control returns from the *read_termcap* function.

INDEX